To Julie,

With Best Regards

Joan x

Joan Gibbons & Kaye Winwood, eds.
VIVID/Article Press

Audience members during the *Curation* seminar, 29 January 2005

Preface
Kaye Winwood

Hothaus Papers: Perspectives and Paradigms in Media Arts is a collection of papers presented as part of a programme of four seminars, *hothaus series* (2003–2005), originated by VIVID and developed in collaboration with the University of Central England. This publication contains 21 papers, including some which were not originally presented at the seminar series, but which the editors felt would contribute to the key themes in this book.

The series sat within a strand of VIVID's programme called *hothaus*, which ran 2001–2005. *hothaus* was conceived to accommodate the research and development of media arts and facilitated practice-led R+D, residences, talks, events and commissions. The seminars afforded VIVID an opportunity to discuss and disseminate some of the concerns and issues that arose from the *hothaus* programme of activity such as the use of technology, interaction and participation, curation, distribution and interdisciplinarity.

The objective of the *hothaus series* was to situate media arts within a bigger picture of contemporary visual tradition, and to draw parallels between media arts, visual arts, science, technology and popular culture. The aim was to challenge the widely held assumption that media arts are exclusively digital and/or electronic, principally internet-based, and therefore only of interest, and accessible, to a specialist audience. Key to all of the presentations was a creative and conceptual rigour, a deliberate shift away from the use of technology for its own sake, in favour of a programme that held a similar fascination with, and a regard for, new and old technologies alike.

The intention of the series was to provide a platform for artists, curators and theorists to present research relating to, and located within, contemporary media arts practice and theory. And the series brought together speakers from a miscellany of disciplines to investigate emerging working methodologies and artforms. It was important for the seminars to exist beyond a formal academic framework, thereby providing a space for a diverse audience comprised of artists, arts professionals, theorists, students and technologists.

It was never the intention of the *hothaus series* to provide a definitive or conclusive summary of the position of media arts but rather to proffer a platform from which the varying perspectives and paradigms of this artform could be presented, explored and discussed.

The seminar programme was thematically composed to encourage specific strands of enquiry whilst looking more broadly at the widened discourse surrounding media arts. Issues of innovation, appropriation, authorship and distribution ran throughout the seminars as key concerns. *Reinvention* (25 October 2003) opened the series with presentations looking at artistic practice involving the recycling and appropriation of existing technologies. Research included the relationship between the artist, technology and the artwork in an investigation of creativity and authorship. The role of existing technologies within contemporary arts practice and intent to subvert the original design of an item of technology were key to these talks.

Whilst *Reinvention* borrowed from history, the second seminar *Progression* (2 October 2004) looked at contemporary culture for new ways of working and for the provision of a new set of tools.

Simon Yuill, Matthew Gough and Gregory Sporton in discussion during the *Progression* seminar, 2 October 2004

For many years technology has influenced art production and today the prevalence of the internet, mobile and locative devices in society provide the artworld with new creative possibilities. Fundamental to this discussion was interdisciplinarity and collaboration as a form of distributed learning and empowerment.

The penultimate seminar *Space* (4 December 2004) looked at physical and virtual properties in an exploration of the interface. Here research included the internet as a space for interaction and participation, ubiquitous and locative media, its impact on our social and physical spaces, and the urbanisation of video. This seminar explored how technology, and the transition from analogue to digital, has affected our perception of space, from an actual to a representational space, and altered the way in which space is represented and experienced.

Audience members during the *Space* seminar, 4 December 2004

Caitlin Jones presenting as part of the *Curation* seminar, 29 January 2005

Having explored production within earlier seminars it seemed appropriate that the final seminar *Curation* (29 January 2005) explored some of the challenges associated with the commissioning and presentation of media artwork. The variability and precariousness of media-based work is a significant concern for curators working within this field and critical to conservation and distribution issues. Furthermore media-based work can provide new and innovative ways of engaging with an audience, enabling participation and possibilities for distributed authorship.

On behalf of VIVID and the University of Central England I would like to take this opportunity to thank each of the speakers and authors for their invaluable contributions to the seminar and publication, and without whom this programme would not have been possible, or as fascinating. I would also like to thank the staff at VIVID, and project assistants Emily Luxford and Siân Evans, for their continued enthusiasm and support throughout. Finally, a huge thanks to Joan Gibbons for a series of insightful and contextual introductions in each section of this publication, for her highly tuned editorial skills and for sharing the ambition and vision for the *hothaus series*.

Reinvention

Introduction
Joan Gibbons

When invoked in relation to media arts, reinvention has an obvious affinity with a recurring topic in the literature of the subject, that of remediation, which, at its simplest, can be used to describe ways in which the 'new' media are rooted in older media such as print and film and the way that the former frequently borrow approaches, conventions and genres from the latter.[1] But, as Nina Pope points out in her paper, *Reinventing Ourselves*, reinvention also sits among a cluster of similar words such as reworking, recycling, re-enactment and representation (re-presentation). All of these terms carry a similar sense of remaking or redoing and might readily be invoked to describe the reinventions discussed in any of this set of papers. An obvious question that is begged in the light of this choice of 're' words is why reinvention rather than any of the other closely associated words? The first answer is that reinvention was chosen as the title/theme of this set of seminars to make a point that is dear to Kaye Winwood, Projects Organiser at Vivid and instigator of *Hothaus Papers*. Winwood's point is simply and straightforwardly that media arts are all too often seen in terms of high-tech methodologies and approaches and that low-tech media arts, while just as legitimate and just as inventive, are often overlooked in favour of the ever increasing reach, versatility and novelty of the newer and newest technologies.

The second answer it that while reinvention seems to embrace all of these related terms in some way, it nevertheless carries key notions associated with invention per se, in the sense of something that can be an act of finding out or discovery and/or a matter of the creation, production or devising of new ideas or things through ingenuity or imagination. Reinvention suggests that, while the starting point may not be new, as for instance with Duchamp's infamous readymade objects, the defining features of invention are nevertheless present and redeployable. In other words, reinvention presupposes the potential to produce something that is sufficiently ingenious in its reworking to constitute an original thought or artefact. A term such as remediation, while similarly suggesting appropriations of form, convention and genre, does not necessarily imply the same creative input as is required by reinvention. Moreover, while remediation is usually framed as high-tech translations of well-recognised features of 'older' media, a term such as reinvention opens up the field of practice to include approaches that use what might be perceived as quite clunky or even redundant technologies. The artists in this first set of papers variously combine old and new in their choice of medium or subject matter and the six papers that follow offer a range of approaches for this blending of old and new. In this, they give an indication of the wide scope and rich potential for reinvention to be found in the field of media arts. Addressed in different ways by different technologies and according to very different aims and objectives, time and history are key elements in the process of reinvention that is related in the papers written by artists Nina Pope (in collaboration with partner, Karen Guthrie) Paul Ramírez-Jonas and Jem Finer. For Pope and Guthrie, history and its reinvention provide a pretext for a performative use of new media that enables both artists and audience to bring the past into the present. For Paul Ramírez-Jonas, time can be either elusive or relentless and is arrested and reconfigured in works that bring together different histories of technology to make understated but nevertheless provocative political and social allusions. In Jem Finer's work, past, present and future history have been rolled into one ambitious project in which time and history are shown for the abstractions that they ultimately are. On the evidence of these cases alone, it seems that reinvention has almost necessarily to go hand in hand with some sort of reconsideration of time and history and that the defining features of reinvention may exceed those of invention described above. Moreover, the reinventions of these artists evoke wistfulness for other times or other ways of being that can be broadly described as nostalgic, a quality which also permeates the work of Paul Granjon and Brian Duffy. While history and time are not self-consciously expressed in the work of these two artists, this possibility of other histories, other ways of being, nevertheless underpins Granjon's low-tech robotics and Duffy's transformation of period toys. In the final paper of this section, James Wallbank describes the reinvention of recently redundant new technologies and, in doing so, speaks ultimately to the acceleration of our sense of history and time that new technologies are said to bring.

Both historically canonised literature and actual historical events have been recurrent preoccupations for working partners Nina Pope and Karen Guthrie who have reinvented themselves (and, in some cases, given others the opportunity to reinvent themselves) through the stories that are offered by each of these sources. Pope and Guthrie's reinventions are achieved through re-enactments of the events of their chosen 'stories' rather than their passive consumption, so that in undergoing a process of self-reinvention, Pope and Guthrie can also be said to be reinventing traditional methods of story-telling. In reinventing stories, whether fictional or historically-based, the two artists eschew traditional narrative and engage interactively and non-linearly with both their material and their audience through a mixture of technologies that includes television broadcast, webcast,

----

1   A key work is Jay Bolter and Richard Grusin's, *Remediation: Understanding New Media* (Cambridge, Massachusetts and London, England: The MIT Press, 1999). See also, Anders Fagerjord, "Rhetorical Convergence: Studying Web Media", in Gunnar Liestøl, Andrew Morrison, Terje Ramussen eds. *Digital Media Revisited: Theoretical and Conceptual Innovations in Digital Domains* (Cambridge, Massachusetts and London, England: The MIT Press, 2003), 293-325. For example, the non-linear organisation of the newspaper or magazine has provided a prototype for the organisation of both time and space in web design, which builds on the sort of interactivity offered by such print media and expands it through the use of hyperlinks.

hyperlinks and mobile phones. The flexibility of such technologies allows them to reinvent their stories in a way that part actualises them and part renders them contemporary. Time and history are not only reconfigured, undermining the gap between past and present, but they combine to become a new form of recognition (literally re-cognition or re-knowing) and, in this sense, a form of memory. Here memory is not, of course about the accurate recall of events or experience, but a reminding through subjective interactions with the past. From this point of view, memory can be said to occupy the sort of liminal position that Susannah Radstone has identified at the threshold of subjectivity and objectivity, of the self and the social.[2]

Pope and Guthrie's *Hypertext Journal – A Journey to the Western Isles* (1996) provided just this sort of liminality, not only for the artists themselves but also for its web-based participants. Poised between the actual and the virtual, between history and the present, between artist and audience, the *Hypertext Journal* reinvented a journey into the Western Isles of Scotland originally made by the renowned essayist and raconteur, Samuel Johnson and his biographer, James Boswell, in the autumn of 1773.[3] Rather than merely reconstruct the original journey, Pope and Guthrie invited their audience of web-browsers to participate by offering suggestions concerning how the journey should proceed, making the journal a live event rather than a record to be consumed in retrospect. As Paul West has pointed out, The *Hypertext Journal* stood at the threshold between an online community of web-browsers and the off-line community of the Western Isles, in which Pope and Guthrie occupy an intermediary position.[4] In reinventing the journal in this way, the two artists not only reinvigorated a historical text, but also provided a model for the reinvigoration of methods of engagement with literary texts in general. The knock-on effects of this sort of development are culturally significant, as Peter Ride put it, "it also reminds us that our awareness of collective experience, present and historical, factual and anecdotal, contributes to our comprehension of cultures – which is represented and referenced by the multi-layering of information in an art project."[5]

The two other major projects described in Pope's paper develop the modes of reinvention set in *Hypertext Journal. /broadcast/(29 pilgrims, 29 tales)* (1999), was based on a literary text of a different order, which, while of immense historical value because of the time in which it was written, is fictional in essence, as opposed to Johnson and Boswell's more historically-based account. This time, Pope and Guthrie chose to reinvent Geoffrey Chaucer's *Canterbury Tales* (1387–1400) in order to explore the forms that a contemporary pilgrimage might take, given the potentials offered by new technologies such as webcasting and mobile phones. In this complex reinvention of Chaucer's tales, fiction is not just incorporated into the lived experience of the participants and the vicarious experiences of the webcast audience, it becomes both history and memory at once. Their more recent project, *TV swansong* (2002), shows Pope and Guthrie still in the process of reinventing their practice and still seeking to reinvent an older medium through the reinvention of narratives. However, in this case, the two artists decided to invite a number of other artists to take part in the project, which was to examine a 'site or situation made famous by TV.' As Pope's description of the project shows, some artists deconstructed the original site/situation by changing the terms of engagement with or transforming the terms of a genre or form, producing a thought-provoking dialectic between the inventions and conventions of the older broadcast medium of television and the potentials and reinventions of newer medium of webcast.

A different sense of history underpins the reinventions made by Paul Ramírez-Jonas, who has faithfully restaged historical inventions in his own work for his own purposes, as witnessed in his reconstruction of Edison's first recording machine and his reconstruction of the kites that served as prototype flying machines in the late nineteenth/early twentieth century. As is suggested by the title of one of the sections in Ramírez-Jonas' paper, 'Trying to follow in someone else's footsteps and getting to exactly the same point they got to,' the business of reinvention is, at one level, a literal retracing of history in which Ramírez-Jonas foregrounds the symbolic or ideological significance of the inventions he singles out, addressing the ways in which they embody a political ordering of the world. In fact, as Gregory Volk has noted, the inventions that Ramírez-Jonas has recovered and remade, although iconic, were often visionary but 'failed' utopian projects.[6] Yet, on another level, and despite the difference in approach, Ramírez-Jonas' work is, in its own way, as much about story-telling as is Pope and Guthrie's. For instance, in *Men on the Moon* (1992–ongoing), he brings together the separate narratives of two historically distant examples of technological and scientific achievement. In this work, Ramírez-Jonas both augments and compounds the history of Edison's first recording machine by using it to record conversations from another highly significant historical event, that of the moon-landings in 1969.[7]

This unexpected combination of historically disparate objects or events is also to be seen in *A Better Yesterday* (1999), in which the time-honoured and sophisticated time-keeping mechanisms of the Utrecht church tower were co-opted into a comparatively low-tech automated

2 Susannah Radstone ed. *Memory and Methodology* (Oxford and New York: Berg, 2000), 11-12.

3 For transcript of original account, see Samuel Johnson, *A Journey to the Western Isles of Scotland*, edited by J. D. Fleeman (Oxford: Clarendon Press, 1985).

4 Paul West, "In the Digitised Footsteps of Boswell & Johnson", *The Herald*, 15 March 1996. <www.somewhere. uk/hypertext/journal/press/Paul Welsh.html>.

5 Peter Ride, "Hypertext Journal - a Journey to the Western Isles", *Mute* M4, September 2002, <www.somewhere. org.uk/hypertext/journal/press/ mute.html>.

6 Gregory Volk, Paul Ramírez-Jonas, Ricci Albenda, <www.zingmagazine. com/zing3/reviews/040_jonas.html> 1996.

7 *Men on the Moon* is a project in four parts, *Tranquility* (1992), *Eva* (1996), *Rest Period* (1998), *Return* (ongoing). See, Sofia Hernández Chong Cuy, *Paul Ramírez-Jonas*, (Manchester: Ikon Gallery/Cornerhouse Publications, 2004) 56-63.

artwork (through the adaptation of a tricycle, which had been transformed into a musical organ with drums that played every hour immediately after the tower's carillon and that mapped out time as Ramírez-Jonas rode it through the city). In both *Men on the Moon* and *A Better Yesterday*, an original, historically validated, invention is not only reconfigured but also recontextualised through its coupling with another history from another time. But, it is the thoughtfulness behind these conjunctions of normally separated histories and the ambiguities that emerge that is perhaps their most engaging feature. In *Men on the Moon*, the aforementioned combination of two iconic signifiers of scientific and technological progress is rendered impotent by the fact that the recoding machine erases the recorded material as it replays it. In the installation, the wax recording cylinders, as Ramírez-Jonas puts it, form a "monument that keeps the story safe", but this is a fragile and ironic security because the content of the recording cannot be realised without its loss.

In *A Better Yesterday*, Ramírez-Jonas plays on the cultural significance of towers and technology, simultaneously alluding to the Tower of Babel, which has stood for division and punishment in Christian mythology, and to Tatlin's *Monument to the Third International* (1919–20), which, conversely, stood for unity and solidarity in the rhetoric of early twentieth century Socialism.[8] To borrow a term from photography, this sensitivity towards unexpected but nevertheless apt juxtapositions creates a 'third effect' that often adds a particular poignancy to the work.[9] In *A Better Yesterday*, a 'third effect' is produced not only by the unexpected juxtaposition of disparate technologies of the clock tower and the tricycle in the service of marking time (not to mention the extension of the piece to form a 'clock' in the cityscape), but also by the ironic combination of *It's a Small World*, theme tune from Disney World, with the socialist anthem, *The Internationale*. The result is a disassembling of established meanings that encapsulates the ambiguities, ambivalences and contradictions of our times, in which the 'grand' narratives of science and progress no longer command the same blind faith as they did even fifty years ago.[10] Another example is found in *Ghost of Progress*, a video piece in which Ramírez-Jonas had placed a scale model of the Concorde into the handlebars of his bicycle with the camera placed to film to give the illusion that the bicycle journey (through a third-world city) was the fight-path of the Concorde. Again, the piece thrives on contradiction, the coupling of privilege and underprivilege in which, "The artifice is always evident, the sound of the pedalling is constantly present, and the discrepancy in scale is unavoidable."

The intertwining of *It's a Wonderful World* and *The Internationale* that is a feature of *A Better Yesterday*, is also a feature of Ramírez-Jonas' musical 'spacecraft,' *Rocinante* (2003), named after Don Quixote's horse. In chivalrous gesture worthy of Don Quixote himself, Ramírez-Jonas decided to construct a musical satellite for those countries without a space programme and, in typical Quixotic fashion, the project was inherently doomed to failure due to an obvious lack of finance and technical expertise, destined therefore, to take its place as a work of art rather than science. The choice of *Rocinante* as the title for this work is telling in respect to almost all of Ramírez-Jonas' work, founded as it so frequently is on anachronism and informed as it often is by the naïve optimism of the original invention. More than this, however, it is perhaps Ramírez-Jonas himself who is Quixotic in the continuously valiant and disingenuously simple address of hugely complex political or philosophical issues in his works. On a philosophical level, for example, the impossible but, nevertheless, consistent desire in our culture to chase or capture time is encapsulated in *Longer Day* (1997) and *Another Day* (2002). In *Longer Day*, for instance, Ramírez-Jonas sets out on "a futile attempt to make the day last forever" by driving as far as he could in a westward direction until sunset, under the conceit that the change in time-zones would extend his day (which it did by one minute).[11] In *Another Day*, Ramírez-Jonas' portrayal of the elusiveness of time and attempt to regulate it are more ambivalent. Just as the times of take-offs are counted down on video monitors in airports, the sunrises of 90 cities around the world are mimicked on video displays, marking the relentlessness of time. Time is continually decanting from one side of the present to the other and what the viewer makes of it philosophically depends on their propensity to think optimistically or pessimistically about time, future and past.

The fusion of past and present also underpins the reinventions discussed by Jem Finer. Noting that reinvention is everywhere once you start looking for it, Finer interprets it in terms of "playfulness", "experimentation" and "curiosity", emphasising the originality and inventiveness of reinvention. Finer gives three examples from his own work that demonstrate these qualities. The first, a radio broadcast, *disobey the manual* (2002), consisted of a number of musical pieces that had been composed "through the abuse and reinvention of existing instruments, notation and technology." The piece embodies a blending of old and new that is also characteristic of the other two works that he discussed. As will be seen in the two other works under discussion, Finer typically trawls the past for source material and 'reinvents' it with the aid of a range of electronic technologies. As Finer notes, whole genres of music have sprung from this ability to see beyond the face value of prevailing or historically established conventions – to find and release new potentials in a pre-existing musical form.

----

8   For thorough iconographical analysis of Tatlin's *Monument*, see John Milner, *Vladimir Tatlin and the Russian Avant-Garde* (New Haven and London: Yale University Press, 1983), 151-180.

9   For instance, the third effect was the term given to the ironic juxtaposition of images that were formally or compositionally alike, but different in subject and context, often making a visual pun. See, for example, the (often politically loaded) juxtapositions in the early photomagazine, *Lilliput*, founded by Stephan Lorant in 1937.

10 I refer to 'grand' narratives in the sense that Lyotard speaks of the metanarratives that have governed Western culture since the Enlightenment. See Jean Francois Lyotard, *The Postmodern Condition*, (Manchester: Manchester University Press, 1984).

11 Cuy, op. cit. 7.

Such an approach underpins *Longplayer*, a musical piece designed
to play in a 1000 year cycle, and which so far has been playing
since midday, December 31st, 1999.[12] The piece has been eloquently
characterised as a response to the start of a new millennium and an
attempt to transcend mortal time.[13] Like any other piece of music, it
can only be realised or experienced in a forward unfolding of time but,
like any other piece of music or any other cultural production for that
matter, it also embodies a relationship with the past that, in this case,
again calls up a sense of reinvention rather than remediation. The
elements of old and new, past and present, are conspicuously there.
The instruments, Tibetan Singing Bowls, are ancient in their technology
and the methods of recording and replaying the music are necessarily
forward-looking. While *disobey the manual* was an eclectic reworking
of a number of sounds and their original technology or composition,
Longplayer organises a single score in such a way as to produce a piece
of music that has the potential to play indefinitely on a 1,000 year loop.
The desire for transcendence that this signifies is signalled in Finer's
first choice of musical score, which was Judy Garland's rendering of
Over the Rainbow "chosen not only for its optimism for an uncertain
future but also for its familiarity."[14] And, just as the title of *disobey
the manual* signifies an anarchic reworking of pre-existing forms and
content, *Over the Rainbow* can be said to represent the gap between
need and want that the French post-Freudian Jacques Lacan sees as
the basis of human desire or aspiration.[15] In this case, nostalgia for
a never-never land beyond the rainbow is further underscored by
its association with Garland and all that she has come to represent.
As it happened, the vocal elements of *Over the Rainbow* presented
unsatisfactorily and Finer had to look for alternatives, settling finally
on a score of his own rendered by Tibetan Singing Bowls. Although this
change brought a considerable shift in signification, from the nostalgic
to the esoteric, the 'ancientness' of the Singing Bowls occasioned a
'reinvention' of another sort which brought a sense of transcendence
rather than optimism. As Kodwo Eshun has noted, *Longplayer* not only
transcends future time but also forms a connection with a past that
is outside of the 'given' chronicles of history.[16] Produced at a point in
history when our awareness of time was heightened by the turning
of the century, *Longplayer* represents far more than the reworking of
sound and its technologies. In lengthening the time-base of the work
so extensively, Finer has both reconfigured time and responded to a
yearning for larger unattainable abstractions such as the eternal or the
sublime. In this, *Longplayer* becomes almost inherently Romantic, with
Finer striving for something that in reality is beyond our capacity to
experience in its entirety. What we experience in actuality by listening
to *Longplayer* may be an almost infinitesimal fragment of that entirety,
but in the course of that experience, we are able to both conceptually
and symbolically transcend our physical limitations. In this Finer
invokes the German Enlightenment philosopher Immanuel Kant's
notion of the sublime as a sensation of extreme pleasure that allows us
to conceive of things far beyond our physical constraints.[17]

In contrast to the transcendentalism and outward reach of *Longplayer*, Finer lurks in the nether regions of a pinball machine in his more recent project, *Pinball*. However, this does not preclude a visionary take on the inner landscape that he encounters, which he describes as resembling the flashing lights of a futuristic city. The reinvention here is in turning a pinball machine into a musical instrument, a reinvention that will again facilitate invention of new musical forms and contexts. As previously, Finer shows a respect for older technologies and a desire to not only to conserve them but to reinvigorate them, respecting that there is already "too much stuff in the world." In converting the pinball machine into a musical instrument, Finer not only conserves its function as a form of play but reinvents the game, so that numerical scores are obtained through the force of the sound or 'music' created by the flippers, not the usual force of a travelling ball. As Finer notes, this apparently simple shift in the rules of engagement opens up an enormous potential for new musical experiences in which machines may be orchestrated on a grand scale in elaborate installations.

Play also forms an important aspect of artist Paul Granjon's work which consists largely of performance and video pieces that provide arenas for his ingenious experiments in low-tech robotics. Granjon employs a DIY aesthetic which aligns with the notion of bricolage, a form of 'play' associated with the postmodern strategy of deconstruction advocated by French post-structuralist philosopher, Jacques Derrida in his seminal essay, *Structure, Sign and Play in the Discourse of the Human Sciences* (1966).[18] Essentially, the bricoleur is a DIY practitioner who has the ability to make inventive use of the means at hand and to therefore find creative solutions. Although initially deployed in the field of linguistics, the wider relevance and transferability of deconstruction to other arenas of cultural production is evident in the way that Derrida has subsequently expanded his reach to take in the visual arts and in the direct influence he has had on leading architects such as Bernard Tschumi. Derrida's paradigm of

---

12 Artangel is a London-based contemporary art commissioning agency that supports the production of site specific works, see <www.artangel.org.uk>.

13 Hari Kunzru, "Marking Time", *Mute* 17, July, 2002.

14 Jem Finer, "October 1995-31 December, 1999" in Jem Finer, *Longplayer*, (London: An Artangel Publication 2000), 23.

15 Jacques Lacan, "The Subversion of the Subject and the Dialectic of Desire in the Freudian Unconscious" in *Ecrits; A Selection* (London, Routledge, 1977), 311.

16 Kodwo Eshun, "An unidentified audio event arrives from the post computer age", in Finer, 10.

17 Immanuel Kant, *The Critique of Judgement*, (1790; Oxford: Oxford University Press, 1952), 61-4, 82-9.

18 Jacques Derrida, "Structure, Sign and Play in the Discourse of the Human Sciences", 1966, in David Lodge, ed. *Modern Criticism and Theory: A Reader* (London and New York: Longman, 1988). This essay is of key importance to postmodern thinking as it is the first in which the term deconstruction is employed as a strategy for challenging the centrality and rigidity of traditional structures of knowledge. In recognising the contingency and mutability of language, Derrida called for the introduction of playfulness as a means of opening up the constraints of conventional linguistics and he recommends bricolage as an appropriate method for these purposes.

creative production as bricolage fits Granjon's art almost perfectly in the way that he takes old technologies and reinvents them to create installations and performances that, in their eccentricity and faux-naivety, serve to undermine the everyday pretensions of human beings.

While Granjon obviously addresses the relationship of the human to the machine in his robotics, the non-human is not contrived in the more conventional terms of robots as mechanical human surrogates, but in terms of robotic animals. Early functioning autonomatons or robots such as Jacques de Vaucanson's life-size *Flute Player* (1737), The anonymously manufactured *Steam Man* (1865) and Professor Campion's *Boilerplate* (1893), were most often formed in the image of man and both the physical and psychological anthropomorphism of robots is deeply ingrained in the history and literature of robotics, notably in Karel Capek's *RUR (Rossum's Universal Robots)* (1921) and Isaac Asimov's collection of short stories (1940–50) subsequently published as *I Robot*.[19] In cases such as these, the push is towards the sophistication of robot capabilities, including the potentials for complex emotional responses. Granjon's robotic animals, on the contrary, cultivate the sort of emotional simplicity that has its roots in the French Enlightenment philosopher Jean-Jacques Rousseau's view of animals and children as representative of the innocent and morally uncontaminated state of raw nature to which humankind should aspire (except that Granjon's robotic animals are, of course, all artifice). Through the use of simple mechanical prostheses such as tails or moving ears, for instance, Granjon's robotic performances and videos allow us to re-identify with or even reinvent our more innocent, playful selves. In effect, Granjon's quirky combinations of animal characteristics and mechanical prostheses produce a hybridisation where the opposite of anthropomorphism is achieved, in which the human adopts the simplicity and innocence of animals, producing a uniquely enchanting form of artificial intelligence.

Nevertheless, Granjon's robotic animals can be situated among several other related inventions that use animals as the base for their robotic projects. These include *The Robot Zoo*, a travelling exhibition of the biomechanics of robotic 'wildlife' that has been touring the US and captivating both adults and children for around five years, and robots that are produced to mimic animal intelligence in order to perform particular and vital tasks, such as Brooklyn College's research into robotic lobsters for the purposes of identifying underwater mines. In the domestic sphere, interactive robotic animal toys have recently increased in popularity, for example Sony's well-known *AIBO* puppy, which requires the owner to assume responsibility for the 'life' of the puppy as if it were real. Granjon's mimicking of animal characteristics can be aligned to the same emotional base as the *AIBO*, grounded as it is in his own experience of the human/pet relationship and his continuing feelings of affection towards and appreciation of the dog that had been his companion from the age of six to twenty three.

While the 'animals' that Granjon introduces into his work are usually quirky and rudimentary in their pastiche of real animals, there is a sense that Granjon is being both ironic and disingenuous and that their endearing simplicity belies his sensitivity towards the complex emotional basis that often underpins the sentimentalisation of animals.[20] This sensitivity was evident in the performance that Granjon gave to bring the seminar to its conclusion. It was here that Granjon spoke of his family dog and took the audience on a similarly affectionate journey back to the growing pains of adolescence in his anecdotal account of the sprouting of body hair – a phenomenon which Granjon also suggests underlies the bond between animals and humans. The robotics in this performance consisted partly of Granjon wearing a pair of furry 'ears' and a long thin dog's 'tail' which acted as accessories in the rendition of a short song or ditty that he had written about the making of mechanised animal parts. This was followed by a song about a mass produced cherry pie that he associates with Wales (he teaches at the Cardiff Institute) and a second example of animal robotics in the form of a mechanical 'bird,' accompanied this time by a whistled ditty that mimicked birdsong. All of this was done with the complete lack of affectation that is often attributed to children and animals. It is in pieces such as these that Granjon's work becomes highly nostalgic, recalling the less complicated emotions of childhood and reinventing the sort of innocence and delight that, according to Rousseau, is the essence of our natural state.

Brian Duffy's short paper represents only one half of his seminar presentation, which was accompanied by a musical performance based on period toys that he had converted into instruments. Duffy is both a sound artist and an accomplished musician, who has much of the dreamer, the Romantic and the magician about him. In a recent work, *Optophonic Lunaphone* (2005), for instance, Duffy almost incredibly managed to harness the sound of stars in an outdoor musical performance that became a video installation in the Ikon Gallery, Birmingham: "My Mum told me that it was possible to hear the stars sing if you listened hard enough.[21] So I'd go off to the local garage roofs, lie down and stare at the stars. It was my first meditative experience, where language and thought stopped and were replaced by wonder and awe," recalls Brian. "There's a world and universe that we can't see or hear or feel. My work attempts to bring some of that within our sense window."[22]

It was, however, Duffy's earlier *Modified Toy Orchestra* that formed the subject of his paper and performance for the Reinvention seminars. Donald Woods Winnicott has referred to toys as transitional objects that help form a bridge between internal and external life and assist in the recognition of difference and similarity. They provide an

19 Isaac Asimov, *I Robot*, (first published 1950, London: Harper Collins, paperback edition, 1996).

20 For a recent overview of cultural significance and complexity of human/animal relations, see Erica Fudge, *Animal* (London: Reaktion Books, 2002).

21 Commisioned by VIVID, mac and Ikon

22 See profile on NESTA website. <www.nesta.org.uk/ourawardees/profiles/5067/02_profile.html>.

intermediate arena of experience that Winnicott claims is retained in the intense experiencing that belongs to the arts, religion imaginative living, and creative scientific work.[23] Rather than personal reminders, Duffy's 'orchestra' consists of electronic toys such as Speak & Spell or a Casio Keyboard that, following in the tradition of Alberto Giacometti and André Breton's forays into the fleamarkets of Paris, are readymades that Duffy has found in rummage or car boot sales. In this, they are more generic objects of transition, part of a shared childhood world of make-believe. The toys have had their circuits 'bent' in order to draw out hidden potential as musical instruments – demonstrated, for instance, to the great amusement of the audience by having the keyboard play Wham's *Wake Me Up Before You Go-Go*. Or, at the end of the presentation by performing a ten-minute set, beginning by making a series of vocal grunts into the front panel of the realistic keyboard and then spiralling off into 'another world,' ending with a demonic hula dancing Barbie doll singing "I'm a Barbie girl in the Barbie world. Life in plastic, it's fantastic."

Duffy's circuit bending work shares similar elements of bricolage and nostalgia with the work of Granjon. Yet, while the critical content of Granjon's work is due to deceptively simple forms of parody, Duffy's critical practice is in the distortion of the original cultural meaning and intent of toys that he reinvents and in his ability to use them as metaphors for the limitations that we allow objects to set, "For me it's a philosophical thing, circuit bending is a perfect metaphor for showing human sensory experience is limited. We've a limited window on the universe, yet we think we see everything. There's a lot we can't see like radio waves. I use the toys as a metaphor to explore that notion."[24] Here, reinvention can be seen in terms of both a remediation and recontextualisation of the original object in which there is a deeply felt ironic contrast between the character of the 'instrument' and the accomplishment of the music. With his blend of accomplished music and low art form of the modified toy, Duffy is almost satirising our tendencies to create hierarchies and, in doing so, produces a rather special mixture of wonder and burlesque.

Finally, James Wallbank's paper on the Redundant Technology Initiative (RTI) is a poignant reminder of the speed at which history appears to accelerate in an age of high-tech media, seen by some as signalling the collapse of history.[25] Yet, in contrast to this scenario of rapid advancement, the creative possibilities of low-tech take on a more directly social and political significance. Wallbank's initiative, in particular, encourages us to think less materialistically and less narcissistically about computers as a desirable commodity that signifies advancement and affluence. In doing so, it allows us to see the potential for the reinvention of 'redundant' computers not just as a cheaper but equally viable route to the 'information highway' but also as a medium for art and, in some cases, as the material components of works of art. There is no doubt that, in addition to their indispensability as corporate tools, computers rank highly among the objects of desire of the early twenty-first century. And, there is no doubt that the technology they embody has both expanded and altered the marketplace, changing the understanding of the internet as an arena for the free-exchange of knowledge into an arena that just as frequently provides information for the purposes of financial gain.[26] The Redundant Technology Initiative challenges the notion that computer technology has to be high tech and expensive in order to function effectively and, in the provision of free facilities and equipment, seeks to widen the access to information technology and digital media. As Wallbank emphasises in his paper, it is important to understand the context of the Redundant Technology Initiative, that of a largely impoverished post-industrial city where unemployment has had a crippling psychological and material effect on the lower echelons of society.

Yet, despite the historical specificity of its context, the Initiative is not alone in this remit of empowerment through the recycling of redundant computers. For example, Computerbank in Australia has a major ongoing project to supply low income individuals, community groups and disadvantaged schools with cast-off computers and cite similar organisations in Canada, France, Belgium, Thailand and the US on their website <www.computerbank.org.au>. However, the provision of computer equipment is not enough on its own and initiatives such as the RTI and Computerbank depend on the availability of Free Open Source Software (FOSS). FOSS is founded on the principles of shared knowledge that governed programming in its early days before the corporate dominance of Microsoft and Apple (although, as Simon Yuill notes, Apple and IBM are beginning to embrace FOSS in respect of its ready usability)[27]. At this point, it becomes evident that the 'reinventions' or reinvigorations fostered by the RTI are part of a larger and more complex political effort that seeks to build a more efficient and democratic internet. For example, in an inverse of normal corporate licensing restrictions, the Open Source Initiative has been set up as "a non-profit corporation dedicated to managing and promoting the Open Source Definition for the good of the community."[28] The Definition is explicit about shared distribution and redistribution of software so as not to discriminate against persons or groups, or against any field of endeavour. The source code is to be readily accessible and in a form that allows easy modification and the license that comes with the software is to be transferred openly between users, who are not allowed to build in any added restrictions. In a similar spirit

23   Donald Woods Winnicott, "Transitional Objects and Transitional Phenomena", *International Journal of Psychoanalysis*, 1953, vol. 34, 89–97.

24   <www.westmidlands.ideasfactory.com/performance/features/feature22.htm>.

25   Andreas Huyssen, *Twilight Memories: Marking Time in a Culture of Amnesia* (London and New York: Routledge, 1995), 6 and Pierre Nora, "Between Memory and History: Les Lieux de Memoire", *Representations* 26, Spring 1989, 7–8.

26   Julian Stallabrass, *Internet Art: The Online Clash of Culture and Commerce*, (London: Tate Publishing), 68–81.

27   Simon Yuill, "Your machines: Your Culture?", *Variant*, issue 20 <www.variant.org.uk>. <www.opensource.org/docs/definition/php>.

28   <www.tdlp.org/manifesto.html>.

of sharing, GNU/Linux have a large well-established documentation project to develop manuals as guides for their software.[29] While the community referred to in the Definition has not tended to included the commercial world, open source software is "now seen to be breaking into the commercial world, and... changing all the rules." As Simon Yuill has noted, the political implications of such a move are enormous, "a government run on Microsoft is, in some ways, a government run by Microsoft... choosing FOSS technologies in this context not only prevents vast sums of money going into private corporation but also raises many issues around the relationships between governance and private business."[30]

The philosophies and attitudes engendered by FOSS are clearly mirrored in the manifesto issued by the RTI's website, <www.lowtwech. org>. First declared at *The Next 5 Minutes* conference in Amsterdam (1999), the manifesto advocates the ideas and practices spoken of in Wallbank's paper. After the championing of free software and access, the notion that high technology does not mean high creativity rides high in the list, as does a fine scepticism at the 'consumerist frenzy' associated with information technologies where there is a constant push in the corporations to develop new software and constant pressure on users to upgrade.[31] As Wallbank explains in his paper, an emphasis on the inventive use of recycled computers – in other words their reinvention – became evident in the RTI's first major installation piece, *Redundant Array* (1998). This piece embodies both a philosophy of recycling (that it can so readily be a creative activity) and an expansive philosophy of art (in which boundaries between the social, economic and aesthetic aspects of the work are interwined in the creative process).[32] The model is not that of the self-contained artwork but one of the contingency. In this case, the work began as a workplace exercise in recycling for students from the local technology training centre which soon became an exercise in the creative adaptation of the machines. The creative skills developed on the project then provided a further return by augmenting the transferable skills of the students who Wallbank claims became instantly more employable. Reinvention became far more than the redeployment of the machines' socio-economic function, but provided with the technical an opportunity for self-reinvention as creative producers. Moreover, *Redundant Array* led to the establishment of the RTI's Access Space that provided a public access media lab which, in addition to providing an arena for creativity, was intended to have economic and social effects by providing a means for the development of computer skills.

---

29 Yuill, op. cit.
30 The Redundant Technology Initiative, *Lowtech Manifesto 1999* <www.lowtech. org/projects/n5m3/>.
31 The norm, of course, is for the gallery presentation of the artwork to mask or neglect the social context and conditions that surround the production of the work. See, for instance, Chin-tao Wu, *Privatising Culture: Corporate Art Intervention since the 1980s* (London and New York: Verso, 2002) for discussion of business machinations that underpin the artworld.

Reinventing Ourselves
Nina Pope

To me reinvention feels like a grand term: something groundbreaking, in some ways in itself a contradiction (arguably you can only truly invent something once?), something maybe to aim for, a difficult status to achieve... a daunting term. Thinking through our own projects didn't, at first, help me, I could think of lots of instances where we've reinterpreted or represented information or visual material but not actually reinvented it.[1] Thinking through other projects more and more connected themes came up – reworking, recycling and most significantly re-enactment – a theme common to much of our work which recently we've been trying to address very directly (and I'll say more about this later). Finally by thinking about all these other themes I realised the way I could most comfortably address the idea of reinvention was in the context of our own practice, this being the only thing we really do try to constantly reinvent by way of many of these other related ideas or themes.

In terms of representing I thought initially of two projects; *An Artist's Impression of a Text Based Environment* (1999–) and *Homemade Heroes* (2002).[2] In *An Artist's Impression* we slavishly attempted the impossible task of constantly representing or in fact reinterpreting players descriptions of the objects and buildings they made in a text-based online game onto a real 'scale' model of the island environment we'd initially created online.

An Artist's Impression of a Text Based Environment 1999-

1   Nina Pope & Karen Guthrie have worked in collaboration for the last 10 years, and more recently as the organisation, Somewhere, for more details, see <www.somewhere.org.uk>.

2   <www.somewhere.org.uk/artistsimpression>.

With *Homemade Heroes* we approached sewing circles we found online to reinterpret our own text based descriptions of well known computer games characters without revealing to them the identity of their specified 'super hero'. So, in both cases we used a familiar technique of representing, as a way to understand or question the 'source' material. To expand on this I'm going to talk about three projects and focus on how all of these look to re-enactment as a way of reinventing our own practice through the experience of producing particular pieces of work.

The first of these projects, *A Hypertext Journal*,[3] dates from 1996 and was one of our first collaborative projects. In many ways it has remained one of our most successful pieces both in terms of the development of our own work and outside 'acclaim.' So, what was it and why do we now see it as so significant to our practice? In simple terms it was quite literally a month long journal written in hypertext on the web. This doesn't seem now in any way remarkable or unusual – there are many models from the Guardian's 'Netjetters' to TV travel programmes and holiday photos emailed home to worried mums, which take this instant-journal approach.[4] However, in 1996 the web, certainly in the UK, was a different place. It felt like you could know most people with an email address but, as yet, still-pictures were quite a new addition to the previously grey and text-based world of web pages. We began the project as a challenge to ourselves to reinvent what the (much hyped at that point) idea of interactivity could mean for our work. Early interactive art had taken the (to our way of thinking) rather lame 'CD-ROM click-here' approach and we thought there must be more at stake than this. As it turned out we ended up reinventing not only what interaction could mean for our work but most of what we then understood as the rules of engaging with our audience and indeed the idea of what making work could actually be for us. During our month on the road retracing Boswell and Johnson's *A Journey to the Western Isles* we opened our 'studio door' at the stage of production, for the first time we made work live and we allowed our actions and, to a certain extent, our focus to be directed by a small but intense and enthusiastic 'first level' audience who followed our progress.

A Hypertext Journal 1996

My clearest memories of this trip are those of confusion and frustration – but in a positive sense. With a couple of notable exceptions we were working in an unprecedented field and there were no rules for how the work should look or how the story should unfold. There was nothing to directly copy, only a previous model to reinterpret (that of a journal written a long time ago by two men) which gave us a structure and form to spring from but no real idea of where we should take it. The small steps we did take towards putting actual work rather than documentation onto the site may not seem that significant now but at the time they felt very hard won. Using current technology gave us a path through which to reinterpret an existing form. Writing a journal, even in its simplest form, can't be conceived of in the same way when your readers look over it every night and email you back what they think. This brings me on to a point about old or new technology. Looking back over our projects we've always been interested in current technology and what that can offer, the small windows of creative opportunity set up by each advance before it becomes commonplace, widely used or accepted. We've never experienced the 'if only the resolution was better' effect or conversely the 'but webcasting just doesn't have the same feel to it as film' scenario. For us, each new point along the line has its own interests and aesthetic and its own challenges. By mixing regular familiar forms like a mobile phone call or writing a diary with an unfamiliar or current technology we have been able to use this space to create an intimacy with our audience maybe enhanced by this temporary unfamiliarity. I'll come back to this point with other project examples.

The second project I'd like to talk about was made in 1999 as a commission for the soon-to-be Tate Modern and was a one-day annual event in a short series commissioned as part of their pre-opening programme. Called /broadcast/(29 pilgrims, 29 tales), the project took Chaucer's Canterbury Tales as its inspiration or text to reinvent – we chose this text as Chaucer's fictitious pilgrims departed from the Tabard Inn, Southwark – a stone's throw from Borough Market, the designated site for the annual event.[5] By re-approaching the idea of what a contemporary pilgrimage might be, but also, and perhaps more significantly, how a set of stories based on these journeys might be told using current 'technology', we devised the framework for the project. We then advertised for 29 modern day pilgrims who could make any journey of their choosing, secular or religious and we would support it. In return the journeys all had to be made at the same time and during a 24hr period and each pilgrim had to relay their 'tale' back to a live audience both at an installation in Borough Market and onto a webcast via mobile phone. Whilst they travelled across the UK and beyond, Karen and I 'hosted' what resembled a very long live chat show installed in the market with 29 remote guests. Footage on the webcast cut between us introducing each pilgrim then playing footage from their interview, explaining why they wanted to make their trip

3 <www.somewhere.org.uk/ hypertextjournal>.

4 <www.guardian.co.uk/netjetters>.

5 <www.somewhere.org.uk/broadcast_ intro>.

/broadcast/(29 Pilgrims, 29 Tales) 1999

and going over to a live audio stream from their various destinations overlaid with imagery we'd gathered with them prior to the journey. At their destination most pilgrims were alone delivering a personal tale via a current yet familiar technology (their mobile phone) but these stories were in turn broadcast out to a diverse audience either in the market or more unusually sitting (often alone) at home listening via their computers.

At this time webcasting was very new outside of academic experiments and much hyped occasional pop extravaganzas and this 'novelty' of the medium really inspired the experimental structure for */broadcast/* in the same way as hypertext had done for us with the journal. */broadcast/* built on what we had learnt from *A Hypertext Journal* and helped to us to really focus our ideas of how we could develop different 'circles' of audience for our work. In many ways in terms of the most 'intimate' circle of our audience the project reinvented this very idea as the pilgrims were not only in the work but, you might argue, were the work. The experience of collaborating with so many individuals on a project was both inspiring and exhausting and certainly influential on our future practice. Again, we felt as though we were working without any real precedent we could point to... we would describe it as a 'little bit like TV' a 'little bit like radio', 'quite performance based' etc, etc. All of these accurate, but only in part – using webcasting gave us a chance to reinvent for ourselves the actual scope of what we could call our practice.

If we skip forward by three years we come to the next project I want to look at, *TV swansong*, which we developed in 2002.[6] An interesting 'by product' of *A Hypertext Journal* was that we appeared in a BBC Horizon programme which looked to the possible future of TV. Called *Long Live TV, TV is Dead,* the programme tried to address what might happen to our ideas about narrative and interactivity through our TVs and (as the programme makers correctly projected) many of the influences on the structure of TV would come from the web.[7] At the time we had no interest in their agenda, but in retrospect, and particularly in relation to our later project *TV swansong*, the facts that we were trying to reinvent our own practice and they were trying to reinvent TV were not completely unrelated. In many ways, when we came to make *TV swansong*, we had more idea of what we might be getting into than on previous occasions. Webcasting was now at a point where it was much more 'available' as a technology for artists to use and viewing figures for some highly publicised events had crept up into the hundreds. On TV in the UK the Big Brother phenomena was just settling down and UK viewers were starting to get used to the idea that their cosy national Sunday night shared TV conversation maybe on the way out.

In 1996 when we made *A Hypertext Journal* lots of artists seemed to be approaching this territory and we wanted to see what it might mean for us – how might TV be changing and what might webcasting offer as a particular means of artistic production and distribution? This time we decided we'd like to approach the area with some other artists – still with the same open-ended, experimental approach but we wanted to speed up our ability to process what we'd learn from the project and we thought we might be better off doing this in collaboration with a small group of other artists whose work we were interested in. *TV swansong* looked to TV itself as an inspiration and site for reinvention but we never claimed that it (or in fact webcasting) would be the future of TV. Rather that it offered a particular window of opportunity for making work in this specific medium around a common theme. The 'brief' that we asked all the artists to respond to was to look 'at a site or situation made famous via TV' although many of the projects did seek to reinvent the artists' personal ideas of what TV or maybe more accurately broadcasting might be.

In the case of Giorgio Sadotti's *Virtual Bootleg* – a live webcast from cameras attached to ballroom dancers in Blackpool tower's magnificent ballroom – Sadotti wanted to reverse the traditional 'viewpoint' of the broadcast camera. He spoke of giving the power back to the performers who, as they danced, literally directed the cameras rather than having the cameras trained on them. Jordan Baseman's *The Last Broadcast* looked to the 1976 film *Network* and its central character Howard Beale who threatens to commit suicide on air, as its starting point. Baseman re-wrote Beale's soliloquies to be 'delivered' by an actor for the webcast looking to place the new work in the context of a very different broadcast environment. Graham Fagen's piece *Radio Roselle* again took an existing broadcast genre (in this case pirate radio) and looked to

---

6 <www.swansong.tv>.
7 <www.acmi.net.au/aic/baird_chitty.
   html>.

how this might be transformed through the webcast. His DJ, *The Owner of Broadcasting,* played a set from the 'good ship Roselle' anchored mid way between Scotland and Jamaica. The set comprised of alternate records of Robbie Burns and Jamaican Reggae and with each new piece of music *The Owner of Broadcasting* downed another culturally appropriate drink of whisky or Red Stripe.

Chris Helson's *The Act* took a more predictive response to the brief – switching round the idea of a famous site or situation to a soon-to-be-famous place. Working with the already incredibly current medium of rolling news he proposed to travel to the location of whichever story was top of the rolling news on the day of the webcast. Interested in the 'performances' of newscasters and the ever more 'current' status of reporting, like Fagen and Sadotti he looked to reinvent the role of the author in his piece – the source of the news. Based on a BBC World News report he eventually ended up travelling to Corihuayrachina in Peru and the remains of a 'newly discovered' Inca settlement. Broadcast live via satellite phone from the top of a mountain it had taken him four days to climb, his piece for me was one of the most moving and strangely intimate webcasts or 'reports' I've ever seen. Despite the lack of dynamic 'news' (he simply showed us the view from the top of the mountain and described what had happened to him) and maybe because of the clunky technology you felt really amazed at the sheer fact he had achieved the broadcast in a way that with TV I think one rarely feels surprise about any more. His piece looked to reinvent the idea of what 'reporting' might be for him and, like much of the other work in *TV swansong*, it reflected both an old and yet currently very volatile type of storytelling.

After a recent talk I gave about *TV Swansong*, a student commented that many of the pieces in the project (despite its overall technical and contemporary 'theme' and delivery medium) look to a pre-television era for inspiration – to 'light' or even 'home-grown' entertainment. I thought this was an insightful observation and in relation to the idea of reinvention particularly pertinent. Often we find that to try and reinvent our own practice (never mind anything outside of that) we have to look beyond old or new technology and to popular forms of story telling or entertainment, forms which are always in a constant process of reinventing themselves.

Seven Reinventions
Paul Ramírez Jonas

Artists are always trying to replicate objects and situations that have already taken place. We often try to give permanent form to ephemeral acts, through automation, representation, and repetition. It might have something to do with a fear of death and dissipation. Trying to take a temporal process and making it permanent reveals a tremendous amount of anxiety with regard to death. The most extreme case of this condition might be Wim Delvoye's piece entitled *Cloaca* (2000). The artist succeeded in taking our digestive process and turning it into a sculpture machine that has to be fed twice a day and that defecates in equal measure. The machine's excrement is chemically indistinguishable from ours. *Cloaca* is the ultimate automaton, replicating our most basic functions: consumption and elimination. And in turn, *Cloaca* is but the reinvention of *Merda D'artista* (1961) by Manzoni. And *Merda D'artista* is but the continuation of Duchamp's *Fountain*. In the game of art (history), we are always copying and repeating things that have been forgotten or ignored. It is not too different from the technological world. My own work has precedents. My reinvention strategy is but a reinvention of other reinventing artists, Chris Burden, for example, who made pieces that recreated famous experiments such as the proof of the speed of light.

Location	Time to Sunrise
Satuimalufilufi	00:42:18
Baker Island	00:43:18
Beru Atoll	01:14:17
Uluinggalau	01:16:17
Enajet	01:22:17
La Roche	02:11:17
Oroluk	02:24:17
Poum	02:25:17
Honiara	02:28:17

Another Day 2002

Another Day
In 2002, I completed a work called *Another Day*. The piece mimics the arrival and departure video displays found in airports and train stations. Three monitors display the names of 'destinations' on the right and a time for each on the left. The sculpture tracks the time left before the sun rises in 90 cities around the world. The chosen cities are evenly spaced along every fourth meridian. The displays count down the time left to the next sunrise – with the next location having a sunrise at the top of the list and the last one at the bottom.

When the sun 'arrives' to the top city/location, in other words, when the countdown for the city in the top row reaches zero, after a short pause, and just like at the train station, that city name is erased. At this time, all the destinations move up one row to fill the empty top row and a new city name appears at the bottom. The arrival of new days is relentless.

Depending on your attitudes towards the future, this piece can be either optimistic or pessimistic. The piece itself remains neutral. It is cruel, pragmatic and utilitarian. All it states, for example, is that in a few minutes the sun will rise in Greenwich, located at degree 0, and a few minutes later in Toledo at –4º, then Marrakush –8º, and moving further west:

-4°	TOLEDO		176°	BERU ATOLL
-8°	MARRAKUSH		172°	ENAJET
-12°	FONGOLEMBI		168°	LA ROCHE
-16°	ADEANE		164°	POUM
-20°	DANEBORG		160°	HONIARA
-24°	PATREKSFJOROUR		156°	OROLUK
-28°	SANTA CRUZ DA GRACIOSA		152°	KUOP ATOLL
-32°	KAP EDUARD HOLM		148°	TUMBA RUMBA
-36°	CARUARU		144°	LALIBU
-40°	ITAJI		140°	FUNABASHI
-44°	BELO HORIZONTE		136°	UTA
-48°	TAGUATINGA		132°	TEMINABUAN
-52°	VITORIA		128°	WONJU
-56°	MONTEVIDEO		124°	MOLIGABU
-60°	MANAUS		120°	CHANGZHOU
-64°	MONTEAGUDO		116°	SILKA
-68°	VALENCIA		112°	KEDIRI
-72°	CUZCO		108°	KON TUM
-76°	CANAS GORDAS		104°	SINGAPORE
-80°	ROANOKE		100°	NAKHON SI THAMMARAT
-84°	MARYVILLE		96°	MANDALAY
-88°	SAN PEDRO SULA		92°	BAJAN HOSUU
-92°	LAFAYETTE		88°	DHULIAN
-96°	TULSA		84°	SAMBALPUR
-100°	SAN JUAN DEL RIO		80°	JABALPUR
-104°	MARFA		76°	KASHI
-108°	ASCENSION		72°	KUVASAJ
-112°	PHOENIX		68°	AHTAKOR
-116°	TWENTY NINE PALMS		64°	SEVERNYJ
-120°	LAKE TAHOE		60°	NIZNIJTAGIL
-124°	RIVER JORDAN		56°	RAMKAN
-128°	KITAWANGA		52°	ATYRAU
-132°	ALLIFORD BAY		48°	AL KUWAIT
-136°	TENARUNGA		44°	TA IZZ
-140°	HAKAHAU		40°	KARAKOCAN
-144°	CIRCLE		36°	OREL
-148°	TIKEHAU		32°	SMOLENSK
-152°	MAUPITI		28°	JOHANNESBURG
-156°	KANATAK		24°	TUBRUQ
-160°	JARVIS ISLAND		20°	KRAKOW
-164°	UNIMAK		16°	TOLE
-168°	WALES		12°	GOTEBORG
-172°	SATUIMALUFILUFI		8°	AGADEZ
-176°	BAKER ISLAND		4°	TIBIRI
-180°	ULUINGGALAU			

There is another day always waiting to come out – it is another day ad nauseum. On one side there is future, future, and more future, and on the other side there is past, past, past. Time is just decanting from one side to the other. If you believe that the world is getting better and believe in progress, then all these sunrises mean something different than if you believe that it is just one thing after another, neither better nor worse.

The actual order of the sunrises is dictated by several factors. In this previous example I just listed cities in their geographical order. In reality, the piece uses an algorithm that takes into account latitude, longitude, date and year.

A Better Yesterday

I was asked to make a piece in the city of Utrecht, Holland. There is a church tower there that stands in the center of town. At the time of its construction it was the tallest structure in Christendom. The building provoked a debate in town as to whether the tower was being built for the glory of god or the city's. The debate made repeated references to the myth of Babel and its lessons.

Precedents:

> The ziggurat. European ideas of what the biblical tower of Babel might have looked like were based on the ziggurat.
> The Tower of Babel. This was a technological object that might have outdone God. God punished humans by making us speak different languages (the punishment endures, as specialized languages and technical jargon continue to multiply).
> *Monument to the Third International* (1919–20). During the Russian revolution people like the artist Vladimir Tatlin thought that since God was dead, man would be able to build the tower of Babel. No longer an act of hubris, this would be a triumphal act. Tatlin's design for the Monument intentionally references the shape of a ziggurat.
> The Utrecht tower is an enormous musical automaton. A clock dictates the playing of the carillon every hour on the hour. The carillon is automated and new tunes can and are programmed frequently.
> Utrecht has one of the best collections of musical automatons in the world; the museum is situated near the base of the church tower.
> Tatlin conceived of the *Monument to the Third International* as an automaton. In the first level, the soviet congress hall would rotate at a rate of once per year. The second level would house the executive chambers, and would rotate once a month. In some versions, the top level would contain a radio station and newspaper that would rotate once a day. Like a church tower, the top of the tower is broadcasting; but instead of religious melodies, the tower would disseminate secular ideas.
> Tatlin's tower can be seen as a response to Gustave Eiffel's tower, which embodies both republican, and implicitly capitalist values.
> Bicycles are a popular means of transportation in Utrecht.
> Utrecht has a tradition of ambulant musical automatons. Thus, a static giant automaton dominates the center of town, while around it small moving automatons meander through the city.

All this lead to an object that referenced both the tower of Babel and its ziggurat shape, and Tatlin's tower with its slanted double helix. The piece was a bicycle (actually a tricycle). It was also an organ with drums. It was a musical automaton that played music every hour on the hour. Its melody began as the religious tune of the church ended. It was a secular response made up of the intertwining of *The Internationale* and *It's a small world after all*. Capitalism and socialism merged into one melody.

It's a small world / L'Internationale

Arise ye workers from your slumber
Arise ye prisoners of want
It's a world of laughter
A world of tears
It's a world of hopes
and a world of fears
There's so much that we share
Arise ye workers from your slumber
That it's time we're aware
It's a small world after all
Arise ye workers from your slumber
Arise ye prisoners of want
It's a small world after all
For reason in revolt now thunders
It's a small world after all
And at last ends the age of can't
It's a small, small world
Away with all your superstitions
Servile masses arise! arise!
We'll change henceforth the old tradition
Though the mountains divide
And the oceans are wide
And spurn the dust to win the prize
It's a small world after all
So comrades come rally
And the last fight let us face
There is just one Moon
And one golden Sun
And a smile means
Friendship to ev'ry one
The Internationale unites the human race
There's so much that we share
That it's time we're aware
Arise ye workers from your...
Small world after all
Arise ye workers from your...
Small world after all
Arise ye workers from your slumber
Small world after all

Meanwhile, the cityscape was turned into the face of a clock. The 12 hours were painted on pavements, buildings and awnings forming a circle around the city. 12 was due north, 6 was south, 3 was east, etc, etc. The bell tower was at the center of the circle, allowing the viewing of the hours from its viewing deck. Every hour, the tricycle moved and parked on top of the number corresponding to the upcoming hour. On the hour, the cathedral's bell tower chimed in the hours and played a religious song. The tricycle organ responded with its secular tune. For example, at a few minutes before noon the tricycle would park on top of the number 12. At 12 the bell tower chimed and the tricycle responded. The tricycle acted as the hour hand of a giant clock and it circumnavigated the city in 12 hour cycles. The tricycle became a clock within a clock, a loop within a loop, a moon orbiting a planet orbiting around a sun.

The automaton is an interesting object. The automaton performs better than we can even with no one present, it remembers, it plays the music, and sounds the wake up call.

Men on the Moon

Since 1990, I have been casting wax records that I record onto with my homemade replica of Edison's first recording machine. My reproduction was based on Edison's initial drawings. I sought to re-enact the moment of discovery, not to improve on it, but to stop as soon as I was able to record sound. After several tries I succeeded in recording onto the handmade cylinders.

Men on the Moon, Tranquility 1990–

Trapped as I was in a reinvention game, failure was not an option – I knew that what I was trying to do was possible, as it had already taken place. Since then, I have been re-recording the audio communications of the 23 hours men spent on the Moon during their first mission on July 20 and July 21, 1969. Each wax record can hold up to 60 seconds of sound. Each cylinder is indexed to the second and its contents are transcribed onto a 'lyric' book. Some of the recording contains static and silence.

July 20 1969 11 PM E.S.T

00:01	LMP	Okay. Don't hold it quite so tight.
00:02	CDR	Okay.
00:17	CDR	Looking up at the LM, I'm standing directly in the shadow now looking up at Buzz in the window. And I can see everything quite clearly. The light is sufficiently bright, backlighted into the front of the LM, that everything is very clearly visible.
00:55	LMP (TRANQ)	Okay. I'm going to be changing the ***
00:58	CDR (TRANQ)	Okay.
02:23	CDR (TRANQ)	The camera is installed on the RCU bracket, and I'm storing the LEC on the secondary strut.
02:53	CDR (TRANQ)	I'll step out and take some of my first pictures here.
03:05	CC	Roger. Neil, we're reading you loud and clear. We see you getting some pictures and the contingency sample.
04:19	CC	Neil, this is Houston. Did you copy about the contingency sample? Over.
04:26	CDR (TRANQ)	Roger. I'm going to get to that just as soon as I finish these picture series.
05:25	LMP (TRANQ)	Okay. Going to get the contingency sample there, Neil.
05:27	CDR (TRANQ)	Right.
05:30	LMP (TRANQ)	Okay. That's good.
05:58	LMP (TRANQ)	Okay. The contingency sample is down and it's ***. Looks like it's a little difficult to dig through the initial crust.
06:12	CDR (TRANQ)	This is very interesting. It's a very soft surface, but here and there where I plug with the contingency sample collector, I run into a very hard surface, but it appears to be very cohesive material of the same sort. I'll try to get a rock in here. Just a couple.
06:54	LMP (TRANQ)	That looks beautiful from here, Neil.

This is a story that was put into an object. It is a monument that keeps the story safe, but can store it but for one retrieval. For the player and the recorder are one, and at the moment of playing back you would record over what you are listening to. In fact, you would record yourself listening to the story.

Ghost of Progress
In this video piece, the future appears as a nostalgic symbol and the present as a place where progress is an uncertain direction. The video was shot from a camera mounted on the handlebar of my bike as I traversed a city in the Third World. At the opposite end of the handlebar was a scale model of the Concorde. The resulting video gave the crude illusion that the plane was flying through the city. The artifice is always evident, the sound of the pedaling is constantly present, and the discrepancy in scale is unavoidable. The utopian hopes, and ultimate commercial realities embodied by the Concorde were juxtaposed against a background of street commerce, stores, new and old cars, public transport, noise, decaying historic buildings, smog, aging modern buildings, dirt, and people going about their daily life. The future personified by the Concorde is a future that is already obsolete. And yet in many parts of the world we cling to that future, without any real belief in it, perhaps out of ritual.

Ghost of Progress 2002

Tatlin (again)

Tatlin's *Monument to the Third International* was never built. It existed and continues to exist as a latent building. In that sense, it resides permanently in the future. Perhaps that is why so many artists have attempted to remake the model, the suggestion, yet no one's ever attempted to build the actuality – that would negate its strength. Tatlin's next project was a flying machine. Curiously, planes already existed at the time. There was airmail, air travel, plane factories, etc. In contrast, Tatlin wanted his plane to be powered, like a bicycle, by the human body. Thus, the wide use of his flying machine would have resulted in extremely fit citizens, as well as in providing the people with incredible freedom and mobility. It is not altogether clear if his was an artistic gesture, a utopian suggestion, or a mad attempt at realization. His remains an interesting object, trapped between being a model and a reality, a work of art and a functional object. It never flew and found its final resting place in a museum.

Heavier than Air

Between 1993 and 1994 I re-built kites that were used in the early 20th century to prototype flying machines. I limited myself to inventors that failed to invent the airplane but managed to make heavier than air flights. Each of my remakes was equipped with a camera. During flight, the camera took a picture of the tether leading back to my hands. The resulting photographs document the ability of these objects to fly, as well as my performance. Since the laws of physics appear to be immutable, an object that flew a 100 years ago can fly just as well as it did back then. Such an object can be resurrected and used to re-tell an overbearingly male history from an emasculated point of view. This would be the point of view of the failed, the forgotten, and the ones who did not quite get it up. The announcement card for this project was a reproduction of a photograph taken by a U2 spy plane. The photograph revealed that the soviets were placing nuclear missiles in Cuba.

Radial Winged Kite, after Alexander Graham Bell 1994

Rocinante

Not everyone can put cameras in space. Therefore, I made a little spacecraft called *Rocinante* (Rocinante is Don Quixote's old run down mare, which he of course saw as a glorious stallion). *Rocinante* is a musical automaton that pretends to be a satellite. It is being proposed as the first object to be put in orbit on behalf of countries without a space program. The flags of all those countries are painted on its body.

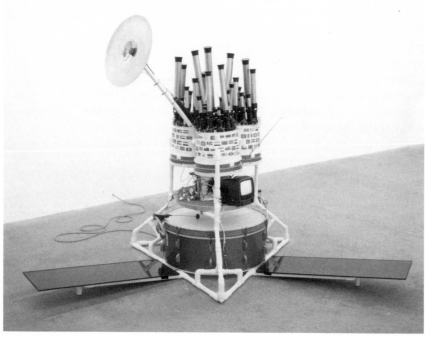

Rocinante 2003

Because of severe budgetary constraints and overall lack of know how the satellite's only function will be to play a mixture of *L'internationale* and *Small World After All*. Although the craft is musically functional it still lacks a proper launch vehicle. Please note that the small television screen on its side displays the countdown to the next launch. Once *Rocinante* begins to play, the screen flashes the lyrics of the song. 4, 3, 2, 1, 0, sing along:

It's a small world / L'Internationale (reprise)

Arise ye workers from your slumber
Arise ye prisoners of want
It's a world of laughter
A world of tears
It's a world of hopes
and a world of fears
There's so much that we share
Arise ye workers from your slumber
That it's time we're aware
It's a small world after all
Arise ye workers from your slumber
Arise ye prisoners of want
It's a small world after all
For reason in revolt now thunders
It's a small world after all
And at last ends the age of can't
It's a small, small world
Away with all your superstitions
Servile masses arise! arise!
We'll change henceforth the old tradition
Though the mountains divide
And the oceans are wide
And spurn the dust to win the prize
It's a small world after all
So comrades come rally
And the last fight let us face
There is just one Moon
And one golden Sun
And a smile means
Friendship to ev'ry one
The Internationale unites the human race
There's so much that we share
That it's time we're aware
Arise ye workers from your...
Small world after all
Arise ye workers from your...
Small world after all
Arise ye workers from your slumber
Small world after all

Reinvention: Music, Turntables and Pinball Machines
Jem Finer

Once you start looking for reinvention you see it everywhere. One could say that we are born as reinventors. If you watch a child at play no object has a fixed meaning and purpose. A box for example could be endlessly reinvented – as a house, as a hat, as a pet. Within playfulness I would identify two other elements that are the basis for a more rigorous reexamination of the world, experimentation and curiosity (with often a touch of necessity) and it is through the prism of these two facets that I am going to look at reinvention.

disobey the manual

The idea of *disobey the manual* was to collect together examples of music made through the abuse and reinvention of existing instruments, notation and technology for a radio programme broadcast in May 2002 on Resonance 104.4fm.[1] The problem was not where to find them but what not to include. The history of 20th century music is one in which experimentation grows hand in hand with the emergence of new technologies, notably electronics and the computer, and extends across the whole broad sweep of creating music from compositional forms and tuning systems through to instruments and equipment. Whole genres of music that have come to permeate music the world over have sprung from the simple act of not taking pieces of equipment at face value. To take a couple of well documented examples:

> Drum machine technology was originally developed by organ companies in order to be able to produce home music machines that could make the music of an entire band. When programmable stand-alone drum machines started to be produced they began to be used by Chicago DJs and house music was born.
> Turntables and records have a long history of transcending their original function, to simply play back a record. In the middle of the last century John Cage used records of test tones played back at variable speeds as instruments, he used cartridges of records to play objects other than records. By the end of the 1970s turntables 'misused' in the Bronx spawned hip hop, while Christian Marclay was starting to use multiple turntables and to create his first sonic collages.

Taking the example of turntables to the present day, their structure is being modified in diverse ways. Janek Schaeffer[2] builds multi arm turntables that will play a record at multiple points, Calum Stirling's *Longplayer* (2000) is a turntable system that can play – and cut – records up to 53cm in diameter.[3] Another *Longplayer*, my own thousand year long composition,[4] takes inspiration from both of these developments and merges them together as the basis for one possible means of it surviving.

Longplayer Trinity Buoy Wharf, London, December 1999

Longplayer

In the autumn of 1995 I began to work on composing *Longplayer*. The idea to make something one thousand years long, and deciding to realize it as a piece of music, gave rise to several questions. The first, and seemingly most pressing question, was how to compose it, but this was to be further complicated by the question of how to keep it playing for the duration of its performance.

Initially I concentrated on the 'composition'. I write this word in inverted commas because it could never be composition in any traditional sense of the word. Consider writing it as notes on sheets of manuscript paper. Even at the rate of one sheet of paper per day the score would stretch to 365,243 pages. Some way had to be discovered not only to somehow grow the score, to reorganize the organization of sonic events, but also to allow the sounds themselves to have evolutionary characteristics, to somehow resynthesise themselves. So I began to explore ways of using various systems to allow the composition to emerge from their application. I borrowed ideas from Artificial Life and Chaos Theory: cellular automata, genetic algorithms, swarming, equations... and mapped their results onto musical parameters, notably pitch, duration and touch.

1   Resonance is an art radio station run by the London Musicians Collective, <www.resonancefm.com>. The playlist included:
Jukebox Capriccio, Christian Marclay, multiple turntable and record abuse.
Ruglen Holen, Aphex Twin, prepared piano.
Study #51, Conlon Nancarrow, impossible piano compositions realized on the player piano.
Version 78 Style, Glen Brown and King Tubby, recording studio as instrument, de/reconstruction of existing recording.
Bonobo Beach, Hans Reichel, guitar built with a bride each end.
And on the Seventh Day, Petals Fell in Petaluma, Harry Partch, handmade instruments made from found objects playing a composition composed using Partch's 43-tone scale.
Naiades, Jacque Dudon, converting light into sound.
Eloj du Piqueupe, Pierre Bastien, invented mechanical instruments and turntable abuse.
Store Cheque, Oval, cd abuse.
Hafen, Pole, sound processed through broken equipment.
Babbachichuija, Tom Waits, creaking door machinery.
2   <www.audioh.com/>.
3   <www.calum.clara.net/longplayer/player.html>.
4   <www.longplayer.org>.

Eventually I ended up with a system that took an existing recording as raw material and created a new one thousand year long version. This system works by simultaneously taking six sections from the raw material and playing them all together, while changing the playback rate of five of these sections, so that all six sections are playing at different pitches. Rules as to where and when to play these sections work in such a way that no combination ever repeats until exactly one thousand years have passed – at which time the composition returns to the point at which it first started.

This was all well and good as long as the computer was the means of playing the music. As a means of realistically keeping the music playing though, the computer was not the best bet. For one thing computer technology is always evolving. The mortality of the computer means replacing machines every time one dies. New processors and new operating systems may necessitate rewriting the program.

Even adopting the strategy of space programs and 'freezing' technology doesn't get around the mortality problem – and what if there's no one around to buy a new computer.[5] *Longplayer* has been playing for less than three years and I have already had to contend with screen burn out on one computer and the arrival of a brand new operating system that has meant rewriting the program. The best strategy seemed to be making *Longplayer* in a form that could last as long as possible without attention and suggest by its simplicity and design how to get it going again.[6] Not a computer then, but something mechanical or played by humans. At the very least if the music was going to start its life being played by a computer it had to be composed in a form that would allow it to be transferable to other technologies.

The problem posed by the initial version of *Longplayer* was not the system but the question of how to deal with the source material. The system was, in essence, an emulation of a physical system. It can be imagined in the form of multiple record players playing copies of the same record, each at a different speed. Theoretically then it could exist in such a form – six record players modified to implement the rules of the system through lifting and lowering their arms, playing copies of the same record, the raw material.

The question then was what if one wanted to make it in some other mechanical form, how would one store the source music. Initially I was using old recordings – the first being *Over the Rainbow* sung by Judy Garland. No problem to store this in digital form or on vinyl but what if one wanted to make a machine that played the music in some other way. In this form it's still tied down – to either the computer or the record player. Of course one could make a machine that recreated the lush score of *Over the Rainbow*. Musical automata of extraordinary complexity exist, playing all manner of instruments, but one has to question how long they would last. The answer has to be, 'not very long'. The amount of maintenance and upkeep is enormous; let alone the considerations of tuning. This then leads to the question as to what mechanical means of storing music there are. Might there be some way of storing music mechanically in a digital form?

I pondered this question for a while and then a very obvious answer suggested itself to me – the player piano. Here a piece of music is stored by splitting it into two parts, the score and the sounds to be played and the instrument itself. The score is stored as binary information, holes punched into a roll which when fed over a mechanism attached to the piano plays the appropriate notes at the appropriate time. A hole means play the note, the absence of a hole means don't. This elegant scheme gave birth to the notion of modifying the roll mechanism to emulate the system described above and having six such player pianos, one for each copy of the source music. It also changed the way of thinking about the source music. This new approach called for a simplifying of the source music itself. The demands of reproducing an orchestra on any scale were unrealistic. The player piano model suggested simplifying the source music to a piano piece. This led to a period of experimentation from which it soon became clear that a piano was still too complicated. Strings break, they go out of tune.

In the end I landed on the idea of using Tibetan Singing Bowls. These hand held bell like instruments are extremely strong and eliminate tuning problems. Furthermore, the nature of their sound being sinusoidal lends to a form of synthesis. Played together one doesn't always hear them as individual sound sources, rather they combine together to produce new timbres. The solution then was to use a system analogous to six turntables playing copies of the same record, with the source music being made from Tibetan Singing Bowls. This is then no longer dependant on any single technology.

I've recently started to think again about going back to the idea of using turntables and records to make a *Longplayer* machine. Janek Schaeffer and his multi armed turntables suggest a way to get around one limitation of a conventional turntable. In the system each time the point at which one begins to play a segment of the source music is updated, there is no gap in time between the end of one segment and the beginning of the next. If one has a turntable with only one arm though there is a problem. There will be a gap in time as one picks up the needle and replaces it at the next start point. However, this is easily solved by having two arms on a turntable, one in the conventional position, in the top right hand corner, and the other in the bottom left hand corner, diametrically opposite. As one is playing the other can move to the next start point hovering above the spinning vinyl. At the appropriate moment this one gently lowers itself into the groove while the other lifts off – no gap.

---

5   Consider sending a probe into deep space. It's not realistic to run down the shops and upgrade the computer systems while the probe is on a voyage that might last for tens - or even hundreds - of years. The simple way round this is to adopt a working computer reliable system and stick with it, 'freeze' it.

6   Danny Hillis's design for the *Clock of the Long Now* was very informative and inspirational in this regard. <www.longnow.org>.

That problem solved there is one other pressing difficulty: the gearing to make the arms move to the right places on the record. The design of the gearing is not too hard but the sizes and precision are, due to the existing dimensions of the turntable. Scaling it up though to, say, six times the size, removes this problem though creating another! How does one cut a six foot diameter record? This is where the inspiration of Calum Stirling's *Longplayer* comes in. His turntable will play and cut records just over 20 inches in diameter. The answer then is to take this approach and make it bigger.[7]

So through a long process of experimentation the turntable emerges from its already spectacular history of reinvention, with an extra arm and blown up in size to something maybe six to twelve times its original dimensions. In so doing it proves to be a possible answer as to how to play a millennium long piece of music.[8] It's interesting to note that in beginning to think about how to keep something going for a very long time, the answer, in this case, proves to be the reinvention of something already 'old'. Not to invent something totally new, not to embrace state of the art technology. And this begs the question, 'Is there too much stuff in the world?' Do we really need new things? Why can't we just use what we've got? And then, when we don't have something that does what we want, try to reinvent something to fit the role. ...*and sometimes an object just sits up and says, 'abuse me!'*...[9]

Pinball 2003, in collaboration with Franko B and Dominic Robson

Pinball

One evening at a friend's house, playing on his pinball machine I became curious to see inside it, under the playing surface. I knelt down and opened the door at the front of the machine, where money is inserted. Inside was the underside of the playing surface and all the circuitry, switches and cabling, laid out like a futuristic city, lights blinking and switches triggering, punctuated by blue sparks. I played a few games without looking at the ball and flippers, lost in the pyrotechnics inside. I became interested in possibilities of using this hidden space and started to make films of it. Gradually a thought emerged that it would be interesting to somehow change the sounds or better still, to use the machine as an instrument in its own right.

One way to do this would be to attach triggers to various points inside the machine so that when the ball hit them they could send information into a computer. Once inside the computer the information could be mapped onto any kind of output one wanted. Before long these ideas led to the formation of a three way collaboration. I would program the music side, Dominic Robson would handle the wiring side and Franko B, whose machine I'd originally become lost inside, would visually customise the machines. The finished prepared pinball table could then be used in many different situations. At its simplest it could be a one off piece in a room, alternatiely a number of machines wired into a big sound system and projecting live footage of their insides and playing surfaces, could be installed in a larger space.

We found one in *Loot*, and Dominic and I drove up to a village near Northampton one evening to buy it. It then sat for a while in his front room until it was rewired at which point I took it away to start programming it. We had triggers on the flippers, on the hole where the ball goes out of play and on a number of the objects that register a score when the ball hits them.[10] I wanted to create a framework, in software, that would allow any one to compose pieces for the machine.[11] My approach was in the first instance to keep track of the score. This means that, if one wishes, musical events can be linked to various scores or given as 'prizes'. Events could be mapped onto any combination of triggers by testing for their unique i.d.[12] From a combination of these tests and the score, rules can be created and sounds triggered from the source. This could be a sound synthesised by the software, a sample, the sound of the machine fed into the computer by a microphone and processed in some way, or any combination of the three.

In the first game I programmed, the flippers trigger a short sine wave whose frequency is chosen at random from a harmonically related collection spanning seven octaves.Each time the ball hits one of the triggers a longer sine wave is triggered, again with a frequency chosen at random from the same harmonically related collection. Each time the score for an individual ball hits a multiple of five thousand the player 'wins' an arpeggio which is made up randomly from the same notes as above. Every successive five thousand triggers not just a new arpeggio but doubles the speed at which it plays.

---

7   I'm not suggesting blatant ripping off and appropriation of other artists' ideas here. Ideally this would become a collaboration.

8   There are of course other problems to be solved like wear and tear and dust. These are being considered!

9   J.F. Sloane, *Ethos, Pathos: The Dual Poles of Existence* (San Francisco: Flower Press, 1974).

10 It quickly became obvious that this was not the best way, nor the simplest way to have proceeded. A far better plan is to put triggers on each score wheel and none on the playing surface (save for the flippers, the ball exit and entrance points and game start and game over). This way every scoring event becomes a trigger and a totally accurate score can be tallied.

11 I used the programming language SuperCollider2. <www.audiosynth.com>.

12 Each trigger sends a unique midi note into the computer.

To begin with the music is very gentle but as one racks up the score and hits more and more triggers it becomes at first more dense, chords emerging from the harmonically related tones, and then also more frantic as one wins arpeggios. Every game creates a new piece of music. For the second game, I created different banks of sounds for the flippers, the ball exit point, the rest of the triggers and for general background sounds. I loaded them up with samples from a kung fu movie. The flipper bank consisted of short impact sounds, whelps and shrieks as did the trigger bank while the rest were longer samples, some musical, some speech, some sound effects. Each hit of the flipper would choose a random sound from its bank, the triggers likewise. This time the score rules were created to generate a more complex sequence of possible combinations of sounds, gradually building up as the score increased. At the time of writing this is the point at which the project stands on the cusp of realisation.

I've talked about music, touching the surface of innovation fuelled by reinvention, by ignoring preconceptions, by experiment, by curiosity and, on occasion, no doubt by accident. I've talked about how necessity in long term planning can throw us back into looking at older technologies and reinventing them, combining different features from different things to create a new function from old ideas and technology. Lastly I've talked about a more playful reinvention in the shape of the pinball machine extending its function to become a creative force in vision and sound. This is just the tip of an iceberg. Like I said at the beginning, once you start looking for reinvention you see it everywhere.

A Personal Story of Art and Technology
Paul Granjon

In the following text, reinvention is examined throughout the development of my electronic art practice as an attitude characterised by three main aspects: 1) The construction of artefacts aiming to produce a comment on a given context. 2) A transformative use of existing resources, including discarded and recycled elements. 3) A critical approach to technological progress.

Premises

I was about 5 years old when my godfather offered me my first Lego kit, a fire engine. The toy's success lasted far beyond the Christmas holiday, unlike the Zorro outfit I received the same year. Soon after that, I started customising bicycles, the parts of which were collected from the local dumpsite (in those days, one could just walk in the site and explore at will the hills of garbage). Aged 8, I received a Meccano box set no. 5 that provided endless hours of involved toy scale engineering.

A few years later I saw a picture of a work of art involving recycled parts of technology. It was *Head of a Bull* (1938) by Picasso. Although the piece is made of bronze, it was cast from a bicycle saddle and handle bar, arranged together so as to approximate a bovine head with curly horns. Art made with bicycle parts was bound to have an effect on me at that time, and the image stuck solidly to my mind. Although, when I discovered Duchamp's *Bicycle Wheel* (1913), my pre-teen brain and taste were left largely nonplussed, probably because the piece was not a representation.

Being indecisive about my career choice, I ended up doing a Maths and Technology Baccalauréat (A-Levels), which was supposed to lead to a career as an engineer. It did not develop that way and I started a Fine-Arts course instead. Thanks to a thorough programme of lectures on contemporary visual art, I got to understand Duchamp's *Bicycle Wheel* better and learned to appreciate its radical freedom and lateral inventiveness much more than Picasso's illustrative bronze object.[1] During my foundation year I visited a retrospective show by Jean Tinguely in Geneva. The show featured a huge amount of recycled mechanical parts, including bicycle wheels and chains, integrated in a quasi-organic nonsensical world of handmade machines. I could see

---

1   "It had more to do with the idea of chance. In a way it was simply getting things to go by themselves... To help your ideas come out of your head. To see that wheel turning was very soothing, very comforting, a sort of opening of avenues on other things than material life of everyday. I enjoyed looking at it, just as I enjoy looking at the flames dancing in the fireplace...".

that the man had a fine taste for the junkyard and relate to the playful
absurdity of some of his creations.[2]

Nowadays my art practice stems from the same roots as my
childhood playtime. It involves a basic playfulness very similar to that
I felt when spending afternoons building Lego superplanes for my pet
mouse or assembling armoured cars from damaged toys and other bits.
Technology as a tool, a subject and a method is always key.

Influences and technological explorations
After making several short films about junk food, my first moving
robots appeared in *Euronutrifood* (1992), a self-produced and directed
pilot episode for a science fiction series. Two of the robots were actors
wearing costumes chiefly made of recycled aluminium printing plates,
another being a used remote-controlled toy car fitted with a cylindrical
body of the same material. Video, with its various editing and special
effects tools, was a way to bring to existence fictional worlds featuring
creatures and situations that I could not otherwise have created.

At the same time I explored in some depth the work and life of Nam
June Paik. I found the South Korean artist highly inspiring and a true
visionary. I was impressed by his relentless inventiveness and his
hands-on approach. Paik combined the technological know-how of an
engineer with the openness of the Fluxus movement, enabling him to
explore and exploit the artistic potential of contemporary technology in
a true pioneering fashion.[3] Not only was he the first video artist to own
a portable video unit (Sony Portapak, 1965), he also staged *The First
Accident of the 21st Century* (1982) where his female robot K-456 (1963)
was run over by a small Honda car at a crossroads in New York City.

Getting started with computers
In 1994, after years of squatting in friends' computers, I bought my first
machine: a Macintosh Quadra 660AV, brand new and almost cutting
edge with its 16mb of RAM and video digitising capabilities. Using
various applications for sound, image and DTP, I grew progressively
more frustrated with the virtuality of the output, the physical
limitations of what I called the screen-keyboard-mouse trilogy. I
also found the use of pre-written, high-level, specialised software
increasingly limiting. At some point I realised that the printer on my
desk was a sort of robotic device. When printing, a two way cybernetic
dialogue was taking place, producing results in the real world. I wanted
to tap into that potential, but had no idea where to start.

The BBC microcomputer
I moved from France to the UK in 1995 for professional reasons. I quickly
discovered the local Maplins electronics shop, of which there is no
French equivalent. During one of their sales I bought three outdated
magazines featuring a series of articles entitled *Practical Robotic
Techniques*. The author explained in full detail how to get control of an
electric toy car with a BBC microcomputer and some basic electronic
circuitry. It was not long before I got hold of one of these machines and

started to follow the instructions. Coming from my point of view as the end user of pre-written applications, the BBC microcomputer[4] was an invaluable eye opener on the workings of a computer. The old machine had lots going for it: an open and simple architecture, an educational vocation, the fact that it had to be programmed to get anything done. And its financial value was close to nil. The 15 year old computer offered an accessible insight into the principles governing current systems. The access was also facilitated by a large collection of educational and technical printed material.

From video to robots

My first experiments in interface techniques involved electric toys, VCRs and printers, prime materials sourced from skips and car boot sales. I devised a system of communication which allowed me to use the controlling and sensing capabilities of the BBC micro in conjunction with the massively superior audio and graphics solutions offered by the Mac. Once in control of the basics, I built machines to be used in the *2 Minutes of Experimentation and Entertainment* video series I was making at the time. Each episode described an invention from conception to demonstration, the inventions' capabilities being sometimes enhanced with video special effects. Introducing machines such as *The Cybernetic Parrot Sausage* or *The Hamburger Duplicator*, the films observed the effects of technological progress with an amused distance.

Cybernetic Parrot Sausage, video still, 1997

2   Marcel Duchamp interviewed by Arturo Schwartz in Arturo Schwartz, *The Complete Works of Marcel Duchamp*, (New York: Delano Greenidge Editions, 2000).
Billy Klüver reports a conversation he had with Jean Tinguely in 1960. They were driving to a dumpsite in Newark, looking for material to be used in *Homage to New York*, a self destructive piece for the Museum of Modern Art: "If he [Tinguely] could find a willing girl (which he admitted would be difficult), this would be a place where he would like to live. "I could, you know", he said. He would spend his days in the dump as a completely free man." In Pontus Hulten, *Tinguely-Meta*, (London: Thames and Hudson, 1975).
3   "Everybody knew - a million engineers across the world knew - that if you place a magnet close to a TV screen the image will be

distorted. That was written in every physics book... Nobody had done it. I placed a small magnet around the cathodic tube: the effect was so powerful that I lived for 4 years from this invention." Nam June Paik interviewed by Irmeline Lebeer, December 1974. In *Paik, du cheval à Christo et autres écrits*, Editions Lebeer Hossmann, 1993
Alan Packard, Maplins magazine issues #42 to 44.
4   The Acorn BBC microcomputer model A was commercialised in 1982. It was closely followed by the model B which was my interfacing machine of choice until recently. The BBC micro model B was fitted with a 6502 processor running at 2MHz, 32kb of ram, 8 colours display, and a host of interfacing possibilities including a user port, a function that is completely absent in contemporary machines.

I completed the 7th and last episode of *2 Minutes of Experimentation and Entertainment* in 1998 with *The Fluffy Tamagotchi* (1998), a fully functional robot with a real body, moving parts and physiological functions emulating the popular virtual pet.

Fluffy Tamagotchi 1998

My creature was made of disparate recycled elements, the only new parts being the fur and some of the components in the interfacing circuit. *The Fluffy Tamagotchi* raised questions about the effective worth of a virtual creature and the long term impact of 'intelligent' toys (caricaturised in the excretion function, where the machine cries until the owner cleans the sticky poo it produces once a day). The piece was a breakthrough in my practice. From then on my machines could exist in the physical world, the techniques involved being sufficiently developed for them to operate without the crutches of video effects.

Influences
Among others, two artists and a writer I researched contributed to the development of my reflection on the meaning of art with machines:

> Stelarc with his robotic prosthesis, cyborgisation and theories of the obsolete body. Stelarc's vision of post humanity is made convincing by the man's engagement and the clarity of his discourse. Unfortunately he might have been born a little too early to fully benefit from the hybridisation/enhancement of human with machines he's been advocating since the mid eighties.
> Mark Pauline, founder of Survival Research Laboratories. This group of artists working with army surpluses and other large mechanical

parts, putting together an apocalyptic world where machines with claws, fire-throwers, jet engines and other threatening elements run amok with huge noise and destruction. Pauline has a little smile when he talks about scaring the human audience with a display of barbarian machines, thus making a point about the threatening destructive potential of our technological times.[5] He also revels in the quality and power of the discarded kit he can access, mentioning the way in which military machines are becoming too fast and sophisticated for human operators to control.[6]

> Kevin Warwick and his book *March of the Machines*, a prospective essay describing from a knowledgeable scientific point of view a future where machines exterminate the redundant human race, thus becoming the next step in evolution on earth.[7] The book also provided a good insight into state of the art autonomous robotics.

Lowtech heaven

In 2000 I got in contact with Redundant Technology Initiative, a group from Sheffield. I had found one of their leaflets in a festival.[8] It featured a photograph showing a massive collection of obsolete computers, with a short impactful slogan that said "(3000) computers are discarded daily in the UK", followed by the icon of a computer cursor stuck between two options: 'Delete' or 'Recycle'. I contacted them and found out that they were an artist-led organisation collecting obsolete computing equipment from schools and businesses in order to put it to good use in the hands of artists. Thanks to their generosity, my studio was soon crammed with lots of BBC micros and many other computer related relics from the eighties. A year later they contacted me, asking if I wanted more kit. They had to move to smaller premises, and discard the older and bulkier items of their collection. I brought back a smaller, more carefully selected load than the first time, and serious thoughts about high-tech trash and related environmental issues.[9]

---

5   "How far can you play around with the power of this kind of technologies without hurting people. How much does it take before the fun of it turns into, like, just panic". Mark Pauline interviewed in the documentary film, *Pandaemonium*, directed by Richard Curson and Leslie Asako Gladsjø.

6   "The only kind of technology we can get access to... is what is at the bottom of the bucket. It's just that the bottom of the bucket now is swimming with all sorts of industrial equipment that only a few years ago was out there producing lots of [kit] for killing people very efficiently. The fact of its obsolescence leads us to possess it and manipulate it." Ibid.

7   The following extract from Kevin Warwick, *March of the Machines*, is representative of the general tone of the book: "There appears to be absolutely nothing to stop machines becoming more intelligent, particularly when we look towards an intelligent machine network. There is no proof, no evidence, no physical or biological pointers that indicate that machine intelligence cannot surpass that of humans. Indeed, it is ridiculous to think so. All the signs are that we will rapidly become merely an insignificant historical dot." See, Kevin Warwick, *March of the Machines*, (London: Century, 1997), 256.

8   ‹www.lowtech.org›.

9   The extent of the problem caused by the disposal of obsolete high-tech material is exposed in *Exporting Harm, the High-Tech Trashing of Asia*, a report prepared by The Basel Action Network (BAN) and Silicon Valley Toxics Coalition (SVC), downloadable from ‹www.svtc.org/cleancc/pubs/technotrash.htm›.

Developments

I started to work on *Toutou* and *robotHead*, two robots for live performances. *Toutou* is a singing modified toy dog, centre of a cybernetic audio visual display controlled by a BBC micro and an early Powerbook.

Toutou 1999

robotHead is a concept wearable robot that questions the extent of the delegation of human activities to machines and it is programmed to override the user's speech and motion. Once in control of the interface, the user can free up significant mental space and time by delegating routine daily tasks to the robot.[10]

robotHead 1999

The next stage was the construction of installations for a gallery context. The solo exhibition *Z Lab 2001* comprised three pieces focusing on the relation between nature and machines. The show was run by a total of 5 BBC micros. The audiences' favourite piece was *Automated Forest*, a cybernetic environment complete with photorealistic forest wallpaper, robotic birds, rustic bench and artificial day/night cycle. The show opened in the UK at the height of the foot and mouth crisis, when access to the countryside was difficult. It was of particular interest for me to observe families bringing their sandwiches for a picnic in the *Automated Forest*, somehow endorsing the simulative power of my crude robotic version of woodlands.

Robotic Bird in *Automated Forest* 2001

10 More on robotHead at <www.zprod.
    org/zLab/robotHead.html>.

View

I have now moved on to more recent technologies (microcontrollers) to control my machines.[11] I also use less toy parts and recycled motors as some of my machines must run for weeks on end in a public context. Nevertheless, my understanding of and attitude toward technology, continuous learning process and awareness of the significance of making machines in the 21st century are strongly influenced by what I learned from obsolete kit. An important aspect of such a hands-on approach is the empowerment it provides. Understanding and taking control of some tools and techniques, even at a fairly basic level, contributes to a demystification of our increasingly technology-mediated world. It also allows the artist/inventor to bring to existence ideas and constructs that not so long ago would have been the fruit of magic or at least of prohibitively expensive and inaccessible high-technology. Through both regular presentation of my machines in festivals, galleries and performances and the running of robotic workshops, I am attempting to share this positive, generative and critical position.

My work originates from an ambiguous relation of attraction and concern with the possibilities offered by contemporary science and technology. I am attracted by the possibilities offered and simultaneously concerned by what the place of the human is becoming in a hyper-technological world. My work questions the omnipresence of technological systems and objects, the ever increasing range of human activities delegated to machines and the potential helplessness that might occur in case of crisis. The reinvention involved in the work might be that of a more active, empowered, playful and down to earth attitude towards technological progress, more in touch with fundamental needs of the human being, embracing life instead of promoting doom or immortality.[12]

- -

11 In terms of *Doom*, Theodore Kaczynski, also known as the *Unabomber*, who killed 3 and injured 23 scientists and engineers in the USA between 1978 and 1995 is another revealing example. *The Unabomber Manifesto* clearly explains his dark vision of technological and social developments of contemporary society ‹www.unabombertrial.com/manifesto›.

12 On the other hand, many technologists and other visionaries are looking forward to a future where they will merge their minds with an artificial intelligence (the Singularitarians, at ‹www.yudkowsky.net/sing/principles.html›, want to do just that in order to save the world and live forever), or solve the problem of ageing and mortality by transferring the content of their brain onto a machine (Hans Moravec from the Robotic Institute at Carnegie Mellon University goes into the details of such a transfer in his book *Mind Children, the Future of Robot and Human Intelligence*, (Harvard University Press, 1990).

The Modified Toy Orchestra
Brian Duffy

When I was first invited to talk about reinvention I wondered 'why me?' It's not as if I'm an expert in reinvention – my own work is more about re-purposing, enabling an audience to look at something familiar in a new way. But the more I thought about it, the more I came to realise that this is exactly what happens if you strive to reinvent – you are trying to look at the same thing in a new way in which the process and the end result are the same phenomenon.

I work in many different fields involving sound, and one of the things that I've been doing for the last few years is called *The Modified Toy Orchestra*. As Paul Granjon has mentioned in his paper, there is an underground movement across the world of people re-purposing old technologies called 'circuit bending'. I don't really like this phrase because it sounds a bit destructive and macho. Destruction and machismo aren't things I'm particularly motivated by. I prefer to see myself as revealing hidden potential – potential which is implicitly there, but that has not been placed there by the designer.

To explain a little about this process: first of all you open up a circuited object – a toy in this case – and make sure that the toy is battery powered and not plugged into the mains supply! You explore the circuit by taking a piece of wire that has been stripped at both ends and while the toy is making a noise use it to join two points on the circuit together, two points that were never meant to be joined. Often this short-circuiting results in the toy crashing. If this happens simply removing then replacing the battery will usually bring the toy back to perfect health. It's very rare that this process causes any harm to the toy, although over the years I have managed to kill a few of them. If an effect happens while exploring the toy in this way then you simply hard wire a toggle switch between the two points and this allows you to access this new function.

One of the first things like this that I did was to make 14 modifications to a bright orange Speak & Spell toy. In 1978 Texas instruments packed human speech for the first time ever into a chip inside this design classic. Before then electronically generated human voices where incredibly complicated to produce. Vast amounts of computational power and huge computers were required. It was a technological miracle that they managed to put it into this toy. Its got a nice carrying handle and a headphone socket on the side, just in case you need to do some spelling while you're waiting at a bus stop or something like that. Any Kraftwerk fan will recognise this sound as it was used on their wonderful album *Computer World*.

Speak & Spell was a toy that I coveted as a kid. Then, five or six years ago, I bought one for a couple of pounds from a garage sale in Cornwall and I was absolutely thrilled with it. I started sampling it and using the sounds to construct drum kits and as a source of new sounds to include in the music that I was writing at the time. I became convinced that there must be a kind of voice synthesiser inside it and wondered if there was anything it could do besides generate phonemes. I was wrong. It's actually a digitised human voice, which is very different. Anyway, I opened it up and started blindly stumbling around the circuit without any knowledge of what I was actually doing, hoping to find new sounds. Friends started saying "Why on earth are you doing that? You're going to blow it up and destroy your beloved Speak & Spell, and it's the only one you've got". Luckily I found another at a market in Birmingham and thought "aha here we go, now I can really take some risks".

So I began to explore this one. I'll show you what the basic toy can do. It can say a word from a list; you can play various word games; and it can say the letters of the alphabet. People tend to think that you can write a word onto the toy and it will say it back but that is not true. It has a wonderful, but limited, set of sounds, the potentials of which I was able to reveal by circuit bending that allows the toy to produce a loop of electronic pulses. This modification produces a loop of sounds, but the interesting thing about it is that it never repeats itself. The sounds that make up the loop will be different every time. You can predict the process but not the outcome. This next modification freezes a syllable – by pressing the letter 'w' and the toy says double yoooooooooooooooooooooooooou creating a droned note.

Next along is this little brass sphere. Touching this leaks electricity off the circuit and into my body. The result of this is that the toy changes its pitch down about two semitones. If, while my finger is in contact with the brass sphere, I place my other hand on the front of the toy, where the letters are printed, then the pitch will drop another semitone. The next modification alters the pitch via a three-way switch and a potentiometer. This lets me pre-set the pitch up or down about an octave. Using these modifications together lets me access nine notes – moving my hands all over the toy produces a melody running up and down a strange scale and sounds a little like a theremin. The next modifications are to four switches on the side of the toy. The first reveals this little rhythm [the toy clicks and chirps] only when this connection has been made, do other connections become possible. The state of the circuit is changed, and this is what makes the next connection possible – and another rhythm more complex than the last. Once these two have been made, a third becomes possible etc.

I often have the feeling that I'm walking around in the dark in an alien landscape, blindly bumping into things. Sometimes I wander around a circuit for days hoping to find something. A toy will sometimes go off into this little random poem all of its own that I particularly like. You would assume that this is completely random but it's not. I've made many of these now, and you can make them sing this same poem all slightly out of phase with each other. Once, I'd watched this keyboard over about two months at a local car boot sale. It was covered in felt pen that looked like baby vomit and seeing it being rained on every week was such a shame. It was going down in price by about ten pence every week and it had gone down to twenty pence. I had once tried modifying a little Yamaha keyboard but it blew up, so I didn't go near these again for a while. But this one was a Casio.

The first thing that I do with toys in this state is to take them apart and give them a good clean. Late one night I decided that I'd explore this one, so I took it apart intending to just clean it. The case was so dirty that I had to leave it soaking in hot water, and while waiting I decided to poke around the circuit. I turned it on, and it's got a wonderful demo – *Wake Me Up Before You Go Go* by Wham. I found a connection that threw the toy into a strange chaotic state, that never repeated itself. It then produced a series of sounds, rhythms and melodic phrases that weren't in the toy to start with. You can imagine my surprise. Where was the music coming from? Where was it stored – maybe in a field of future potential or possibility? How was it being accessed? Why was it random? Who wrote it if the designer of the toy didn't put it there? Where would the music be now if the connection had not been made? Why is it now making a rhythm track that I'd have to be a genius to have intended? What's the point in me writing music if this toy is now more inventive than I could be with an instrument and my monkey hands? I made a single record using just this toy. It was a 7-inch released by Static Caravan, and included instructions on how to make the toy yourself. The irony being that you could buy the single for £3.50 or you could make it yourself for about a pound

These then are a few of the things that I use for live performances – just a small selection from the orchestra. In addition, we have the Playskool saxophone. This is controlled mainly by skin resistance and touching these brass spheres changes the pitch in several ways. This allows you to rewire its circuit using yourself as a kind of biological patch bay. Or you can patch the information/voltages between different toys. There is also the electone jazz drum, a realistic sampling keyboard that you could buy at Tandy's in the 80s. And finally this young urchin is 'hula barbie'. The springs you can see coming out of the top of her head serve two functions. The springs themselves are the body contact points for this circuit, and they also serve to hold the control switches away from her body. I built her so that she would run all over the floor bumping into things, which meant that I had to chase after her in order to play her. But I needed to be able to do this without restricting her dancing and putting the switches on springs and using the springs as the body contacts solved this. I gave her an elbow joint that now controls what sounds like a nuclear explosion, and rotating her right arm controls over all pitch, because ergonomically it seemed like the right thing to do.

At the end of his paper, Brian
performed a ten-minute set using the
toys. He began by making a series
of vocal grunts into the front panel
of the realistic keyboard, that then
spiralled off into another world, and
ended with a demonic hula dancing
Barbie doll singing "I'm a Barbie
girl, in a Barbie world, life in
plastic, it's fantastic."

Redundant Technology Initiative
James Wallbank

Introduction

In the mid 1980s I studied photography in Birmingham. One of the things I'd like to consider is the way that in that intervening time, the city of Birmingham has reinvented itself. One of themes of all the work I've been doing in the last fifteen or so years has been about cities and the urban environment – about Birmingham, about Sheffield. I moved to Sheffield in 1986. Coming back to Birmingham now I see huge changes – Birmingham used to be an industrial city – those of you who can remember the 70s will remember the awful time the city had with the destruction of the car industry and so on. Then this huge energy pushed the city forward, and the city reinvented itself as the convention capital of Europe, with the National Exhibition Centre, the expansion of the airport, the International Convention Centre and so on. This has a huge contrast with Sheffield. If you have seen Peter Cattaneo's, *The Full Monty* (1997) you'll have a sort of comic-book idea of Sheffield as a post-industrial city. The tragic thing about that rather sad film was what could the unemployed steelworkers actually do? How could they join the information economy? Well, they could take their clothes off, and that was about it. Moving straight from industrial work into... can we call it a service industry? I don't categorise stripping as a vibrant part of the information economy. But it does beg the question, 'what is value?'

Redundant Technology Initiative was founded from a very simple premise. We really wanted to get involved with 'media arts'. My friends and I saw the role of the artist not just as to make exciting, creative things, but also to help all that creativity to have a wider impact – social and economic effects. So our single decision which created the organisation was, 'We're going to get creative with technology, and we're not going to pay.' This was quite a convenient decision if you happen to be unemployed, as I was at the time.

Some science

Rather than start by showing you some artworks made by Redundant Technology Initiative, I thought we should start with some science. Here are some diagrams! First, a very simple one:

```
Value...
     ^
     |
     |
     |
     |
     |
     |
     +--------------------------> Time
```

Time goes forward. I think we can all handle this one! The vertical axis in this case is going to be about 'value' – the higher, the more.

Price

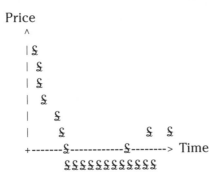

This diagram is about computers. Computers are really expensive – but they're only really expensive for a very short time – quickly the price drops off. There are adverts for the latest G5 or whatever in *Mac Format*, and if you buy one in the first three months you're regretting it weeks later as prices plummet. Prices even out a little after a couple of years as second-hand dealers start to recycle them, but very shortly it all goes horribly wrong. Second hand dealers aren't selling them any more, you can't get spares, and we get into 'the valley of valuelessness'. This is the point, possibly after only three or four years (this is your computer, remember, that you paid good money for!) that a machine is worth absolutely nothing! Or, and this is the important distinction – it costs absolutely nothing. In fact, you'll see that I've actually put the price below zero. Even though you, as an individual, may be able to realise fifty quid for your machine (by flogging it in through a small ad in the paper, perhaps) institutions that are disposing of hundreds of computers actually have to pay to have them taken away. Notice that in the far future the value starts to creep up again, although not all that much. This is the moment when the machines acquire a new value as collectables of historic interest, rather than as tools of production. That value's never going to get that high – there are huge quantities of this waste material around.

The bit that we at Redundant Technology Initiative are interested in is 'the valley of valuelessness' – the huge area (that accounts for much of a computer's lifespan) in which computers cost nothing. They aren't cool, they're not a lifestyle statement, and you can't even get any money for them second-hand. They're just nothing... or are they? This came out of my work as a trash sculptor, doing what many artists do – yank things out of skips and recreate them into some kind of artwork. The reason we focussed on computers was the fantastic potential of technology – the possibilities inherent in the machine. What we'd call 'art', would be described in network industry parlance as 'content'. The computer is the vehicle in which to move from post-industrial wasteland into the information economy. The potential for personal empowerment attracted us – surely the possibility to communicate with people all over the world for next-to-nothing is hugely valuable to people producing valuable information.

Utility
```
 ^
 | uuuuuuuu
 |      u
 |      u
 |      uuuuuuuuuuuuuuuuuuu
 |                  u
 |                  u
 +------------------------u--> Time
```

How useful is a computer? It's really useful! In physical terms a
computer will carry on being as useful as it ever was for a considerable
time. Eventually, perhaps after five or six years, you'll get a major
component failure – usually the CD-ROM drive stops working, which
significantly reduces its utility. But then again, one of the things we've
found is that they just carry on. They keep going for ages before there's
a critical component failure, perhaps the motherboard goes wrong, and
it really doesn't work any more. That's all very well, but physical utility
isn't the same thing as practical value, or real-world usefulness. I guess
a computer which has had a critical component failure can still be used
as a step to reach a high shelf, and there may be many other uses for
computers that the manufacturers' certainly didn't intend.

Chance of Failure
```
 ^
 | f                    f
 | f                  f
 | f                  f
 | f                  f
 |  f                f
 |    fffffffffffffffff
 +------------------------*--> Time
```
(Bathtub Curve)

This is a bathtub curve. It's about the likelihood that something in
a computer will go wrong. In fact, when you first get a computer it's
actually quite likely that something will go wrong. Perhaps you have
experienced this yourself – you buy a new computer, and you might
well be sending it back to the manufacturer within a week, or a month.
But after about three to four months you're really pretty safe. Once you
know you've got a good one the chances of a component failure are
really low, and if you treat it well, the flat bottom of the bathtub will go
on, and on. But then, time, age and decay set in, and it becomes more
likely that something will go wrong. Then, quite quickly, you'll get to
a point where they're very unreliable indeed. The computer that I'm
using for this presentation is about six years old, safely on the bottom
of the bathtub, lurking like some kind of ghastly spider. However, we
still have the question of practical, real-world utility to deal with.

Practical, Real-World Utility

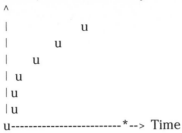

```
^
|                    u
|             u
|       u
| u
|u
|u
u------------------------*--> Time
```

When you first get a computer, it's pretty useless. In minute one, it's still in the box. And even when you unwrap it, you know the situation, you get it on your desk, and you can't do all the things you were just doing – you haven't configured your email, you don't have your data, which is still on your old computer, and you're not sure how to use it. Quite quickly you orientate yourself and the machine becomes pretty useful. But the machine becomes more practically useful the more you know about it. And in theory, this upward gradient of practical usefulness can go up, and up, and up. Now have a think about the shape of these curves compared with the first curve we saw, the one about the falling price of computers. Look at the difference:

```
u = practical, real-world utility
£ = price
    ^                    u
   |£                u
   | £         u
   | £   u
   | u£
   |u    £
   |u    £            £   £
   u-------£-----------£--------> Time
          £££££££££££
```

There's a huge area of opportunity opening up – in which computers cost far, far less than their real-world utility – and the bounds of this territory are getting larger and larger as computers become more and more powerful. This new, and expanding, continent of opportunity is the landscape which Redundant Technology Initiative is exploring.

You can argue that in fact, the real world utility curve looks more like this:

```
u = practical, real-world utility
£ = price
    ^
  | £                    u
  | £        u      u    u
  | £   u    u   u          u
  | u£       u             u
  |u    £                  u
  |u    £                    £   £
  u-------£------------£--------> Time
          £££££££££££
```

A shape that quite neatly and, perhaps appropriately, makes a factory. The first drop-off would indicate a component failure, perhaps the CD-ROM drive failing. The moment when the utility curve comes up to meet the level of that peak again might be, for example, the moment that you've worked out how to load software across a network, making the presence of a CD-ROM drive much less necessary.

```
u = practical, real-world utility
£ = price
    ^
  | £                    u
  | £        u       uXXXXXu
  | £   uXXXXu    uXXXXXXXXXXu
  | u£XXXXXXXXuXXXXXXXXXXXXXXXu
  |u    £XXXXXXXXXXXXXXXXXXXXu
  |u    £XXXXXXXXXXXXXXXXXXX£  £
  u-------£XXXXXXXXXXXXX£--------> Time
          £££££££££££
```

In effect, the area we're interested in is huge, and the vertical scale of power and utility is getting larger almost daily. We haven't even talked about hardware repairs (which can make the territory even larger) and, with a strategy in place to acquire free IT on an ongoing basis; every failing computer can be replaced with a newer model that's much more powerful. Currently we're finding that it's possible for us to replace computers with more powerful models acquired for nothing after only twelve to eighteen months – even before the first major component failure!

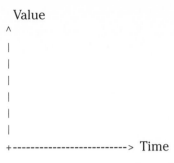

Value

+-------------------------> Time

I haven't filled in this diagram – which is the nub of the matter
– because I'm not sure where the lines should go. What's the
actual VALUE of computer technology over time? We can establish
quantitative things, like practical utility, price and the user learning
to do new tasks. We can understand and quantify these things – but
what about the 'overall value' to the user on a personal level to the
economy and to the health and diversity of culture and society? In the
end that value is much more to do with the user than it is to do with
the computer. If you have the expertise and the technology and the
opportunity to communicate all over the world, the real question is,
'Have you got anything to say?' Similarly, if you have an old computer
that all the PC mags are telling you really have to upgrade, because
it's totally useless, then as an artist – filled with 'content', filled with
things to say, filled with ideas – can you not play with this value
curve? Can you not push it upwards, using the powers of imagination
and creativity, into all sorts of areas that make a total nonsense of
the concept 'valley of valuelessness'? This was what Redundant
Technology Initiative set out to do. Our methodology was very
straightforward: we asked people to give us their old PCs – the stuff
that was really rubbish that they couldn't find anything useful to do
with – by saying that we could do something with it.

Redundant Array
The first major installation the group did was *Redundant Array* (1998)
made with the help of artists Paul Matosic and John Denaro, and a
number of students. Essentially, it's a process artwork. The previous
year we had a small exhibition which generated some publicity. During
that show we were given about 200 PCs. More publicity followed,
and four months later we had 600 PCs! The phone was ringing about
five times a day, with people saying, "Please, please, come and take
this stuff away!" What we did was to recruit some 'IT Installation and
Maintenance' students from a local technology training centre. We
asked them to fix the machines, as part of a work placement scheme
– so they were getting value out of the fact that many of the machines
didn't work, they were all of different specifications, and didn't have
manuals. These things which might have been problems actually
added value, if you're learning about computers. An added advantage
was that, if they accidentally broke them, then there were plenty more
where they came from. Essentially what we did was to challenge the

idea that if a machine doesn't work as a computer, as the manufacturer says you have to use it, you can't use it in a communicative manner. As the students ripped these machines apart, tried to work out what was going on inside them, and sort them out, if a machine worked, we reprogrammed it to show these 'X's.

Redundant Array 1998

X was the letter that was written on many of these computers – a kiss of death. People have a lot of respect for computers, until the moment when they get really bored with them, at which point they want to deface them with marker pen. Or is 'X' ten? Or is it Christ, as in X-mas? Or is it a vote? Or Factor X? Formula X? Doctor X from Planet X? X is the unknown factor. This unknown factor of value, of whatever that creative thing is that makes reinvention possible. I'm struggling to articulate what this 'mystery value' is, but I put it to you that it's about creativity, it's about imagination, it's about art, and it's enormously hard to pin down. So we had this rippling X-wall, of functioning computers, but meanwhile, anything that didn't make the cut (the computers that we couldn't repair) was disassembled and laid out in a plane, forming a science fiction landscape of microtechnology.

The whole thing has become part of a larger 'art process'. If you like, you can simply understand the installation as a self-contained artwork in itself – but you can also see a larger artwork in progress, continually changing and evolving. The installation itself started to have interesting social and economic effects. Not only did the students who came for a crash course in brain surgery suddenly became significantly more employable, and were a lot more excited by technology, but also, because people saw this picture, they, too, became excited with the process, and started giving us more and more computers. It actually became ludicrous quite quickly – at this stage we had only one warehouse – three months later we had to move into a complex of underground store rooms in order to store the stuff we were being given. This point, in mid 1998, was the point at which we realised that our deficit was not, as we'd initially thought, a deficit of access to technology, the opportunity to get involved with this empowering medium... It wasn't even access to skills... Our true deficit was 'factor X', creativity or, indeed, invention.

It's all very well to be inventive with lots of computers (there are about 200 machines in this artwork) but you can't do that more than once a year, and people are going to get bored fairly soon. Maybe we could devise new and creative ways to use fifty or sixty new machines a year, and we tried pretty hard, but how could we use five or six hundred machines per year? As an arts group we had the awful realisation that we just weren't creative enough.

Landfill
We got desperate, and tried crushing up the machines that we were unable to revive. This artwork, *Landfill* (1999), represents just that.

Landfill 1999

It's created in four glazed panels, each with panes of laminated glass held about 7 centimetres apart. Each one holds about 200 kilograms of crushed technology. This was a desperate statement – could we find any more intelligent purpose for these machines, or did we have to simply smash them to pieces to keep pace with the sheer volume of disposals? "We're not creative enough – all we can do is destroy this stuff!" In fact, this artwork very much reflects what's really going on outside the art world. Most computers aren't getting recycled – instead they're being crushed up and buried. Imagine it a section through a layer of future archaeology. We found some statistics, and realised that about 3000 computers were being thrown out in the UK every day. A 0.1% success rate netted us three new machines per day – more than a thousand a year, while being 99.9% unsuccessful in our mission to give new life to machinery only three to five years old.

So in our desperation we decided that we had to set up some kind of participatory process by which more people could come and be inventive with the technology we were recovering. We set up Access Space, a public access media lab with the proposition that anyone can come in and try to be creative with the machines. There's a huge sea of these powerful tools available. We intend Access Space to have economic and social, as well as creative effects. Sheffield is in one of the poorest regions of the EU, with high levels of employment, low levels of literacy, and one of the lowest levels of uptake of information communication technology in the UK. It's really struggling to move from an industrial economy and an industrial mindset into the information economy. There are some interesting statistics about Sheffield: it's an industrial city without being a commercial city – before the Meadowhall Centre was opened it had the lowest number of retail square feet per head of population in the UK.

Lowtech Video Wall (1)
Throughout this process we made a conscious effort to try to get cleverer with the way we used the computers. This was one of our early video walls which used colour and black-and-white monitors together, making huge scrolling texts across each screen. At the time we were researching all sorts of things on the internet, searching for an answer to what could be achieved with these machines. We came across forbidden and unusual information, for instance a fragment of the word 'virus' on one of these screens, which we encoded into this piece. If you stare at one of these thirty-six screens for about fifteen minutes, you'll be able to see the source code of a 1990s computer virus (now thankfully impotent). However, by that stage you'll have missed the other thirty-five scrolling messages containing who knows what subversive secrets? We felt that looking at this piece encapsulated the sensation of looking at the internet – you can only see a tiny part of it, it's continually changing and developing, and the information contained within it is often so abstracted as to be entirely incomprehensible.

We could have gone on making these pieces over and over – but the larger idea here, was not just to be sculptural, but to get more involved with the technology and get a better understanding of it. With higher levels of skill we could unlock huge amounts more of the potential of the machines. There's a huge amount to learn about computers.

Networked Lowtech Video Wall (2)
This piece has been shown in several high profile venues including Tate Britain. The innovation and the exciting thing about this is it's

real video – five frames per second of real-time streaming ascii art synchronised across 36 screens. ('Ascii art' is the original digital picture format – every image is made up not of pixels, but of text – so a capital 'W' is a light colour, whereas a full stop is a dark colour.) This was probably the most technically demanding piece that we've made – and I can't say 'I am the artist' because there were people drawn into the process at Access Space with prodigious levels of skill. Technically speaking (if you really want to know) this is a 37 machine 10-base-T IP network, and the data is streamed across the network to each display client machine, which has a different IP number, as an oversized UDP packet... if that helps.

We managed to get 15 minutes of video at a magnificent 480 x 150 resolution onto a 486 DX 66 server, with twin 300 megabyte hard disks. At the time of writing, a newish computer might be a Pentium IV running at not 66 but 2000 megahertz, with a 50000 megabyte hard disk. The manufacturers will say you can't do streaming media with a 486. Is this because (a) it's true or (b) because they want you to dump that old 486 and buy their new product? (Actually, it's 'b'!). But with 'Factor X' all of a sudden you can get all sorts of exciting new possibilities out of the computer you already have. Anyone with a computer science degree could have created the *Networked Lowtech Video Wall*, but no-one did. Thinking about the people who came and helped out with this project (I'd particularly like to thank Tony Goddard and Matt Palmer, whose help was extremely expert), they got involved because of the way that this creative project fired their imaginations. What was the factor that diverted them from developing products for a market, into doing a trash technology project that 'seems kinda cool'? 'Factor X'.

A conclusion

So, after three and a half years of running Access Space in central Sheffield, getting all sorts of people involved, learning ICT skills, developing their own projects, employability, and in some cases, their own business startups, what's happened in the Cultural Industries Quarter? The National Centre for Popular Music (something like £36 Million of public investment) has closed – it went bankrupt within 6 months – and the flashy bar next door, which was going to be a meeting point and cultural hub, is now Spearmint Rhino. So perhaps our economic strategists are taking their cues from *The Full Monty* – move straight from steelworks to low-level prostitution, as a way for a low skill population to join the information economy. They say it makes 150 jobs... tell me about the transferable skills. I feel there's an urgent need for more creativity, more lateral thinking, more 'Factor X' – more reinvention.

Progression

Introduction
Joan Gibbons

Standard definitions of progress include "an act of journeying, moving onwards," "the course or process of a series of actions or events, a narrative etc," "advancement to a better state or condition, growth or development."[1] While imbued with a clear sense of direction, such definitions are constrained by a sense of linearity, reflecting an ethos of singular purpose that is deeply inscribed in many religions and in scientific methodologies. Such purposefulness gained particular purchase in the West with the advent of the industrial revolution and the preoccupation with technological and economic advancement that accompanied it. Moreover, in the visual arts, the weight of the notion of progress has been made even heavier by the value given to it through the avant-garde's embrace of new technologies since the early twentieth century. In the name of social progress, for example, the Russian Constructivists developed seminal ideas for screen-based mass communications, including travelling film shows and outdoor film projections that, in various ways, have a continuing legacy in both mass culture and media arts in the twenty first century.[2]

Yet, despite the continuing relevance of ideas developed in those heady days of media utopianism, the avant-garde has shifted its terms of reference and lost its ultra-heightened sense of progress.[3] Walter Benjamin and László Moholy-Nagy's claims concerning the emergence of a lens-based culture have not only been fulfilled but have become commonplace.[4] And, of course, analogue forms are now largely accompanied, if not overtaken, by digital forms of representation, further confirming Benjamin and Moholy-Nagy's prophesies of deep cultural changes in the production and consumption of visual material. But, while it is true that the pressing imperative felt by the early-twentieth century avant-garde has been largely defused and technological changes in visual culture have been so amply realised, many of the issues and debates that were raised concerning the authorship, control and ownership of publicly consumed cultural forms are still ongoing. The texts that make up this section of *Hothaus Papers* respond to these issues, but in a manner far distant from the ethos of stridency and forward advancements associated with conventional understanding of progress. Instead, they push at various edges of current thought and technologies, effecting a lateral as much as a forward movement – progress in an expanded field. Accordingly, progression for Michelle Kasprzak is not in the least to do with linearity, rather the cross fertilisation of interdisciplinary practices and the opening up of governing systems of knowledge. For Simon Yuill and Matthew Gough progress is in the potential offered by computer programming systems for the opening up of new methods of artistic invention and exploration. Building on their research into the use of supercomputers, Gregory Sporton and Robert Sharl have experienced the value of cross-disciplinary rather than interdisciplinary practices. They see collaboration as involving not only technologies but, as importantly, people as a creative way of progressing knowledge. The last paper in this section, by Martin Rieser, speaks to the progression of narrative forms, examining a range of forms and media through which narrative has been spatialised in history and mapping out the legacy of these practices in a number of new media artworks.

Kasprzak neglected to mention her own practice in the paper she gave on the relevance of systems and interdisciplinary practices as a way forward. However, a brief look at her practice shows that she has inherited much of the ethos of subversion associated with the historical avant-garde. In the spirit of the open source software movement, for example, Kasprzak has been active in an underground movement known as 'warchalking' that controversially promotes the notion of 'free' internet access by the unauthorised raiding of wireless networks or, more popularly, Wi-Fis. This includes the social dimension of avant-garde art as Warchalking involves the sharing of information through the marking out of Wi-Fi zones for other potential users in the way that itinerant hobos in the American Depression would mark out places that provided hot meals or friendship.[5] As Kasprzak notes, the ability to "move from hotspot to hotspot" that Wi-Fi brings allows a freedom of movement that opens up new possibilities of social relations (and which also resonates with Situationist practices of *dérive*).[6] Here, Kasprzak reveals an anarchic attitude of openness and experimentation which permeates her own practice and is as characteristic of the practices and practitioners she speaks of in her paper. Above all, she prizes the sort of practice that subverts systems or challenges prescribed rules. To illustrate this point, she refers to practices as diverse as Hawaiian Slack Key guitar playing, *Bumplist*'s approach to mailing lists and the work of

1 See, for instance, *The Shorter Oxford English Dictionary*, Vol. 2.
2 For Example, Vladimir Tatlin's project *Monument to the Third International*, 1920, Gustav Klutsis' mixed media designs for information kiosks, 1922, or the agitational trains that spread the revolutionary message through the posters they carried and films that they showed.
3 For a discussion of the demise of the avant-garde which takes in major commentaries, such as those of Hal Forster and Rosalind Krauss, and gives particular reference to digital media, see Rachel Schreiber, *The (True) Death of the Avant-Garde*, August 8 2002. <www.mica.edu/schreiber/aboutRS.html>.
4 Walter Benjamin, "The Work of Art in the Age of Mechanical Reproduction," Hannah Arendt (ed.) *Illuminations* (London: Fontana, 1992) and Moholy-Nagy, László, "The Future of the Photographic Process," 1929, *Creative Camera*, June, 1986.
5 While this practice may be seen as the stealing of someone else's paid internet access and even an invasion of privacy, the ability to tap into existing radio signals has immense social potential as rural populations are readily connected and communications in so-called 3rd world countries can be empowered. "Wireless World: Inside the Warchalking Movement," CBC MARKETPLACE: YOUR HOME - TECHNOLOGY. Broadcast Feb 24, 2002.
6 A hotspot is the term often used to describe a Wi-Fi zone. Michelle Kasprzak, "Where art thou, Wi-Fi?" *Spacing Magazine*, 2004. *Dérive* (the practice of roaming) was a strategy by which Situationists felt the city could be experienced in an ad hoc and more creative manner. See Simon Sadler, *The Situationist City* (Cambridge, Massachusetts: The MIT Press, 1998).

Nicolas Fleming, in which perfomativity, conceptualism and landscape painting become conflated practices.

The embrace of weblogging is another manifestation of Kasprzak's search for ways of creatively exploiting systems. As Rebecca Blood has pointed out, weblogs are often constructed from free resources such as *Pyra's Blogger, Winer's Edit This Page* or *Campbell's Velocinews* that offer an alternative to the corporate control of such media. They also offer a sustainable alternative to the one way traffic of broadcast media, allowing participation much more readily.[7] Kasprzak's weblog, *The Hive*, is a testimony of the scope of her interests and ability to make wider connections, from comments on art that she has recently encountered to reflections on Anglo-Francophone relations in Montreal; from watching the Superbowl on TV in a family setting to an appreciation of falconry.[8] The commendable lack of hierarchical distinction Kasprzak shows between such diverse topics is consistent with the interdisciplinarity of her art practice, which includes and integrates photography, sound, video, and digital technology. All of this seems to add up to a typically postmodern paradigm that accommodates the vagaries of subjectivity and privileges plurality over singularity. This sort of paradigm is especially encouraged by the inherent openness, flexibility and interconnectedness and interactivity of new media. As many new media theorists have noted, these characteristics precede digital technology and were fundamental to the aspirations of the early twentieth century Russian avant-garde in particular.[9] What has progressed, therefore, is not so much the close relationship between the characteristics of a particular technology and a particular mindset, but the wider availability and ever-widening potentials of technology. This mindset, which is characterised by a flexibility or mobility of thought and understanding, cannot only be said to come readily to contemporary artists such as Kasprzak, but, partly due to the ever increasing role of computers in the everyday, is becoming ever more widely characteristic of the general culture in which we now live.

The understanding that progression resides in the inventiveness and creativity of the mind as much as in the available technology is at the heart of Simon Yuill's paper, "Programming as Practice: A Comparison of Old and New Media", which discusses the ways in which programming, both pre-digtal and digital, operates as an artistic practice. Yuill notes several contexts in which programming has traditionally served as a basis for creative production, from architectural plans to music notation and textile patterns. In doing so, he draws attention to the fact that programs not only have an identifiable aesthetic, but that the sort of context or discipline that programming operates within will produce its own set of conventions that particularise and authenticate the aesthetic, which can be "disseminated within larger social groupings." While the particular aesthetics of the mathematics that go into the algorithmics of computer programming have been recognised at least since the 1960s, and while, as Yuill shows, several traditional arts are founded on mathematical principles, the recognition of their potential as medium or language for the making of art in the modern era is far more recent.[10] Given early exceptions such as Donald Judd's use of the Fibonacci system or Sol LeWitt's use of modular series, the use of programming in contemporary art has been slow in uptake, especially in light of the seemingly inevitable infiltration of digital technology into so many aspects of late twentieth/early twenty first century culture.

As Richard Right has shown, however, the computer has gradually become legitimised as a means of producing art so that the central question no longer concerns the relationship of machine to art or the status of machine art, and now addresses the scope and quality of computer-based art.[11] Right also notes the emergence of a new type of media artist, the artist-programmer who regards "software not as a functional tool on which the creation of the real artwork is based, but software as the material of artistic creation."[12] Here, Right is pointing to a shift away from subservience to commercial software to artists who are capable of transcending the prescriptions of existing software or of writing their own programmes, identified by Manovich in his 2002–3 essay, "Generation Flash".[13] Alongside the emergence of this new type of media artist is the emergence of a new sensibility that has already been noted in relation to Kasprzak's paper, symptomatic, in the context of programming – as Manovich has claimed, of a "generation that does not care if their work is called art or design. This generation is no longer interested in 'media critique' which preoccupied artists of the last two decades; instead it is engaged in software critique."[14]

Yuill comes to a similar conclusion in his paper, further suggesting that "the distinction between program and artefact is dissolving," negating the artefact as discreet object and replacing it with a process of "continuous re-creation." As Right has done, Yuill also suggests, the issue of commercial versus 'free' or open source software is again significant, as the manner of licensing or packaging software can be a restricting or liberating factor. Implicit in Yuill's championing of programming as an aesthetic strategy with distinct properties is the idea that programming can provide a range of syntaxes of its own which facilitate creativity in any number of cultural practices (he

---

7   Rebecca Blood, *Weblogs: a History and Perspective*, 7 September, 2000, <www.rebeccablood.net/essays/weblog_history.html>.

8   <www.michelle.kasprzak.ca/blog/>.

9   See for instance the prologue to Lev Manovich's *The Language of New Media* in which he singles out Dziga Vertov's *Man with a Movie Camera*, 1929 as a clear forerunner of the new ways of thinking, looking and communicating that are now associated with digital technologies. Lev Manovich, *The Language of New Media* (Cambridge, Massachusetts, London, England: The MIT Press, 2001), xiv-xxxvi.

10 For an early appreciation of the aesthetics of algorithms, see Donald E. Knuth, *The Art of Computer Programming, Volume 1: Fundamental Alogrithms* (1962) 3rd Edition (Reading Massachusetts, Harlow, England: Addison Wesley Longman, Inc. 1997).

11 Richard Right, "Software: Art After Programming", *Metamute: M28*, 6.07.04. <www.metamute.com>.

12 Ibid.

13 Lev Manovich, "Generation Flash", 2002-3, <www.manovich.net/TEXTS_04.HTM>.

14 Ibid.

cites the music of John Cage, Daniel Libeskind's notational drawings of impossible structures and Jodi's use of raw computer data as an expressive medium in its own right). This chimes with what David Green has termed "the serendipity effect," which he sees as a property of the complexities of programming, arguing that the more complex or deviant the programming becomes, the more opportunity is created for the unexpected or the unpredictable.[15]

For Yuill, it is at this point that programming becomes artistic practice which both "enables the reproduction and distribution of the actual processes of production," a shift in conditions of production and reception that has the potential to suggest different social structures. With respect to the theme of progression, therefore, programming offers a creative approach that can open up new vistas of understanding and corresponds to the type of multivalent practitioner that Kasprzak represents and, by implication, the emergence of a more multivalent audience or 'consumer.' This approach is reflected in Yuill's game-based project, *spring_alpha*, which is an "exploration of software and social governance in relation to Free Open Source Software practice."[16] Based on a drawing, *Spring*, by Chad McCail, part of the series *Evolution is Not Over Yet*, the point of the game is to change the rules in the society represented in Yuill's electronic version of McCail's world, which is done through "hacking and altering the code that stimulates that world, creating new types of behaviour and social interaction."[17] The result is a potent combination of the highly immersive conventions of gaming with the creative manipulation of programming devices that transforms gaming into art and art into a socially relevant practice, in which altered or newly created forms of coding correspond directly with an altered vision of society.

The potential for the serendipity that programming allows is at the heart of Matthew Gough's paper which, located in the arena of dance rather than art, discusses methods of algorithmic choreography. The use of algorithms to plot movement is already practised in science and industry, with a view to more efficient use of robots in the processes of production. However, the emphasis, as in the research on human gait at MIT, is on successfully emulating or extending the functional movements of the human body. Conversely, in Gough's scenario of computer generated dance, the stress is firmly laid on the potential for unknown or unexpected combinations of movement. The method that Gough espouses is termed 'Epikinetic Composition,' a term which encapsulates the mechanics of pure motion that "autonomous algorithmic composition" facilitates. This willingness to relinquish authorial control to the algebra of algorithmic programming is already a recognisable feature of avant-garde dance. Merce Cunningham's famous embrace of chance in choreography comes immediately to mind, which has also been assisted more recently by the use of the computer dance programme, *Life Forms*. It is also a feature of William Forsythe's *Improvisation Technologies*, which, as Paul Groot has noted, creates an almost hallucinatory sphere in which new postures can be generated and overlooked aspects of the body exposed and disordered.[18]

Groot also clearly recognises a potential in digitally assisted choreography that adds to the already existing transformative powers of dance. In the case of the autonomous algorithmic programming described by Gough, transcendence is similarly suggested, not only implied by the use of pure mathematics to produce pure motion, but by the naming of the models that make up the epikenetic system he advocates. For instance, 'vitus,' used to signify epikinetic improvistation, makes obvious reference to St Vitus, the patron saint of comedy and dance, but also to the condition known as St Vitus' Dance, which as an illness is characterised by frenetic, uncoordinated movement that, significantly, has its origins in religious practices developed in Germany in the 16th century. 'Koan,' signifying choreography and composition, is a Zen term for a riddle without a solution that ultimately brings release from the constraints of reason and logic and leads to enlightenment. 'Magnesium' or contact improvisation, a chemical which burns with a white silvery light, was thought to be one of the constituents of the philosopher's stone, a means of alchemic transformation. Lastly 'zanshin,' event perception or memory, again borrows from a far Eastern source for the moments that constitute the in-between of action such as those experienced between moves in Karate in which, rather than relaxation, a state of awareness and anticipation has to be maintained.

From the perspectives that these terms give us, the use of algorithmic programming in dance clearly becomes an expansive rather than reductive practice with transformative powers equal to those of authored choreography. Such transformation lies not only in the movement of the body but also in the space commanded by the body – which is equally subject to the impartial directions of algorithmic programming. The pursuit of the surprising and the unexpected through algorithmic programming has already been applied in psychogeographic walking projects which have sought to develop serendipitous experiences of the environment by the setting of a simple mathematical instruction. The Dutch artists' collective, Social Fiction, for example, has devised a number of applets upon which a walk can be based, one of which is based on the Fibonacci system that, when followed to its logical conclusion, "soon becomes surrealistic, if not downright absurd."[19] While distinct in form and context from algorithmic choreography, algorithmic walks not only share notions of unauthoured, but nevertheless, subjective creative experience that Gough lays claim to, but are also essentially psychosomatic. While, on one level, algorithmic choreography, can

----

15 David Green, *The Serendipity Machine: A Voyage of Discovery through the Unexpected World of Computers* (Crows Nest, NSW, Australia: Allen and Unwin, 2004), 11-24.

16 <www.spring_alpha.org/svs>.

17 Ibid.

18 Paul Groot, *Streaming Video Killed the CD-ROM*, Mediamatic Special, England/Netherlands, 1999. <www.mediamatic.net/article-200.5740.html>.

19 <www.socialfiction.org/dotwalk/dummies.html>.

result in seemingly uncoordinated, unplanned movement implied by 'vitus,' the unexpected changes that algorithmic movement brings to the body can be seen as related to the sort of defamiliarisation mooted by the Russian Formalists, who firmly believed that innovative forms were capable of having an effect on people's cognition of the world.[20] Accordingly, the new forms that algorithmic choreography produces enable changes that open up the mind as well as the body.

In their account of algorithmic psychogeography, Social Fiction draw attention to the issue of subjectivity, striving to produce directions that are unbiased and unprejudiced by devising a set of algorithmic rules informed by the principle of unpredictability in John Conway's *Game of Life*.[21] Such an approach obviously throws up the possibilities of emergent behaviour as contributory factor in the realisation of the work or project.[22] While chiming neatly with Gough's claim to the production of "new narratives" in algorithmic choreography, the notion of emergent behaviours is also central to Gregory Sporton and Robert Sharl's paper, "Ultra Parallelism: the Grid, the Supercomputer and the Creative Artist". In their research into the creative possibilities of supercomputing, Sporton and Sharl are firm in their conviction that the essence of supercomputing is not only in the sophistication of hardware or in the combined powers of computers, but resides equally in human collaboration.[23] Just as Nicholas Negroponte has observed that the technical capability of television is never as important as the content of its programmes, the important factor in supercomputing is not in the accumulation of digital capability for its own sake but in the sort of behaviours and meaning it facilitates.[24]

In flagging up emergent behaviour and the ways in which the bringing together of people from different academic disciplines or backgrounds adds to the creative mix, Sporton and Sharl join both Yuill and Gough in their embrace of the unpredictable and Kasprzak in her related advocacy of interdisciplinary and interactive practices. Again, connections can again be drawn with the principles that underpin Conway's *Game of Life* and also in the realisation of these principles in the fostering of emergent behaviours in the open and improvisational infrastructures of video and computer games, such as Will Wright's *The Sims*. This comparison is not meant as a leveller between two different types of practice, but as a recognition of important cultural trends that cut across hierarchies and categories of practice and which signal new paradigms of behaviour and new models that open up ways in which the personal and public narratives that we live by can be developed and authored.[25]

What is different with Sporton and Sharl, however, is the added intention to develop an 'environment' for creative practice through the forms of supercomputing such as the grid, which as David Green puts it, "differs from the Internet in that the emphasis is on resource intensive applications, rather than data storage and delivery."[26] As is made clear in their paper, the networked environment that Sporton and Sharl are working towards is a social space where the participants can find new ways of working together and new possibilities for development. This ambition resonates with the Toronto School's (led by Marshall McLuhan and Harold Adams Innis) understanding of technology and media as the shaper of "consciousness, social organisation, and cultural expectations" and consequently at the heart of digital communication.[27] Given the claim that the internet is a meta-medium that embraces a wide range of other media, a legion of possibilities is suggested by the networked cross-disciplinary collaborations that Sporton and Sharl have begun to build.[28]

The final paper of this section, Martin Riesers's 'Place, Space and Narrative Forms' also picks up on the theme of narrative, examining the ways in which new media art facilitates the unfolding of narrative in what might be seen as new forms of spatial occupancy. Seeing narrative as diegesis or the unfolding or playing out of a plot or story, Rieser shows how the 'progress' from the linearity of dominant written literary forms to the non-linearity of new media forms fits into an history of alternative narrative expression. Here, diegesis does not have to follow the beginning/middle/end formula, but can be multi-perspectival, as in modernist cinema, or in the ritual journeying through the symbolic meanings given to a sacred space, as with the Hindu Temple or Gothic Cathedral. Progress in this case is in the breaking of the stranglehold of the forms of high literature and the liberation of the story from words on a page or the unities of traditional dramatic performance. As Rieser notes, this does not mean a freedom from bounds or limits, without which you might say the work becomes almost formless for formlessness sake – almost as sterile as art for art's sake.

It might also be argued that progress is not only manifest in the spatialisation of narrative but in what that brings in terms of the production and reception of narratives in terms of authorship and agency. The new media works that Rieser describes, including his own

---

20 Victor Schlovsky, "Art as Technique," in Lee T. Lemon and Marion J. Reis eds. *Russian Formalist Criticism* (Nebraska: University of Nebraska Press, 1965).

21 Social Fiction, *Alogrithmic Psychgeography: The Generic Principle Applied to the City Walk*, <www.socialfiction.org/psychogeography/algoeng.htm>. British Mathematician John Conway devised an enthralling game of solitaire, *The Game of Life*, first publicised in *Scientific American* in 1970. It has since been adapted online, using Java and enjoys continued popularity.

22 Ibid. (Social Fiction).

23 From it's early inception, supercomputing has evolved from the packing of as much power as possible into a large and complex unit to the linking up of and interdependencies of several parallel units of power. See Green, 59-74.

24 Negroponte, 37-8.

25 That gaming has provided important models which encourage the player to move away from prescribed behaviour and towards more independence of judgement is now well-recognised, see, for example, Celia Pearce, "Emergent Authorship: The Next Interactive Revolution," *Computers and Graphics*, Vol. 26, no. 1, February, 2002, 21-29. For games as an expression of more general cultural tendencies, see succinct discussion in Lister et al, 269-272.

26 Green, 71.

27 Leslie Regan Shade, "Is Technology Neutral?" CFP2000, (Computers, Freedom and Privacy) Department of Communication, University of Ottowa. See also, Harold Innis, *The Bias of Communication*, (Toronto: University of Toronto Press 1991).

28 Paul Levinson, *Digital McLuhan: A Guide to the Information Millennium* (London: Routledge, 1999), 37-8.

current project in Bath, all live up to the now well-rehearsed claim that the participatory nature of new media allows for a shift in authorial responsibility, and while tied to the name of the originating artist, the works are eventually the product of interaction between the user/ viewer with the themes, scope and parameters programmed by that artist. As Janet H. Murray has noted, this shift in responsibility might be categorised as procedural authorship in which the artist/author frames multiform plots that can then be developed by the user/ viewer.[29] Moreover, as Rieser's examples show, the narratives generated do not have to relate explicit storylines as might be expected in a MUD or MOO, but can be a sensory and experiential unfolding or diegesis, as in Char Davies' much acclaimed immersive VR pieces, *Osmose* (1995) and *Ephemere* (1998).[30] While the user/viewer cannot ultimately claim authorship, s/he, "can experience one of the most exciting aspects of artistic creation – the thrill of exerting power over enticing and plastic materials."[31] This, as Murray puts it, "is not authorship but agency."[32]

But, perhaps the most notable progress that Rieser speaks of in terms of new media narrative representations is the move from immersive gallery-based contexts to architectural settings and the street itself. Although Rieser is disappointed at the level of content that he feels characterised several of these projects, he nevertheless recognises an advance in the move into public space, especially with projects that involve mobile or locative technology, such as GPS or wireless that works through hand-helds. Among the projects that he considers more successful, Rieser singles out *Urban Tapestries* and *34 north 118 west*, projects that have tapped into or created personal or subjective narratives that connect with the history of a given location. Likewise, personalised involvement and a subjective mapping of history feature large in Rieser's own project, *Hosts*, located in two phases at Bath Cathedral and around the City of Bath.

In discussing the move into public space and the harnessing of mobile technologies for the generation of new narrative forms, Rieser has clearly shown how the definition of progress as a series of events or forward moving narrative is inadequate in a culture and society that is increasingly multilateral and multiperspectival. In this, he prepares the ground for the central thematic of the next set of papers, the deployment of the new media artwork in a range of spatial contexts.

---

29 Janet Murray, *Hamlet on the Holodeck: The Future of Narrative in Cyberspace* (Cambridge, Massachusetts: The MIT Press, 1997), 188-194. Murray also notes the repeated use of well-established plot and character tropes in multiform story-telling.

30 A MUD (Multiple User Dimension, Multiple User Dungeon, or Multiple User Dialogue) is a computer based programme which enables users to log on and explore and experience a virtual landscape. A MOO is a text-based online virtual reality system which enables multiple users to be connected at the same time.

31 Murray, op. cit. 153.

32 Ibid.

Abundance in Scarcity
Michelle Kasprzak

The best condition for fostering innovation is within a system with strict limits. Systematic approaches grow out of a need for a stable framework within which to act, but also to contain and channel creativity effectively. An endless list of options is exhausting and stifling. In a common example, consider the magnitude of brand names, each offering extremely similar products that we confront as consumers on a regular basis. In the face of large quantities of information and abundant choice, we seek constraints on our actions which are necessary to guide our processes, particularly creative ones. In addition, systems that restrict the flow of incoming information or reduce choice need not be engineered, because it may be the case that creators are unintentionally operating with an absence of knowledge. These cases of working within chance limitations can also produce favourable conditions for the development of innovative responses to one's environment. Being presented with fewer options, not more, can offer greater opportunity for original thoughts and actions.

Systems are constantly in use, enabling us to express ourselves for purposes both mundane and sublime. The rules of the English language, for example, allow us to communicate in both oral and written forms every day. Knowledge of the system of musical notation enables a violinist in Austria to read, understand, and play from a score written by someone in England. Rules, systems and conventions permit us to act reflexively, perform according to expectations set by our communities, and transmit an anticipated result. These basic conventions are part of normal existence, and so they are largely taken for granted.

Even though these conventions are now so quotidian that they have become virtually transparent, they did spring from somewhere, and the same ingenuity that resulted in their generation is at play when new systems are being constructed, or old ones are modified to produce a new outcome. New boundaries are built, and old ones are destroyed by those who approach from other disciplines, or by those who are forced to modify a system so that it better serves their needs, or by those who are unaware that a system was already in place for the action they wish to take. A paucity of information and choice, whether self-imposed or unintended, can act as the catalyst in a chain of events that provide moments of beauty and insight, allowing us to better appreciate human innovation.

To return to the notion of musical notation, it functions as a system that allows musicians around the world to understand and perform each other's work effectively. Music could be considered to be a kind of language, and so while the basic structure of the notation that represents it on paper may remain the same, it also must expand to incorporate evolutions in its vocabulary. A graphical system of musical notation, for example, was pioneered by Karlheinz Stockhausen to support his additions to the vocabulary of music. Other conventions in music, such as instrument handling and tuning, are perhaps more mundane. However, the conventions surrounding tuning an instrument were reinvented by musicians who are now known as Hawaiian Slack Key guitarists. In 1792, guitars were brought to Hawaii by Mexican and Spanish cowboys, who were hired to assist with an overpopulation of cattle. When the cowboys departed, some of their guitars were left behind. The Hawaiians who acquired these guitars were left no instructions as to how to tune them, and so each person who obtained a guitar and learned how to make music with it also developed their own individual way of tuning the guitar. These varying methods of tuning became highly prized, and musicians would loosen their strings when they put their guitars down, so no one could steal their tuning. When tuning styles were shared, it was mostly within families, and this created a unique kind of family history, with some musicians able to re-tune their guitars and play in the style of their father, and re-tune again and play in the style of their aunt, et cetera.

The conventions of guitar playing dictate a clearly defined, customary method of tuning, however, in the absence of this information, an innovative variance occurred. The established method of guitar tuning serves musicians who wish to play exactly as others do, and be able to faithfully reproduce melodies from scores. The Hawaiian Slack Key approach allows the instrument to become a conduit through which individual expression and interpretation is privileged over similarity and convention. Even today, with the knowledge of how conventional tuning works, Hawaiian Slack Key guitarists continue to develop their methods, reinforcing the establishment of this parallel system. The conditions under which tuning styles are shared also reveals where trust relationships lie in the social network. Sharing a piece of knowledge such as a method of guitar tuning reveals a significant level of trust in a relationship.

Relationships and behaviour are major components of another project that instead of operating in the absence of accepted conventions, as Hawaiian Slack Key guitar playing does, applies new rules to an existing system. *Bumplist* is a mailing list, created by Jonah Brucker-Cohen in 2003. *Bumplist* provides an open forum for discussion and exchange that any e-mail user may subscribe to, and participate in. One simple added condition makes *Bumplist* unique among the thousands of other mailing lists: the subscriber list is limited to six people. When a new person is subscribed, the person who has been subscribed to the list the longest is automatically removed from the list, or 'bumped'. The *Bumplist* users are never sure precisely when they will be bumped, because it is impossible to predict when the next subscription request will come in, bumping one unlucky user off the list. By adding this unusual rule to a familiar concept, the principle of supply and demand is activated. Because the supply of available spaces on the list is extremely limited, and the demand to be on the list is great, the social manners exhibited are wildly different than on conventional mailing lists. These unique modes of conduct are generated primarily by a singular desire: to be connected to the list continuously, and for as long as possible. The users of *Bumplist* have exhibited territoriality, passive-aggressiveness, and devious behaviour, but most often the users are simply incredibly tenacious, living up to the *Bumplist* slogan, "An email community for the determined". *Bumplist* aficionados have demonstrated their determination not only in their incredibly frequent attempts to subscribe, but also by creating *Bumplist*-related mailing lists and websites, to discuss and chronicle their experiences with the list.

The *Bumplist* website supplies statistics on each user, and a 'Hall of Fame' indicating the most active users by the number of hours they have been on the list, the number of times they have been bumped, et cetera. Making the statistics publicly available is another subtle method of inspiring a different sort of behaviour on this particular list. Striving to become a part of the *Bumplist* Hall of Fame is a long road studded with many subscription requests, and many emails from the system with the dreaded subject line – "You Got Bumped!" Perhaps the most valuable information is the scarcest, however. Statistics are plainly available, but the emails sent out to the list are not archived publicly. When you are off the list, you are out of the conversation, and the more time you spend off the list, the more dialogue is irretrievably lost to you. The unpredictability of when a 'bumping' might happen, and the possibility of missing out on messages keeps the *Bumplist* users on their toes – and by their computers.

Jonah Brucker-Cohen *Bumplist* 2003

The internet is thought of as nearly boundless, with millions of pages devoted to a dizzying diversity of subjects, and seemingly no end to the number of lists and discussion boards one can take part in. Introducing limits to a component of something that is seen as limitless makes our online experience more like our everyday experience, wherein there are more definite boundaries and edges. In daily life, it may seem normal that we can only have a certain number of people on a conference call, while our experiences on the internet are treated differently, and may lead us to believe that there would never be a reason for there to be 'no room left' on a mailing list or online community. Imposing restrictions that are more often associated with physical objects and concrete reality allows our typical conduct in the offline world to become incorporated into these online experiences.

Like the Slack Key guitar example, the modification that *Bumplist* proposes to a system provides insight into social practices. The Slack Key guitarists achieve distinction by their level of ambition in developing their individual styles, and trust is expressed by sharing their methods among members of the community. *Bumplist* users are rewarded for their persistence in pursuing a commodity that has only become a commodity due to a forced scarcity. In each case, the formation of a community around an alternative structure has made the practice a successful venture. Communities may act as valuable conduits for expressing and supporting a modified practice, but individuals sometimes also defy the internal logic of their communities to develop variant personal practices.

In the visual arts, where one may imagine exceptions are the rule, systems and conventions appear, disappear, and then reappear again, depending on factors that run the gamut from the dictates of the art market, to the influence a teacher may have on a group of art students. Certain established aesthetic principles and compositional norms have withstood the test of time and still have some currency today, such as the 'rule of thirds' and the 'Golden Ratio'. Although these norms have a classical appeal, the conventions that are determined to be relevant at the moment can shift depending on a convergence of thinking among tastemakers in contemporary art. Looking beyond trends and movements, the conventions of perception itself dictates which senses are relied upon to convey essential information that is interpreted by the artist. The sense of vision seems an obvious candidate to take priority, and although the interpretation of visual input may change as movements in art shift, inspiration is still often drawn from what a creator sees – whether it is a live model in a studio, or the surrounding landscape.

Recent work by visual artist Nicolas Fleming confronts the traditional reliance on the visual sense to interpret a physical landscape that is later depicted in a painting. Adopting an interdisciplinary approach, Fleming integrates a performative element into his investigation of landscape. In this body of work, Fleming invites colleagues to choose a location that he is not familiar with as the subject. Once his colleague has chosen the location, Fleming is blindfolded and led to the location. At this point Fleming encloses his body in a large canvas bag, and proceeds to drag himself over the landscape, in an effort to read it with his body. When the artist feels he has gathered enough information from his physical sensations of travelling across the landscape, he exits the bag and is escorted away from the scene, still blindfolded. He then retreats to the studio and paints the landscape where he has been, based on memories acquired through his senses of touch and hearing, and the traces of his journey that remain on the canvas bag.

Nicolas Fleming *L'Histoire d'un Vieux Sac* 2004

Fleming's approach is uncommon in its questioning of the investigative methods available to a painter. His use of a performative action to attain knowledge of a landscape discloses a desire for a greater intimacy with both his subject matter and his senses. Where the other examples cited here modify or reveal information about interpersonal relationships, Fleming's experimentations divulge something more internal, about an artist's relationship with his senses and how this relationship may be developed. This work also exposes how an interdisciplinary approach can pose compelling questions to each discipline that is implicated. In the case of Fleming's work, how do his impulses as a painter impact the execution of the performance, and how do the experiences of the performance manifest in the final painting? In an exhibition context, the video documentation of the performance (recorded both inside and outside the bag), the canvas bag as art artefact, and the final painting presented side by side act as separate lines in a complete dialogue about a personal experience of place. The questions about the interaction between disciplines, and the interaction between senses, are answered when the elements of the work are presented together.

As Fleming's work is a highly personal and visceral exploration of landscape from an unusually limited perspective, so the Slack Key guitarists have conducted their personal investigations into sound in a uniquely isolated situation. The style of each Slack Key guitarist is distinctive and belongs to the individual, though tuning styles may be shared. Analogously, Fleming's style of becoming familiar with a landscape belongs to him, and his experiences while in the bag are very solitary ones, but he openly shares his process in the complete installations of his work. For all three examples, the piece of information that is lost or left out defines the singular shape that each project will take. *Bumplist* users join and rejoin the list in an effort to miss nothing of the conversation, Fleming rejects visual information in favour of what his body tells him about a place, and the Slack Key guitarists develop a new style in a vacuum of information. Each case is motivated by curiosity about the human capacity for expression, creation, and self-knowledge, and how these things happen when we induce or endure scarcity. When less information is available, we change our behaviour and discover new subtleties in the information we have. The gaps where the missing information might be take shape as an unfamiliar melody, an unseen landscape, an imagined conversation that may or may not have happened.

> Hawaiian Slack Key Guitar playing: <www.slackkey.net>, <www.slackkey.com>.

> *Bumplist*: <www.bumplist.net>,.

> Nicolas Fleming: <www.nicolasfleming.com>.

Programming as Practice: A Comparison of Old and New Media
Simon Yuill

Programming lies at the heart of what has come to be called 'new media'. Whilst its significance is acknowledged, programming has long been presented as a technical practice that supports creativity rather than a cultural or creative practice in its own right. In part, this is due to programming being defined as a practice exclusively related to, and therefore defined by, computer technology. Here, I wish to outline an approach to understanding programming as an autonomous practice distinct from any specific medium. I shall begin by exploring the root etymology of the term, then demonstrate how forms of 'programmatic practice' are manifest in forms of non-digital media, and end by discussing how such a broadened understanding of programming as practice can inform the analysis of its role within new media arts.

Pro-gram

The word 'program' derives from the Greek programma, combining 'pro' and 'gramma'. 'Gramma' is a mark or inscribed line. The prefix 'pro' has various implications meaning that which comes in front, or in advance, of something, either spatially or temporally.[1] A program is therefore a set of marks that 'comes in advance', anticipates and provides for something. In relation to creative practice (poesis), programming can be understood as a form of mark-making that encodes and guides processes of production – marks which precede the realisation of an entity. As such it belongs amongst other notational, planning and instruction systems used by artists and craftspeople in the design and creation of works, such as architectural plans, music notation and textile patterns. Their use may be described collectively as 'programmatic' practices, in that all employ mark-making systems that encode processes through which particular artefacts are produced.

A set of architectural plans, for example, do not describe what a building will look like but rather how it should be built. A full set of plans not only contains information such as the spatial layout of a building but also how components fit together, how electrical and water supplies are incorporated into it, and also how the manufacture, delivery and assemblage of components can be integrated into the construction process. As well as describing processes of production, programs also, whether explicitly or not, convey particular aesthetics. The extent to which a given programmatic system is able to transmit a particular aesthetic is dependent on how well that aesthetic may be encoded

1   *The Oxford English Dictionary* states that the first use of 'program' in the English language dates from the 17th Century where it referred to a public written notice, a sign placed in front of people to inform them, in advance, of something that is to happen.

within it. Western musical notation can encode the nuances of a Classical or Baroque performance with a reasonably high degree of accuracy, but can be problematic in accurately encoding musical styles for which it was not originally designed, such as Arabic or Hindu music. Programmatic systems may also give rise to new aesthetic forms that might be unthinkable without them, such as Schoenberg's twelve-tone composition technique.[2] Many modern composers, such as John Cage and Cornelius Cardew, have consciously created new notational systems to express new forms of musical process.[3] A programmatic system may, therefore, have significant impact on the evolution of a particular aesthetic. It may also, as in twelve-tone music, imprint aspects of its own formal character on the artefacts created from it. In such ways the aesthetic properties of the programmatic system are imbued in the artworks created from them. They may, in turn, become aesthetic media in their own right.[4] Daniel Libeskind's 'Micromegas', for example, are a folio of drawings which use the notational vocabulary of architectural plans but describe unbuildable structures, and are instead intended as expressions of ideas in their own right. Similarly, in the 'codeworks' of JODI, mez and Alan Sondheim, the syntax of computer programs, or the ascii representations of raw computer data, are used as an expressive medium in which to create forms of poetry or abstract visual structures.[5]

Programming as a self-reflexive, socially-directed activity
In encoding a production process, a program enables that process to be shared and communicated to others. Often this is a major impetus in the development of a particular programmatic system. In many cases the development of programmatic systems is tied to specific social structures within which they are employed, or new demarcations and relations between practitioners emerge as a result of their relationship to a programmatic system. Thus, the distinction between an architect and a builder, a composer and a performer, a designer and a weaver, is based on who creates the program and who follows it.[6]

Programmatic systems also enable dissemination of designs and production methods between larger social groupings, such as the spread of new styles and artforms internationally through pattern books. Mechanisms have also been developed to govern this, such as the guild systems of the Middle Ages or the use of copyright today. Such examples demonstrate the role of programmatic systems in the legitimation of creative practices and production methods. The choice of encoding becomes that which distinguishes one practice as 'authentic' or 'correct' from one that is not. An awareness of this has been crucial to the realisation of the Free Open Source Software movement. The GNU General Pubic License (GPL) is a legal document incorporated into open source code distributions which both encourages the code to be used in particular ways, remaining 'free' and open rather than closed, and legitimises the code as adhering to such principles of production, thereby separating it from proprietary code, such as that distributed under the End User License Agreement used by Microsoft.[7] The Debian project's 'social contract' extends the GPL principle further, outlining a model of how the producers themselves envisage the larger scale social operation of the project and its contributors.[8]

Programming can be considered, therefore, a form of 'socially directed' mark-making.[9] It acknowledges the fact that cultural creativity is not the unique action of an isolated individual, but rather emerges from a dialogue with socially held ideas. This also introduces reflexivity into the process of creation. In encoding a process in an externalised, exchangeable form, it enables that process to be inspected, analysed and critically reviewed. Thus a programmatic system may be instrumental in the transition from poesis to praxis, from the immediate task of making to a more critically aware, self-reflexive interrogation of that task.[10]

Khatt: programmatic practices in Arab-Islamic arts
Kataba is the root from which words relating to writing are derived in Arabic, such as the verb *kitaba* 'to write', *kitab* 'book', and *maktab* 'office'. Sometime between the 7th and 9th centuries CE, a new term, *khatta*, came to be applied to the actual act of writing itself, from which

---

2   Traditonally, Western music has been composed according to the harmonic balance of notes as they are heard, in Schoenberg's technique, however, a composition is developed from the use of all twelve notes of the chromatic scale used in fixed sequences in which no note can be repeated until all twelve have been used, processes such as inversion and reversal can be applied to the sequence in order to generate variations. Such structures can be difficult to perceive aurally and yet are very clear when written in notation and clearly derive from possibilities which the music notation suggests rather than the sound itself.

3   For an analysis and historical discussion of experimental notations systems see Paul Griffiths, "Sound-Code-Image," in *Eye Music: The Graphic Art of New Musical Notation*, exhibition catalogue (London: Arts Council of Great Britain, 1986), 5-11.

4   These drawings, whilst unbuildable in themselves, nevertheless influenced the design of his later buildings such as the Jewish Museum in Berlin.

5   For an analysis of 'codeworks' and the relationships between program code as text and experimental literature see Florian Cramer's essays at <www.userpage.fu-berlin.de/~cantsin/homepage>.

6   This distinction is evoked in Marx's famous story of the architect and the bee in *Capital* (book I): "A spider carries on operations resembling those of the weaver, and many a human architect is put to shame with which a bee constructs her cell. But what from the very first distinguishes the most incompetent architect from the best of bees, is that the architect has built a cell in his head before he constructs it in wax." For a critical discussion of this, and the notion of a "socially directed" practice, see Tim Ingold, "The architect and the bee: reflections on the work of animals and men", in *Man* (The Journal of the Royal Anthropological Institute), vol. 18, 1983, 1-20.

7   A copy of the GNU General Pubic License (GPL) is available at <www.fsf.org/licenses/gpl.html>. For some background on the ideas behind it see <www.fsf.org/philosophy/free-sw.html>.

8   <www.debian.org/social_contract>

9   This notion of 'socially directed' practice is discussed in Ingold, op. cit.

10 For a discussion of praxis in computer programming see Geoff Cox, Alex McLean, Adrian Ward, "Coding Praxis: Reconsidering the Aesthetics of Code", in *read_me: Software Art and Cultures* (Aarhus: Digital Aesthetics Research Group, 2004),160-175.

derives *khatt*, denoting a style of writing.[11] Its introduction suggests the development of a new attitude towards the practice of writing which accompanied the rise of more refined and standardised forms of Arabic script and the growth of Arab-Islamic culture under the early caliphates, which first culminated in the 10th century innovations of ibn Muqlah's *khatt al-mansub* (fig. 1).

Fig. 1 Ibn Muglah *Letterforms* *Khatt al-mansab* 10th Century

Khatt is often translated as 'calligraphy', but the term derives from its use in architecture, where it referred to the marking out of plots of land on the ground. It suggests, therefore, the notion of a marking that organises and structures. The *khatt al-mansub* ('proportional script' or marking) was a system in which the forms of letters were encoded according to a modular proportion based on a single dot. The creation of ibn Muqlah's system was contemporary with a wealth of innovations in the use of notational media that grew out of the introduction of paper-making into the Abbasid caliphate in the 9th Century. These included new forms of notating mathematics, geometry, music, architectural design, and textile patterns. Within mathematics the positional number systems from Sanskrit mathematics, the decimal system from which binary evolved, was adopted and a process of step-by-step mathematical reasoning developed which we now call an algorithm after the 9th Century Arab mathematician Muhammad ibn Musa al-Khwarizmi – 'algorithm' being a corruption of 'al-Khwarizmi'. His text, *al-Mukhtasar fi hisab al-djabr wa al-muhabda*, carried these concepts into European mathematics, along with the principles of algebra, a term which derives from the *al-djabr* of the title. Modern computing would be inconceivable without many of the concepts contained in this book.[12]

Ibn Muqlah's scripts were originally designed to facilitate the creation and use of written documents within the large bureaucratic system of the Abbasid empire. The modular forms of composition and construction on which they are based were designed to increase reliability and ease of reproduction. This facilitates the transference of designs across distance and their continuation in use over time. Similar methodologies were also adopted in architecture and textile manufacture. Where once craftsmen and architects would design directly into the artefacts they were creating, the introduction of programmatic practices enables designs to be produced in one location to be sent elsewhere and realised by other people. New forms, such as the highly complex *murquarnas*, were able to spread relatively fast across Islamic countries. Through the abstraction of design and plan from its realisation in any given medium, the transference of designs between different media also becomes common, and indeed is characteristic of later Arab designers and craftsmen.[13] The nature of such design patterns is analogous to that of digital images, in which the form exists as encoded data, related to a 'program' through which it is realised. The material artefacts that render this data are each simply one instance of its realisation rather than a singular exclusive expression of it. The ability to reflect upon, and plan a design in advance leads to more sophisticated designs, such as the *murquarnas*, or the intricate textile patterns of the Ottoman era which were known as *saz* after the reed pens used to plot them out on paper.[14]

Two general tendencies are apparent in Arab-Islamic art that can be related to the use of programmatic practices. In one, the formal qualities of the notational system itself are imparted to the style of the resultant artefact. We can see this in geometric lettering styles and ornamental patterns that express something of the modular grid on which they are planned. In the other, the reflexivity enabled through 'marking-in-advance' supports the creation of highly sophisticated designs which may play against and obscure their underlying formalism, yet which rely upon that very formalism to achieve their sophistication. This can be seen in the comparison of figs. 2 and 3.

Fig. 2 Islamic tile psttern with geometric lettering design

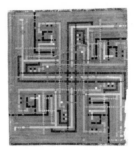

Fig. 3 Book painting, Iran, 15th Century

In the first example, the forms of the text can be seen to derive from an underlying grid structure that simplifies the forms of the letters without destroying their legibility. In the second, the possibility of even recognising that this is a text and not a purely abstract form is

---

11   This section draws on material from: Oleg Grabar, *The Mediation of Ornament* (Princeton: Princeton University Press, 1989); Jonathan M. Bloom, *Paper Before Print: the History and Impact of Paper in the Islamic World* (New Haven and London: Yale University Press, 2001); Valerie Gonzalez, *Beauty and Islam: Aesthetics in Islamic Art and Architecture* (London, New York: I.B. Taurus, 2001), and Renata Holod, "Text, Plan and Building: On the Transmission of Architectural Knowledge," in *Theories and Principles of Design in the Architecture of Islamic Societies,* edited by Margaret Bentley Sevcenko (Cambridge, Massachusetts: Aga Khan Program for Islamic Architecture, 1988), 8-24.

12   See Bloom, ibid., and Georges Ifrah, *The Universal History of Numbers* (London: Harvill Press, 1998).

13   J. Sourdel-Thoumine, in the entry for 'khatt', in *Encyclopaedia of Islam*, Leiden: Brill, notes that many Arabic craftsmen consciously explored the transference of designs across different media.

14   Jonathan Bloom, Sheila Blair, *Islamic Arts* (London: Phaidon, 1997), 374, see also 363-365.

put into question, and yet it derives from the repetition of a single word, the name 'Ali', constructed on a similar modular grid, but scaled, transformed and rotated multiple times in different colours creating an intricate lattice structure. Whilst the superficial appearance of such artefacts may seem quite divergent, they nevertheless derive from similar basic principles and practices.

Pattern books and practitioner communities
Weaving and knitting patterns are forms of program, they encode a process through which an artefact may be created. Anni Albers, in her classic text *On Weaving*, describes the notation system she uses, called 'drafts', in exactly this way: "The construction of a weave can be understood by reading the draft, instead of having to go through the lengthy process of actual execution."[15] And: "This is all that is needed to give an accurate account of the construction of a weave, although, of course, it does not give a naturalistic representation of it."[16]

Albers also describes the use of pattern notations as a means of 'reverse engineering' designs, for analysing existing textiles and working out how they were made by trying to create a notation for them, similar to the analysis of buildings through recreating their architectural plans, or in software through tools which convert compiled binary back into human-readable code. As is well known, the punch-cards used to program early computers of the 1950s were derived from a system of programming patterns into the automated Jaquard looms introduced in the 19th century.[17] In 1925 the Bauhaus purchased a Jaquard loom and the students learned to create their own punch-cards for it. Albers produced designs for her own Jaquard programs (fig. 4).[18] Arguably this made the Bauhaus the first modern art school to consciously teach programming skills to artists.

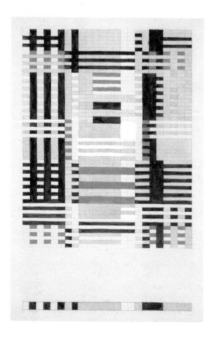

Anni Albers, Design for a Jacquard Weaving, 1926. Photo: David Matthews, copyright Presidents and Fellows of Harvard College

As in the case of computers and the Jaquard loom, programs may often be associated with, or support the development of the automation of a practice. This process is often linked with the de-skilling of human practitioners and the removal of creative and productive control away from those who make into the hands of those who manage. A counter-example can be found in the Fairisles, a small island community off the north of Scotland, one of the few rural knitting cultures to survive the mechanisation of textile manufacture in the Industrial Revolution, effectively resisting the very technologies that made Albers' work possible. Quiet yet successful Luddites, the establishment of the Fairisle Knitters Cooperative in 1980 was merely a formalisation of their long-standing independent and self-managed production methods.[19] The distinctive Fairisle patterns have evolved through processes of copy and recombination that, at least since the late 19th Century, have included the use of self-published pattern books. These have traditionally been hand-produced using matchstick heads to print dot-patterns onto the squared graph paper of school mathematics jotters, with different coloured dots indicating different wools. Local knitters and shop-owners produced and sold such pattern books whose pages would be stamped 'Genuine Fairisle.'[20] The Fairisle example demonstrates the development of a self-sustaining practitioner community that implements its own forms of legitimisation and distribution through the use of notational, programmatic media. Whilst not wrapped in the same strict legal framework as the General Public License (GPL) used in Free Software, they nevertheless represent comparable examples of the ways in which a practitioner community can maintain autonomous control of its production methods. This parallel has been captured in the work of Mandy McIntosh, a Glasgow-based artist who works both with knitting and new media. Internet projects such as *Woolworld* have explored the histories of autonomous knitting communities in the Fairisles, Newfoundland and elsewhere, whilst in others, *Radiant Circle* and *NY Vulture*, she has also adopted a GPL-style license under which she has distributed her own knitting patterns over the internet.[21]

Conclusion: distributed creativity
Programming is not unique to computing, but rather a practice found across many art forms and many of the principle methodologies we ascribe to new media are present in these art forms as well. We

15 Anni Albers, *On Weaving* (London: Studio Vista, 1965), 45.
16 Ibid. 44.
17 On the relationship between weaving and computing see Sadie Plant, *Zeros + Ones: Digital Women + the New Technoculture* (London: Fourth Estate, 1997).
18 Virginia Gardner Troy, *Anni Albers and Ancient American Textiles: From Bauhaus to Black Mountain* (Aldershott: Ashgate, 2002), 74.
19 I use 'Luddites' as defined in E. P. Thompson's, *The Making of the English Working Class* (1963) (Harmondsworth: Penguin Books, 1991). As Thompson explains, the Luddites were not opposed to technology in itself but rather the way in which particularly manufacturers used it to disenfranchise skilled workers.
20 Mary Smith, "A Shetland Knitter's Notebook", photographs by Chris Bunyan, Lerwick: *The Shetland Times*, 1991, 34.
21 <www.hamandenos.com>.

can therefore, place certain developments within 'new media' in the context of a much longer and broader cultural-historical context. The significance to new media of programming as a practice is not so much the simple fact of its presence, therefore, but rather the way in which the media and practice relate. Computing technologies support our ability to work with and use programmatic methods to a far higher degree than previous technologies (such as paper). In this sense the distinction of 'new media' is that of acceleration and intensification of a particular practice, which would follow Virilio's model of technological development. Secondly, the distinction between program and artefact is dissolving, creating a reciprocal loop between creators and users through the medium itself. Whilst there is a clear difference between an architectural plan and a building, it is harder, and perhaps irrelevant, to define the point of distinction between a computer program and a digital artefact. As the arguments of the Free Open Source Software movement demonstrate, such a distinction is only artificially created through the act of packaging and licensing a piece of software. A key principle of licenses such as the GPL is to retain our awareness of this condition of continuous programmability, and, therefore, of continuous re-creation.

In place of the artefact as a discrete object, therefore, programming foregrounds practice as a site of ongoing production. In relation to non-digital media, Tim Ingold's exploration of the epistemic values historically attached to weaving is significant: "The notion of making, of course, defines an activity purely in terms of its capacity to yield a certain object, whereas weaving focuses on the character of the process by which that object comes into existence."[22] The possibility of endlessy modifying an artefact is not unique to digital media but has acquired greater affordance and opportunity. Of greater impact, however, is that the digital medium enables its own processes of production to be distributed and modified within itself, and this, in turn, supports a new type of social structure within which that takes place. Computer programming has not only enabled the emergence of new media, such as software applications and the internet, but these, in themselves, feed back into programming as cultural practice.[23]

The dominant paradigm of artistic production in Western culture, at least since Romanticism, has been that of the artwork as a unique artefact only achievable in an act of direct creation. The economics of the contemporary artworld are still largely based on the commodification of such unique acts of creation. The 'old' reprographic media (print, photography, film and video) challenged this to some extent in enabling such artefacts to be reproduced en masse, but did not really challenge its basic principles.[24] To present programming itself as an artistic practice, or to promote a programmatic basis for such practice, however, provides a far greater challenge. It does not simply make its products a reproducible medium, but rather enables the reproduction and distribution of the actual processes of production. The most significant shifts taking place in current 'new media' are not so much in the formal natures of the artefacts, or their aesthetic styles, therefore, but the ways in which the practice is realised at a social level.

If new media are to have any significance on the development of contemporary culture it will not be in terms of the marvellous things we can get a machine to do, but rather in terms of changing our understanding of what creativity is, and re-socialising and 'distributing' this. Several projects are starting to explore how this might apply to fields beyond computing: the *Creative Commons* project is seeking to apply Free Open Source Software principles to other aspects of digital media and cultural production, *Oekonux* is exploring their application to larger-scale economic models, and *Open Architecture* applies them to urban planning.[25] Just as this has had a history prior to computing so too is it proving to have consequences beyond the technology.

22 Tim Ingold, "On Weaving a Basket", *Perception of the Environment* (London: Routledge, 2000), 346.

23 See, for example, Gabriella Coleman's analyses of the Free Software movement such as "The Social Production of Productive Freedom: Debian and Ethical Volunteerism", <www.mako.yukidoke.org/writing/foss_book_chapter_proposal-final.html>. See also the runme project, a repository for software art and related discussions: <www.runme.org>.

24 The classic text on the challenge of reprographics media to traditional art is Walter Benjamin's "The Work of Art in the Age of Mechanical Reproduction," Hannah Arendt (ed.) *Illuminations* (London: Fontana, 1992), 211-244.

25 Creative Commons: <www.creativecommons.org>, Oekonux: <www.oekonux.org>, Open Architecture: <www.themaze.org>.

Towards Computer Generated Choreography: Epikinetic Composition
Matthew Gough

Whilst dance and technology practitioners embrace computer software for the production of dance works, there is a general desire to retain human authorship in the conceptual and creative process. Artificially creative technologies developed for algorithmic art and music have yet to make an impact on the dance making process other than to provide visual or aural accompaniment. I believe that not only can the choreographic process be simulated and automated, but that such a simulation would present a viable alternative to more traditional methods of dance composition. After examining existing methods of algorithmic choreography, I present an alternative method (epikinetics) that facilitates both algorithmic choreography and autonomous dancing avatars.

Algorithmic options

In 1995, John Lansdown called for "more use [to be] made of the algorithmic approach to choreography" in order to find new 'narratives' and methods of composition.[1] Whilst methods of algorithmic composition have been developed for music and the visual arts, issues such as modelling unique, expressive performance have stalled the development of similar systems for choreography.[2] Yet dance is essentially a motive response to stimuli, consisting of 'movement invention' (concept – ideas/stimulation; movement realisation) and the human body.[3] These elements can be simulated using a combination of neurological and biomechanical models.

For the purposes of modelling we consider choreography (performance and creation) to be a three-part process: 1) Choreography: the organisation of the discrete structures into the larger whole, 2) Composition: the discrete movements and structures, and 3) Improvisation: the navigation between choreographic structures in the absence of instruction and the generation of novel movement invention as it is realised (instantaneous choreography).

Existing methods of algorithmic choreography model one or two processes rather than all three and are achieved by several methods including:

> Choreographic software: for choreographic stimulation
> Performance technologies: enabling real-time choreography
> Human implementation: algorithmic/generative dance
> Simulation and synthesis: autonomous virtual dancers

Choreographic software often takes the form of a multimedia 'sketch book' format such as the *Interactive Choreographic Sketchbook* or *Limelight*.[4] These applications allow the choreographer to enter images, music, dance notation, animation, motion capture data and other stimuli into a timeline based 'stage' and develop the choreography through rapid manipulation and pre-visualisation. Although such programs use a variety of algorithms to 'creatively' filter and process stimuli, they are incapable of autonomous composition and improvisation due to the relatively 'static' format of the data entered. The challenges of animating dance notation and rapid capture, re-targeting and warping of motion capture data severely limit the possibility of sweeping conceptual shifts though generative or emergent means.[5]

A possible alternative to the sketch book concept is a notation based 'pen and pad' model with animated 3D preview and Tanzkurven editing that would allow increased interpretive and transformative freedom through the use of non-deterministic, context-sensitive genetic algorithms.[6] This structure would allow movement scores to be generated from a notational lexis with minimal human intervention. This non-deterministic, syntactical, notation based approach could also be applied to performance technologies to facilitating real-time autonomous composition during a performance. The presence of algorithmic composition and improvisation in rule based performance technologies such as *E-merge* and *ChoreoGraph* would compliment the real-time choreography these 'emergent' systems already provide.[7] Without this capability the advantage of performance technologies over generative dance (accumulation, chance procedures) is minimal due to a reliance on human composition and improvisation. Choreographic 'narratives' remarkably similar to those generated by performance technologies can be found in traditional methods of composition and human implementations of algorithmic and cognitive models.

Davide Terlingo has experimented with 'fractal' choreography with *Nonlinear Generators* a practical application of Genetic Algorithms for composition.[8] Terlingo extends a set of 10 static positions and connecting movements through deterministic, context-free algorithmic

1   Lansdown, J. "Computer-Generated Choreography Revisited", A. Robertson, *Proceedings of 4D Dynamics Conference* (Leicester: De Montfort University, 1995), 89–99.

2   See respectively: Cope, D. *Virtual Music: Computer Synthesis of Musical Style* (Cambridge, Massachusetts: MIT Press, 2001); Roman V. "Epigenetic Painting: Software as Genotype," *Leonardo* 23 (1), 1990, 17–23 and Camurri, A., Mazzarino, B., and Volpe, G. *Expressive Interfaces. Cognition, Technology & Work 6* (Heidelberg: Springer-Verlag, 2004), 15–22.

3   Rainer, Y. "A Quasi Survey of Some 'Minimalist' Tendencies in the Quantitatively Minimal Dance Activity midst the Plethora, or An Analysis of Trio A", Buttcock, G. (ed.) *Minimal Art: A Critical Anthology* (New York: E. P. Dutton, 1968), 263–73).

4   de Lahunta, S. *Interactive Choreographic Sketchbook*, retrieved October 2004 from <www.sdela.dds.nl/sfd/icsketch.html>.

5   Neagle, R.J., Ng, K.C., and Ruddle, R.A., "Developing a Virtual Ballet Dancer to Visualise Choreography", *Proceedings of the AISB 2004 on Language, Speech & Gesture for Expressive Characters* (Brighton: AISB, 2004), 86-97.

6   Nakata, T. *Digital Tanzkurven* retrieved October 2004 from <www.staff.aist.go.jp/toru-nakata/tanz/tanzkurv.html>.

7   Willcock, I. *eMerge performance scripting* retrieved October 2004 from <www.unsafesound.com/Docs/eMergelanguage.doc>.

8   Terlingo, D. *Nonlinear Generators* retrieved October 2004 from <www.choreograph.net/forum/attachment.php?s=edc618fec7b0ccc77d23a527281cd8f9&postid=885>.

composition to generate novel movement sequences. However, the dependence on human creativity results in a movement narrative influenced by the performer rather than the algorithmic procedure. Similarly, Hagendoorn's application of motor control, perception and cognition to dance improvisation has also resulted in techniques and narratives similar to existing methods.[9] The emphasis on organisation in Hargondorn and Terlingo's techniques (at the expense of movement invention) limits the possibilities for a computer based algorithmic implementation as they provide no mechanism for generating movement.

One approach to remove human movement bias and allow new narratives is through the use of virtual dancers. Virtual dancers can be used to pre-visualise choreography generated by keyfame animation and motion capture data. Although these techniques generate fixed movement material, various 'noise' or 'motion texture' functions (layering pseudo-random movement into existing motion data) can be used to synthesise improvisation. Several methods of linking discreet segments of motion data (re-targeting, warping, chaotic selection, motion matching) can also be used to simulate compositional autonomy but do not facilitate a fully autonomous system. To achieve compositional and improvisational autonomy for virtual dancers an algorithmic method for movement simulation is required. Nakata's 'automatic choreography' uses an algorithmic approach to generate life like movement without the need for motion capture data.[10] However, his implementation of a somatically-based coordinated structure (limited of degrees of freedom to enable motive control) is unsuitable for improvised movement generation. Regardless of this limitation, algorithmically generated movement offers a method by which autonomous algorithmic choreography can be achieved.

Epikinetics
epi – on, at, close upon (in space or time)
kinetic – moving, putting in motion

Epikinetic motion simulation is related to Epigenetic Robotics (motion as genotype) but deals exclusively with the generation of raw, unstable movement rather than controlled motion. This raw movement is then processed by a series of algorithmic modules that shape the movement and present it as animation or notation. Generating unstable, rather than stable movement provides a high level of motive agility and responsiveness. Similar techniques can be found in advanced aeronautics where adaptive motion control algorithms are used with unstable platforms (such as the F-117 'Nighthawk') to maintain level flight and keep the aircraft 'in the air'. It is through such adaptive algorithms, with differing methods of intervention that autonomous algorithmic choreography can creative distinct 'narrative' forms.

An epikinetic system models the Somatic Nervous System (SNS) including effectors (muscle) receptors (nerves), and control systems such as the Premotor Cortex, Basal Ganglia and Cerebellum). The system, *chorea,* consists of six principal modules: 1) vitus (epikinetic improvisation), 2) hierarchical skeleton/dynamic environment, 3) zanshin (event perception/memory), 4) koan (choreography and composition), 5) magnesium (contact improvisation), 6) stimuli

vitus

The 'vitus' module is the core of *chorea*. An inversion of Nakata's coordinated whole it replicates the 'moment of movement' in multiple locations as an 'uncoordinated interrelated whole'. An epikinetic algorithm generates movement data by processing each joint and bone of the 'hierarchical skeleton' concurrently, but individually in realtime. These uncoordinated motor images are then passed onto the 'hierarchical skeleton' and dynamic environment where they are bound by the rule of human physics and biomechanics (the related whole).[11] This method of producing motor images without first conceiving the motion to be generated provides a high level of improvisational fidelity and might be considered a simulation of neurological movement disorders such as chorea. The development of our movement disorder influenced method is distinct from recent choreographic research into Ataxia, the inability to coordinate movement.[12]

hierarchical skeleton/dynamic environment

The 'hierarchical skeleton/dynamic environment' is used to process the motor images from the 'vitus' module. Unlike existing approaches, the movement simulation the skeleton does not 'drive' the motion but responds to the motor images. Rather than simulating the mechanical properties of motion we simulate the impulse, or 'moment of movement'. This shift in perspective is reflected in the way the skeleton deals with biomechanically impossible motor images, rather than stopping the movement at the human limitation it will arrange the surrounding limbs to accommodate the desired motion. Such adaptive reconfiguring can be found in numerous dance styles including salsa and contact improvisation.

The motor images are processed by a variety of existing methods for animation and movement simulation. Whilst some of these methods bear little relation to dance practice, other solutions have direct parallels:

> Forward Kinematics – Proximal Movement
> Inverse Kinematics – Distal Movement
> Forward and Inverse Dynamics – Release Technique

----

9   Hagendoorn, I.G. "Cognitive Dance Improvisation: How Study of the Motor System Can Inspire Dance (and vice versa)", *Leonardo* 36 (3), 2003, 221-227.

10 Nakata, T. "Generation of whole-body expressive movement based on somatical theories", *Proceedings of the Second International Workshop on Epigemetic Robotics*, 2002, 105-114.

11 Gallagher, S. *From Action to*

Interaction: An Interview with Marc Jeannerod Institut des Sciences Cognitives web site. Retrieved October 2004 from <www.isc.cnrs. fr/wp/wp01-4.htm>.

12 de Lahunta, S. *Choreography & Cognition: Experiments* retrieved October 2004 from <www.choreocog. net/exper.html>.

By using a range of motion synthesis techniques it is possible to reveal the full range of movement styles available to the human body. Processed motor images are exported as motion data in the form of animation (rendered motion capture data) or notation to enable human performances of the choreography:

zanshin
All events occurring in the performance are stored in the 'zanshin' (awareness) module for the duration of the performance. This allows 'koan' and 'magnesium' modules to 'perceive' events occurring within the performance and react with new motive responses. Data entered into the 'stimuli' module is also passes through the 'zanshin' module, only knowledge of current performance retained, the absence of a long term memory allows greater improvisational freedom.

koan
Algorithmic composition and choreography is generated by the 'koan' module which has the ability to override motor images from both 'vitus' and 'magnesium'. 'koan' utilizes a range of formal composition techniques (cannon, mirroring, unison etc) and is responsible for generating motive responses to internal and external stimuli such as music and limb arrangement. 'koan' defines its own concept(s) for the dance work, ideas for the realisation of concepts, and motor images for processing by the 'hierarchical skeleton'.

magnesium
Points of contact that occur during the performance are monitored by 'magnesium'. This module provides an artificially intelligent method for contact improvisation along with more general touching and lifting tasks. 'magnesium' generates motor images and performs adaptive motion control through a recursive process (based on the principles of contact improvisation) whilst maintaining compositional freedom.

stimuli
The 'stimuli' section may be used to specifically influence the algorithmic choreography of 'koan'. Data entered is flagged with a different level of importance as it passes through to 'zanshin' to become a motive response. Apart from stimuli such as music and images the inclusion of motion capture data is facilitated, this allows *chorea* to 'see' the dancer in motion before creating them a specific choreography.

Algorithmic receptivity
To achieve computer generated choreography (autonomous rather than human assisted) the entire process, from conception, ideas (choreography/composition) to the moment of movement (improvisation) need to utilise algorithmic methods. The ability to create movement without the need for existing movement data (*chorea* reuses motor images) is an essential requirement for any choreographic software designed to automate and or stimulate the choreographic process.

Epikenetic systems deal exclusively with motive responses and are unencumbered by a cognitive or emotive understanding of the stimuli. As with work generated by chance procedures the resultant movement is disassociated from the stimuli, thus 'information – contemporary receptivity – movement' becomes 'information – algorithmic receptivity – movement'.[13]

Whilst stripped of any emotional content the choreography remains embedded in physical reality, allowing it to be mounted on 'real' dancers and via motion capture the computer can coach the dancers' performance. The loss of human ownership in both the choreographic and interpretive processes should allow the deployment of new narrative forms, and physical techniques. These developments may eventually become a part of general dance practice rather than isolated in specific performance works.

Towards the future
Systems such as *chorea* will not replace dancers and choreographers, autonomous choreography virtual dancers can and will exist alongside their physical counterparts, illuminating new 'narratives' and forms beyond our conceptually biased imagination. A loss of authorship to the computer should only strengthen artistic resolve and refresh creative energies.

The simulated sensorimotor system and artificial body intelligence of *chorea* reveals the capabilities of the human body rather than the limitations to which we confine ourselves. If we are to develop new 'narratives' and forms we must let our bodies do the talking, through epikinetics this dialog is technologically mediated.

...Ways to connect [movement] can be algorithmically redefined infinitely. Since we're no longer restricted to the prescribed classical methods of connection, we're open to an extraordinary leap in connection, which is just a matter of defining connective space.

...Where I'd start is with the score. What's been missing so far is an intelligent kind of notation, one that would let us generate dances from a vast number of varied inputs. Not traditional notation, but a new kind mediated by the computer.[14]

With thanks to Bernard Easterford and Anna Jattkowski-Hudson

13 Franko, M. *Dancing Modernism/ Performing Politics* (Bloomington: Indiana University Press, 1995).
14 William Forsythe in Kaiser, P (1998) William Forsythe retrieved October 2004 from <www.kaiserworks.com/ ideas/forsythe1.htm>.

Ultra Parallelism: the Grid, the Supercomputer and the Creative Artist
Robert Sharl & Gregory Sporton

At the commencement of Gregory Sporton and Robert Sharl's presentation, audience members were each given a card. One side of the card had a question mark, and the other an exclamation mark. Audience members were asked to raise the cards during the course of the lecture to indicate a question that might be identified later, or to express a comment about a particular section of the discussion. This was partly to identify emergent behaviours in the community attending the talk, and also to flag up for the presenters moments that needed clarification or were of particular interest.

It has been interesting to note in the preceding papers the absence of something we had presumed in preparing our research for this discussion. The demand for a dialogue between science and art has been conspicuously, and mercifully, absent. As we will discuss later, this is a considerable change in the assumptions about how artists and technology interact, and has had a significant impact on the framework of our project. Instead, we have noticed the extent to which the discourses of cultural studies have come to be the language of the theory of practice in the creative arts, especially where there is technology involved. As will be apparent, we are also involved in invoking concepts from the history of ideas into our current work, but we are also cautious about this. This is not because our practical projects are problematic to us as pragmatic creativity in action. We have seen within the scope of our work very smooth collaboration and very easy communication with technologists and engineers. But, as part of the process of self-explanation, we appear to need to import the concepts of cultural studies into our experience because we are confused about how what we do practically can be explained. Cultural studies, in the context of technological practice in creative fields, has been very successful in insisting that we understand the world through ideas, and yet the ideas we know about sometimes seem inadequate to the tasks we have set for ourselves. In other words, new practice leads to new ideas about practice.

Partly, we are identifying for ourselves a new need to say that what we are doing is not new. Most informed readers can acknowledge the digitisation process of analogue forms has probably reached its limits: even if more processes could be digitised, it would no longer surprise us except by the fact that it hadn't already been done. What remains, and has been the challenge for our group, the Visualisation Research Unit (VRU), at work within the Birmingham Institute of Art & Design (BIAD), has been the development of new processes and new technologies, geared from the outset to address creative agendas. VRU was established by the BIAD in 2004 as an applied research unit to develop the use of digital media in creative practice. The Unit's remit has been to create facilities and produce research outputs in a variety of forms that reflect this new thinking about what and how art could be created through digital media. The emphasis of the Unit's work is on collaboration between creativity and technology, and on putting the technologies we have, and are developing, into creative use. We ourselves are now entering another phase of technological development where the purpose moves away from what we already know into virtual landscapes hitherto undiscovered by the explorers of the analogue.

As creative artists, our relationship with computers usually begins with what they will do for us, by way of expediting a known process or providing easy engagement with our material in digital form. For computing, it seems, creative practice is not an end in itself, and rarely thought of as a market, until after the technology is proven. A normal paradigm in technology development begins with a problem and derives solutions from existing or nascent technologies. This is not true of all these processes, but for the purposes of our discussion a stereotype of this kind offers opportunities to demonstrate more clearly the line of our thought. In this model, white coated boffins with soldering irons sit in computer science labs solving problems defined from outside. They produce technologies that reach creatives via the consumer and prosumer market, sometimes marketed and modelled on existing highly expensive professional processes. In the hands of creative practitioners the original purpose of the technologies can be, and often is, disregarded for creative ends. The subversion of technology is the only possibility available to creative people to get the technology to solve the problems that they need it to. This subversion can be creative and ingenious. It puts into the hands of consumers some level of control over the technologies they have bought that inadequately solve their problems, or stimulates the imagination of creative people to improvise. Yet, this situation also reinforces the legacy of disconnection between the originators of technology and the creative consumer. We have grown used to this chain of production, and sometimes even revel in it.

There are some difficulties with this as a model. Firstly, it tends to privilege the structure of the system that produces it over its creative use, whilst retaining a claim on the fundamental creativity of, say, the mobile phone. The fact that you can harmlessly subvert the technology becomes evidence of what a flexible and useful bit of technology it is. This is because of the inherent problems in this, what we might call, serial model. The sequential chain has many points of possible failure, often related to the currency of the market testing in comparison to the development of the technology. When you include issues like product design, advertising and competition, it is unsurprising that the technology we possess is often as limited as the efficiencies to be gained from the process that produces it. This is not to say that this is all bad, but for creative computing it is eventually inhibiting. This includes the experience of negotiation of technological needs where inevitably we become stuck with thinking in the forms we have to hand, rather than framing questions for our creative activities without the method of mediation that drives them. In our creative practice, often driven by intuitive leaps of imagination and an engagement with tasks rather than language, we can lack the basic constructs to frame the questions that would take us into complex lines of enquiry.

This is not to deny the creative energies of the development of computers. The fields that have come to be called the 'creative industries' have no franchise on creativity per se. It has become commonplace to say that the processes of the sciences can also be determined by intuitive shifts beyond rationality. In much the same way, creative practice can be determined in strongly analytic ways: the cliché of the trained, rational scientist and the intuitive artists have taken a serious battering in recent history, for the benefit of all types of investigators. In fact, it is this now contestable ground of ownership of the means and the possibilities of production that has driven us in the particular direction that our project has taken. The disconnection between the creative act of technological development and creative application of those technologies is slowly, subtly shrinking, and projects like ours are fuelled by a search for new priorities.

It was this type of question we began to think about very much when it became clear that we would have the opportunity to guide the investment of substantial capital explicitly for creative use. The barbaric idea that we would invest in a few graphics tablets and some editing software appeared to leave us hostage to the imagination of the designers of those things, rather than to strike out into new territory. Equally, we lacked the specialist skills to independently commission our own technology, and this was counter-productive to sharing our work: a major principle of our thinking.

The network as model

However, what remains is a serious technical problem. If we can agree that the processes of scientific and artistic practice can be similar, the knowledge base of either discipline is neither easy to ignore or possible to encompass, as if these were discrete and measurable areas of human discourse. In the technological sphere, however, this continues a division of labour that privileges scientific understanding over creative application in the invention of new technologies, and encourages dependence on creative imagination in their exploitation and application. It has been the subversion of assumed uses of technology by the latter that has created a number of applications that we now take for granted: email for example, or text messaging, both originally designed as additionalities to other technologies until in the hands of users they emerged as applications in their own right. The basis of technological change, though, still remains in the possession of those who can create a technology rather than exploit it. Our task has been to reverse the polarity of these relationships. By taking creative responsibility for the technologies themselves, the aim has been to give authority to the practitioner who develops the technologies, and in doing so to make demands on creative practice that it contribute to the primary functions of technology. The range of questions in relation to the development phase of the supercomputer required some structure for our thinking. In particular, we began to aspire to using a network as the basic metaphor for development.

What emerged from our original ideas was the lack of a central point or central focus in the locus of expertise and talent. This was fairly self-evident. Where our project began to diverge from ordinary models was in the distribution of control, in opposition to even the typical process of creativity, with the preoccupation with a unique and individual artist. The distributed network, the creation of many connections rather than relying on single flow, develops parallelism. Its behaviours are emergent and unpredictable, the very features of good creative practice. From the outset it was clear that only a certain type of network would work, and in this, again, we examined the normal processes that accompany development, and realised that there were some unique features. The first was that the economic opportunity had unusual constraints. We found ourselves in line for substantial funding to develop a scientific infrastructure inside an institute of art and design. This meant that we lacked the basic scientific knowledge to do such a thing, but not the ideas on which it might be based.

As a model for the creation of technologies and their application, the network has several important characteristics. The most important of these is that it is *distributed*. This confers the benefits of reliability, the sharing of resources, and the aggregation of computing power. For us, however, the best feature of distribution is the potential for simultaneity. This is important because of the specialist skill sets of individuals referring to the data and the concurrent development of their particular aspect. Rather than eschewing specialism in the popular manner: the belief in transferable skills or portable concepts; we have sought to intensify specialism by layering it through the network, taking advantage of the opportunity of simultaneous operations as part of the creative process. This means the knowledge accumulated by the network might, as happens in life, sharply shift in relation to a new idea, or skip away from its original focus without a net loss to the system. A network, it seems, is robust enough to survive such jolts, and needs to be in response to the creativity of its users.

Decentralisation is another feature of networks, though it may not in fact be a necessary attribute of all distributed systems; it is perfectly possible to conceive systems in which some elements are distributed whilst retaining centralised control. The scalability common to decentralised systems have limits, but they are significantly advanced of those that are centralised. However, for our purposes we consider, and aspire, to a network as a means of distributing control as well as resources; the rules of engagement and the fabric of the interconnections preserve the principles of technological development as creative practice. This is partly because of the article of faith which suggests to us that emergent behaviours can be relied upon as a fundamental feature of a networked system. It should be clear that this is the point in terms of making a creative space through a network. The primary task is to embed within the network the malleable structures of imaginative thinking.

Developing parallelism

Our work takes up a theme that will be well known to many readers. The paradigmatic shift in the use and design of computer technology has moved us from a view of the computer as a stand-alone calculation engine to one where the power of the technology is based not in the raw computational power but in the collaborative effort and community it can build. This is a notion to which we will return in relation to the creative process, especially as it has informed the development of the grid computer and our working structures. Embedded in this process has been a different way of thinking about the development of technology and its application. The purpose of technology, its opportunities and its problems have given rise to a process we describe as *parallelism*.

Parallelism assumes that big tasks can be broken down into smaller ones that can then be performed simultaneously. As a principle, seeking to do such a thing enables us to subdivide tasks and perform them concurrently. In such a distributed system what emerges is a heterogeneous network that can be combined or recombined to approach a specific task. This leads us to the methodology, the working practices of a group of academics drawn from across the university and from outside to examine the questions of creative technology. If the basic premise of a parallel network was to produce complex and unpredictable results, like the flocking patterns of birds, it seemed possible to build a network and to observe emergent behaviour and remain delighted by it.

There is already an acceptance that the future technology belongs to its creative application. This is seen to be key to economic development and educational structures – examples of areas into which the authors come into regular contact. The banality of this often throws people in the creative industries into panic about disintermediation, and the fear of loss of the privileges of specialism. If specialism might be seen by some as redundant knowledge, as a result of a technological revolution in the means of cultural production, the intensification created by overlapping specialist fields looks like a rich source of alternative practice. However, it should be noted that a grid or a supercomputer doesn't necessarily demand specialism as an absolute. The assertion of it in this model reflects a parallel process in our cultural relationships, a subject to which we will return.

Concurrence is a by-product of the network we have created. In a complex network like this one, control is given over to the users themselves, in an attempt not to contrive results. Giving over control of growth to areas themselves means some areas of the network may appear to grow at a different pace, dependent on local conditions, though in taking on tasks that have been subdivided, there are limitations to the extent of any specific area. The sorts of things to emerge from this are diachronic in operation. Having been loosely defined at the point of origin, they are enabled and empowered to come to mean what the users of the network need them to mean. This is a major way to overcome the issues in creating dialogue between scientists and artists. The meaning of the words in play can be used in a flexible way as they are transmitted across the network. It seems that this can be more or less understood in whatever way the user/creator in our network chooses, and they reap rewards or grief, dependent on the substance of their own interpretation of ideas. This aim leads us to the clear conclusion that within creative practice the hardware that reconfigures itself to solve the problem being worked on has more future than something that requires additional software before it will address any further issues.

Tool or environment

Much of the immediate discussion with colleagues centres around what contribution computers actually make, and the process through which those contributions are made. The traditional view, the analogue view, is that computers have replaced an existing skill set, and as a consequence operate in the creative environment as a tool. This is quite consistent with the observations we have made earlier: that, in general, computers have been applied to existing analogue processes, digitising the experience rather than initiating a substantial change in either the work produced or the methods and purposes of production. When applied like this, it is not surprising to note the lack of new types of production, or the banal assumptions that computers in themselves have produced nothing 'new', given that the intention has usually been to digitise the steps already understood in the process of creation. The computer, in these situations, lives up to its purpose of speeding up an existing process that is already understood. A tool is employed.

In the process of development of the supercomputing project it became clear that our own thinking about the computing relationship to production has changed. Effectively, in the search for creative technology, an environment is created of which the computer is a crucial, but not the only, feature. This orientation appears to us as rich in new possibilities, as it moves away from the lone computer user employing a considerably powerful tool towards an environment where creative practice is the main object of production. This situation has parallels with the move in computing from batch processing, where the serial application of technology for individual projects creates a linear narrative like the utilisation of a tool, and the time-sharing simultaneous development of projects and ideas as they emerged in multi-user mainframe computers. The chief distinction to note from one paradigm to the other is that this creates an environment to be populated. The network turns into a social space where ideas and technology can be shared by the participants in it, as they find new ways of working together and new possibilities for the development, rather than the application, of technology.

This process has uncovered and encouraged a number of individuals throughout our university, often working alone and isolated in their particular departments. By inviting them into the network we have developed more than a common facility. There are two points to make about this meta-department as it has developed in the context of the supercomputing project. The first is that the process is driven by an inherently social model of creative production, where ownership of specialism qualifies the individual to participate, and develops a commonality of ownership of the production itself. The contributions of networkers are often difficult to identify individually once the process moves beyond initial stages, and vary hugely, removing some of the personal anxieties often associated with using the computers as a tool. The second is the use of technology as a shield from an older generation of university bureaucrats. A self-selecting group of researchers, often lone, isolated academics in departments flung across the university have found common cause in this project, but not necessarily from a technological perspective. The environment is rapidly becoming a haven where researchers can think and share as much as work, and this stems directly from the different perception of technology, the freshness of the relationships and the opportunity to contribute.

Supercomputers

A supercomputer, or more properly grid computing, embodies these notions of parallelism, networking and time-sharing. In doing so it creates a platform for the creativity of the participants. Artists' access to this level of computing has always been limited, and almost always on the batch-process model, making the artist an interloper amongst technologists. Positioning creative practice at the centre harnesses the energy and ideas generated by the network for artists to develop forms for their work.

The spaces in which the processes of creative development in technology have, thus far, been the domain of the computer science lab. The opportunity to develop a new space for technological development within a creative environment is one the participants are eager to exploit. The shift in emphasis from tool to environment is a critical change in perception about the purpose and application of technology. There is a pressing reason for this, especially considering the efforts that many of us involved with the development of technological solutions or applications perceive as being important. Elements that are not as yet expressible in the technologies, but can be developed by the imagination are awaiting our discovery. The digitised analogue has been an important feature of how to apply technologies, but it should no longer be the limit of our imagination.

> Boden, M. *The Creative Mind* (London: Abacus, 1999).
> Davis, E. *TechnoGnosis: Myth, Magic & Mysticism in the Age of Information* (New York: Harmony Books, 1998).
> Dodge, M. & Kitchin, R. *Mapping Cyberspace* (London & New York: Routledge, 2001).
> Laurel, B. *Computer as Theatre* (Boston: Addison Wesley, 1993).
> Naughton, J., *A Brief History of the Future* (London: Weidenfeld & Nicholson, 1999).
> Penrose, R. *The Emperor's New Mind* (Oxford: Oxford University Press, 1989).
> Plant, S. *Zeros + Ones* (London: Fourth Estate, 1997).
> Stephenson, N. *In the Beginning...was the Command line* (New York: Harper Collins, 1999).
> Wursten, C. *Computers: An Illustrated History* (Koln: Taschen GmbH, 2002).

Place, Space and New Narrative Forms
Martin Rieser

"Modernisation is the process by which capitalism uproots and makes mobile that which is grounded, clears away or obliterates that which impedes circulation, and makes exchangeable what is singular."[1]

New forms

We are entering a new phase in the construction of narrative form – an age of ubiquitous computing and wire-free communication spaces. As always, the political and economic shape of society ultimately decides the dominant modes of narrative. The contradictory pressures of late capitalism seem to offer an opportunity to break the determinist control of narrative vision which dominated in the 19th and 20th centuries, and so promote a more decentred and subtle mapping, based on distributed personal technologies. Unfortunately, that same process of development is simultaneously draining meaning from those real spaces of our lives:

> One of the most exciting possibilities of cyberspace is the uncontrolled, the live, the networked and multiple, and the dynamic and fleeting. For these potentials to manifest there must evolve a place for stories and worlds that are not centered on an ideology based on control. Perhaps we should create designs that give users control in an uncontrolled world as a way to break that paradigm.[2]

I will explore the creative potential of interactive art and narrative forms in a 'free' gallery and in dispersed or public environments. Whilst other emerging technologies are already redefining existing forms of screen-based exhibition and reception (interactive television and digital cinema), they still tie the audience down in relation to the screen. This paper will focus on new forms of public and mobile art, where interaction has become 'untied' and spatialised (mapped onto real spaces/geographies). In my new study, *The Mobile Audience*, I describe and evaluate new modes of audience engagement and participation in such works. I interrogate the potential for the emergence of new visual and auditory languages and strategies of narration. When physical space overlaps the space of diegesis, could this emergent space for art and performance create new perceptions of space and place in an audience?

1   Crary, Jonathan, *Techniques of the Observer: on Vision and Modernity in the Nineteenth Century* (Cambridge, Massachusetts: The MIT Press, 1990), 10.
2   Flanagan, Mary, "Navigating the Narrative in Space: Gender and Spatiality in Virtual Worlds", *Art Journal*, Fall, 2000.

Spatialisation and interactivity

The spatialisation of narrative is not a phenomenon peculiar to new media; it has been manifested in many cultural forms from Renaissance frescos to religious architecture. Indeed Lev Manovich suggests it was the dominant mode of representation until the rise of western science:

> From Giotto's fresco cycle at Capella degli Scrovegni in Padua to Courbet's *A Burial at Ornans*, artists presented a multitude of separate events within a single space, be it the fictional space of a painting or the physical space which can be taken by the viewer all in once. In the case of Giotto's fresco cycle and many other fresco and icon cycles, each narrative event is framed separately but all of them can be viewed together in a single glance... It is not accidental that the marginalization of spatial narrative and the privileging of sequential mode of narration coincided with the rise of historical paradigm in human sciences.[3]

That other precursor of spatialised screen narrative – multi-screen cinema is also not a new concept, being as old as cinema itself. However, when interactivity and mobility are added to these two narrative vehicles we have the embryonic kernel of an entirely new and emergent field. The active participation of audience is not original nor is it disruptive of narrative diegesis; it is merely incompatible with certain narrative conventions, which have become unduly privileged by historical accident. As Manovich points out in his frequently quoted essay on spatial montage, multi-screen and multi-linear may soon once more become the predominant contemporary forms of reception. As Andrew Uroskie notes:

> With the adoption of Cinemascope in the 1950s, the multi screen projection finally became obsolete. Yet precisely at this moment of obsolescence, Warhol chose to recover a path untaken. His multiple screens serve disjunction, not aggrandisement. Rather than increase the illusion of presence, they offer a new means to divide such presence from within.[4]

Its early apotheosis was John Cage's *HPSCHD*, a five-hour 'Intermedia Event' involved 8000 slides and 100 films projected onto 48 windows at the University of Illinois in 1969. More recently, Mike Figgis's experiments with multi-screen, particularly *Timecode* (2000), while not interactive, are revolutionary in their approach to scripting, which takes the orchestration of a musical score and counterpoint as its model, and realises it across four simultaneous strands of action.

Spatial analogues and participatory environments

The participatory aspect of audience as performer is also implicit in most Virtual Reailty (VR) sessions. Long before mobile media drew the public into public performative modes of participation, Brenda Laurel was already exploring these in her *Placeholder* experiment at

Banff in the early 1990s. Participants could create their own stories within the broad boundaries set by the artist. Laurel's work fused improvised theatre with the cutting edge of VR simulation, combining sensor feedback for arms and torso as well as hands and head. The participants could alter their voices electronically to match the mythic characters whose identity they assumed, and could swim or fly through the recorded video landscape mapped onto a computer 3D model. It was a decentered world incorporating elements of shamanism. Similarly Char Davies's *Osmose* (1995) and *Ephemere* (1998) allowed the audience to become physically embodied in virtual space, through a suit which monitored their breathing – a direct correlation between slowness of breath or length of gaze controlled the perception of the work in the two respective installations.

Artificial Changelings (1997) by Toni Dove was an immersive, responsive, narrative installation. It told the story of Arathusa, a kleptomaniac living in 19th century Paris during the rise of the department store. She dreams about Zilith, an encryption hacker with a mission living in the future. As Dove puts it: "Artificial Changelings is more like a conversation with a schizophrenic video android with a history... Things float to the surface and form accretions."[5] A large curved rear projection screen with its curve bowing towards the audience hangs in a dark room like a large lantern. In front of the screen on the floor are three flat black rubber floor pads in a line moving away from the screen. Movement from pad to pad dissolves and changes video images. In close-up a viewer is inside a character's head, hearing interior monologue or seeing from her point of view. Stepping backward leads to direct address and further back to move characters across timeframes.

Jill Scott's site specific installation *Beyond Hierarchy?* (2000) uses a selection of films from the lives of assembly workers from an industrial centre in Germany called the Ruhrgebiet. The space resembled a church in structure, and black and white films of the characters were projected into the arches so that together they look like moving parts of the architecture. The viewer controlled the character's sequences from ergonomic chairs located adjacent to the screens on the floor of the space. At one end of the space on the stairwell, two viewers must shake hands while simultaneously selecting two of the characters in order to cause these characters to meet at the other end of the space on a large screen. The involvement of audience as armchair editor and as a vital link in the circle of projection and reception could not have been more explicit.

3   Manovich, Lev, *Macrocinema: Spatial Montage* <www.manovich.net/macrocinema.doc> (2004).

4   Uroskie, Andrew V., "Film as Film and Cinema: Towards an Expanded Conception of Medium", The Arts in Question, UC Berkeley, Spring 2003 <www.bampfa.berkeley.edu/bca/uroskie.pdf>.

5   Rieser, M, Zapp, A. *New Screen Media: Cinema Art Narrative* (London: BFI 2002), 211.

Paul Sermon and Andrea Zapp's *Body of Water* (2000) was a site specific telematic installation project. This was an interactive ISDN installation, which created a user performance stage through a networked video interface, linking two remote sites and audiences together around the archaeology of the lost workspace of a disused miners' shower facility. Through improvised interaction, the audience became their own actors mapping precisely with remote scenes and objects.

In all these examples, decentred foms of vision dominate, a very different sensation to the usual mode of seeing in VR and a successful strategy in evoking the fullest range of responses in their audiences. The audience's participatory role is related directly to their spatial movements within the installation space.

Story as ritualised landscape: alternative story spaces
The path to the production of deep meaning through spatialised means is a truly ancient one. If we examine the development of early theatre, we have access to other models of social and participatory story spaces. Ceremony, ritual and pilgrimage (symbolic affirmations of spiritual watersheds or transitions, precise narrative codings of resonant moments in a culture's development as well as in individual lives) provide a rules-based and compelling immersive experience. These often embody the primary narratives of adolescence, maturity and death, where the boundary between author and participant, actor and audience was dissolved. But this is far harder to achieve with a modern audience as we may no longer muster the sympathetic animism required for the magic to work. In this description of Hindu Temple we sense the full integration of the physical and spiritual in its architecture. Typical pilgrimages would involve walks around the various perimeters of the sacred spaces:

> The temple is also a microcosm of the Universe. The mandala reflects this aspect of the temple as well. The centre square of the mandala stands for the mythical mountain of Meru, the geographic centre of the cosmos... Around Mount Meru is arranged a symbolic pantheon of gods. Each god occupies its own square and is ranked in importance by its proximity to the centre. To emphasise the temple's role as a crossing place, the mandala also represents the Cosmic Man. The proportions of the square correspond to the proportions of humans, whose heights are roughly equal to their arm spans – these also are the proportions of the Cosmic Man. On this simplistic level of measurement, the temple becomes a cosmic intersection, a trysting place where humans can be in the presence of their God.[6]

A Gothic cathedral such as Chartres is the work of many hands, guided by a shared vision. Its beauty is both in the detail and its overall shape. It is a metaphor of the natural universe in stone: forests, filtered light, soaring trunks and interlaced branches. Immediately recognised, its architecture can be read by the worshipper either as a series of self-directed journeys or as a guided ceremony, for example by tracing the floor maze on their knees as a analogue of pilgrimage or the stages of the Latin Mass. This image serves as a useful model for a spatialised narrative environment – the limits of agency are the fixed walls and the rules-based rituals of Christianity, where the mediaeval mind found a living enactment of religious narrative.[7]

Daniel Libeskind's Jewish Museum in Berlin takes the narrative of architectural space to a new extreme, inducing a physical disorientation in the observer, which echoes the disorientation of the Jewish victims of the Holocaust. Libeskind's work is also highly symbolic: based on the broken Star of David and the void left by the disappeared is echoed by a physical void running through the heart of the building. Spatial narratives in new media have yet to achieve the vertiginous power of such physical narratives. The experience of such a space makes one believe Pallasmaa's contention that "Architecture re-mythologies space and gives back its pantheistic and animistic essence."[8]

Narrative as a spatial metaphor is ubiquitously implicit in a multiplicity of ways. For instance in mythology, Aboriginal Songlines; in the visual arts, the sculptures of Richard Long, and everywhere in architecture and engineered social space. Nor are the currently imagined forms of our digital narrative spaces particularly original, apparently in primitive nomadic cultures such as Australia and Melanesia the story spaces are:

> ...imagined not like trees, but like rhizomes, capable of reconnecting and not necessarily hierarchically organised. Jurg Wassman describes Nyaura knotted cords used in recalling secret relationships between mythical migrations and clan names. He shows interconnections between religious secrecy and myth forms in which time is congealed by being placed in a spatial model of the past, centred on contemporary concerns. Roy Wagner points to the anthropomorphic quality of "maps" that contain stories of how they were made. Here travelling is central to describing place, the landscape is embodied, and the human body projected on the land.[9]

Similarly where cinema is essentially fragmentary and episodic, much of its invented language was concerned with the process of reintegrating disparate elements, spaces and timescales to create a perception of meaning in the audience. Mobile media offers the coherent three-dimensional flow of space along a path, and with its augmented reality, is analogous to a melding together of the two modes of perception described here:

6   <www.mailerindia.com/temples/
    history/>.
7   Lonegren, Sig, *Labyrinths-Ancient
    Myths and Modern Uses* (Gothic Image
    Publications, 1991).
8   Pallasmaa, Juhani, *The Architecture
    of Image: Existential Space in Cinema*
    (Rakennustieto: Helsinki, 2000).
9   Lohmann, Roger Ivar, *Emplaced Myth:
    Space, Narrative and Knowledge in
    Aboriginal Australia and Papua New
    Guinea*, Pacific Affairs, Fall 2001;
    74.3; Proquest Asian Business, 466.

The word 'path' is not used by chance. Nowadays it is the imaginary path followed by the eye and the varying perceptions of an object that depend upon how it appears to the eye. Nowadays it may also be the path followed by the mind across a multiplicity of phenomena, far apart in time and space, gathered in a certain sequence into a single meaningful concept... In the past, however, the opposite was the case: the spectator moved between carefully disposed phenomena that he absorbed sequentially with his visual sense.[10]

The deracination of the image, also identified by Benjamin in his famous essay, *The Work of Art in the Age of Mechanical Reproduction* (1936), can be potentially redeemed through the new technologies of mobility. With its new mobility, glorified in such films as Dziga Vertov's *Man with a Movie Camera* (1929), the camera can be anywhere, and, with its superhuman vision, it can obtain a close-up of any object. These close-ups, writes Benjamin, satisfy the desires of the masses "to bring things 'closer' spatially and humanly," "to get hold of an object at very close range".[11]

A landscape of narrative

Bob Hughes, author of *Dust and Magic* has postulated landscape as a model for new media narratives with each track or journey mapping an individual trajectory through a story space:

To propose that the path is the narrative, is like proposing that the Pyg track is Snowdon, or the Pennine Way is England. Each path is chiefly a route through a particular terrain – and the terrain is the main thing... If that analogy is any good, then the way to create computer narratives is to define the features of the landscape to be explored, and let those define the path.[12]

Here we have the nub of the problem. If we can map a landscape, we fix the narrative in a rigid terrain, which can be traversed by the individual in any direction – what then happens to flow and subtlety? In my own work I attempt to use poetic discourses to rescue the story from fossilisation – the ambiguity and resonance of words ensure that the stories continue to vibrate and hold their numinous sense of lived experience.

If we took Hughes' narrative metaphor literally we would soon be in trouble: the multi-lineal possibilities of new media are not in themselves of any advantage in developing narratives. Economy and compression usually are hallmarks of successful artistic work, and cinematic conventions are based on its powers of visual shorthand and suggestion, with the audience filling in the details – witness the montage practices of Eisenstein.

Locative media narratives

Interactive public art has been with us for over 20 years. Some ambitious examples use locative and mobile media in integrated ways, illustrating multiple approaches to narrative in located spaces. If one examines for example, a famous work by Rafael Lozano-Hemmer, *Re: Positioning Fear Graz* (1997); halogen lights track people and create sharp silhouettes regardless of position. Internet Relay Chat Web Texts are sent by the public and included inside the projections. The work was shown during the third international Film + Arc Biennale in Graz, Austria, a *Relational Architecture* piece, it transformed the courtyard façade of one of Europe's largest military arsenals, the 350 year old Landeszeughaus. *Re:Positioning Fear* used a web site, webcam, 3D trackers, and customised projection technology to connect a very specific instance of Austrian history and architecture with remote and local participants. It was loosely based on the Cathedral's fresco *The Scourges of God*, which depicted the three Medieval fears of the people of Graz: the locust plague (which destroyed the fields in 1477), the Black Death (an epidemic that fortunately never had a devastating outbreak in Graz), and the fall of the city to Turkish invaders (which never happened).

Another architecturally-situated work, *Blinkenlights Interactive* (2002). <www.blinkenlights.de/> by the Chaos Computer Club was installed at the famous Haus des Lehrers (house of the teacher) office building at Berlin Alexanderplatz, which was enhanced to become world's biggest interactive computer display. During the night, a constantly growing number of animations could be seen. But there was an interactive component as well: you were able to play the old arcade classic Pong on the building using your mobile phone and you could place your own love letters on the screen as well. A playful alternative to video walls, impressing by sheer scale, it could not solve the arbitrary nature of the public content.

Increasing the mobility of the participant, Blast Theory's *Uncle Roy All Around You* (2003–4) allowed members of the public to participate as 'Street Players' using a handheld computer. They had 60 minutes to find Uncle Roy, with the apocryphal figure sending directions, giving instructions and makes observations along the way. 'Street Players' could see 'Online Players' exploring the same area of the city on the map on their handheld computer. They could send audio messages to 'Online Players' to ask for help. The game dropped 'Online Players' into a virtual city. 'Street Players' appeared in the virtual city as black figures in a column of orange light. Other 'Online Players' appear as white figures. An uneasy mix of performance and game, its narrative was only accessible to those who successfully complete the quest and found Uncle Roy, ushered into a physical office installation and transported by stretch-limo to their starting point.

Using locative media to 'read' a space with GPS (Global Positioning System) and other wireless technology is now a common strategy.

10 Sergei Eisenstein, *Montage and Architecture*, Introduction by Yve-Alain Bois, *Assemblage*, No. 10, December 1989, 116.

11 Crary, op. cit.

12 Hughes, Bob, *Narrative as Landscape* <www.bobhughes.demon.co.uk/NasL.html> (2004).

In their locative media artwork *34 north 118 west* (2002–) artists Jeremy Hight, Jeff Knowlton and Naomi Spellman (US) used GPS data and an interactive map that triggered live data through movement in downtown LA.[13] The user navigated a few blocks, uncovering oral histories, in a powerful mix of sound landscapes and testimony. The project examined the many layers of city spaces, marking narrative triggers through locative media, they drew multiple lines – from archaeology, fiction, architecture, and design – into the urban terrain. In the words of Jeremy Hight, the project:

> utilises technology and the physical navigation of a city simultaneously to forge a new construct. The narrative is embedded in the city itself as well as the city is read (sic). The story world becomes one of juxtaposition, of overlap, of layers appearing and falling away. Place becomes a multi-tiered and malleable concept beyond that of setting and detail to establish a fictive place, a narrative world. The effect is a text and sound based virtual reality, a non-passive movement, a being in two places at once with eyes open.[14]

In *Urban Tapestries* (2002–4), Proboscis allowed people to author their own virtual annotations of the city, enabling a community's collective memory to grow organically, allowing ordinary citizens to embed social knowledge in the new wireless landscape of the city. People could add new locations, location content and the 'threads', which linked individual locations to local contexts, which were accessed via handheld devices such as PDAs and mobile phones. These new urban narratives appear sharply streetwise and critical, but were more akin to distributed message boards than an artwork

With *Coast: Mersea Circle* (2003) Masaki Fujihata created a new digital artwork inspired by Mersea Island. In response to the island's remarkable shoreline, environment and people, the artist developed 'Mersea Circle'. Using video cameras and GPS devices, 'Mersea Circle' tracked people's flow around the island, creating an alternative map based on human exploration, rather than physical features and true distance. The work is visualised as a series of 3D tracks framing individual photos of the journeys.

Riot (2004), a Mobile Bristol project, depicted the Bristol Riots of 1831, during which the Political Reform Bill had been defeated in Parliament and the vote was denied once more to ordinary people, who rose up and filled Queen Square in the heart of the city to show their fury. The project gives you direct access to rioters' voices as they plunder the surrounding buildings and the noise of Dragoon Guards sabre-charging through the crowds, killing 600 of the rioters. Armed only with a handheld computer and a pair of headphones, anyone connected to the GPS wireless kit could move around an 'interactive sound theatre' in the historic square. Different events happened in different cells, and these were be triggered by people's movements. As well as a new form of experimental art, it was the first GPS radio drama.[15]

Mobile Bristol *Riot* 2004

Hosts

Hosts is my own attempt to evaluate the key questions posed at
the start of this essay. It is a site-specific proposal for Bath Abbey
conceived as a two-phase project. The first phase installation in Bath
Abbey took place between 8th February and 28th February 2006.

Five large screens were placed at strategic points of the interior
space of Bath Abbey. Inspired by the motif of Jacob's Ladder on the
front of the Abbey, it included a direct reference to the story in a single
looping plasma screen set at right angles to the other four projection
screens. Wearing a special badge and FM wireless earphones, a visitor
triggered the presence of a variety of unfocused and evanescent video
characters through the use of ultrasound movement detection devices
and interpretative software. Individual video characters (messengers)
appeared to move forwards and into focus. If an observer then moved
on, they too passed onwards from screen to screen, keeping pace with
the visitor. In this way, once an audience member had entered the

13 *34 north 118 west* premiered
    November 15, 2002 at the Art in
    Motion Festival.
14 Hight, Jeremy "Narrative
    Archaeology", *Streetnotes*, Summer
    2003.
15 Mobile Bristol is a professionally
    coordinated team of business and
    academic researchers from Hewlett
    Packard, Bristol University, UWE
    and digital product experts, The
    Appliance Studio.

installation they became part of the diegetic space and by standing in front of a screen they eventually became paired with and were addressed directly through a series of aphorisms by the individual 'messengers', who followed their chosen person from screen to screen across the spaces.

In the second phase, locative software and GPS enabled phones and PDAs connected to a project website ensure that the meeting and meaning of texts in and through the audience is taken to a new stage. Here location and aphorism are matched to generate new associations and reveal geo-cached histories of the city, which are distinctly 'unheimlich' and can be continuously augmented by public submission. The essence of this phase is that the public can submit a photograph of themselves via a web site together with a short aphorism. Software will create and lip-synch an animated 3D head based on the photograph and read the text via text to speech processing to a third generation technology (3G) or a personal digital asistant (PDA device). The avatars will be hidden across the city and the public invited to discover them through a series of proximity clues on a GPS enable mapping system using aerial views of the city. The idea is that the archive will grow over time and that particular avatars will attach themselves to particular users once discovered.

The technology used is a unique ultrasound location rig optimised to work in a very large interior space. Users wear Ultrasound Chirpers emitting a 100+ decibel 'Chirp' at different rates giving a unique signature to each device. Six receivers mounted on each screen detect 'chirps' which are sent to receivers. Relays pass on the received data to 'Gumstick' (the size of a stick of gum) computers for interpretation, formatting and transmission to Macintosh Laptop Video platforms via Bluetooth, which then translate the data into a logic tree of video clip conditions using Macromedia Director. The Bluetooth transmissions proved to be the most difficult part of the whole rig during tests at the Octagon in Milsom Street, Bath, during July 2005.

Conclusion

The spatialisation of narrative is, as I hope to have demonstrated, not new – but the digital tools and platforms now emerging allow the artist greater imaginative freedom and facility in the mapping process. Lessons from the grammar and meaning of spatialised works are there to be re-learnt from the past and new media is only just starting to explore work with a comparable range and depth. As we have seen, while multi-screen work and even interactive video is also not new, the tools are getting better and only now do the developing forms of mobile media allow such experimental work a chance to become part of mainstream modes of reception. The idea that a real space could become the diegetic extension of narrative is a concept that is as relevant to media artists as it is to architects, cultural theorists and filmmakers.

Space

Introduction
Joan Gibbons

Space is socially produced, culturally constructed and historically relative. In other words, the ways in which space is constructed, occupied and deployed are deeply symbolic and, as Henri Lefebvre and Michel de Certeau have also argued, deeply ideological.[1] Moreover, as Canadian cultural theorist, Marshall McLuhan, has also shown, our experience of space is always that of a body mediated by technology of some sort – the textual space of the printed page is an extension of the eye, the distances made available by the wheel are extensions of the foot etc.[2] McLuhan's claim extends to the idea that the world-view of a culture is determined by the dominant technologies of that culture and that this world-view produces a dominant spatial paradigm (the linearity of printed word for instance goes hand in hand with one-point perspective and rationalist philosophy).[3] What we are faced with in the early 21st century West is a cultural pluralism that has been gaining a greater and greater hold at least since Henri Bergson deconstructed classic notions of time and Albert Einstein developed his theories of relativity a hundred years ago – both of which were reflected at the time in the visual arts by the deconstruction of space and time in movements such as Cubism and Futurism. In line with McLuhan's claims, our cultural pluralism has been accompanied by the development of new technologies that have both exponentially increased the powers of virtual representation and vastly altered the relationship between the virtual and the actual. As Peter Lunefeld has noted, electronic and digital technologies allow for an aesthetic of unfinishedness, the privileging of process or experience over product or object, and give an opportunity for negotiating or experiencing space in a more radical and creative way.[4]

This section of *Hothaus Papers* examines the deployment, production and experience of space in a range of contexts and practices and addresses some of the changes in the aesthetic and symbolic experience of space that the wide range of new technologies has brought. In particular, the papers in this section examine the ways in which either our relationship to the environment or the relationship of the represented to the actual have been altered though new media, creating new relationships between the viewer, audience or participant and the environment. In effect different ways of embedding or embodying art. In discussing the expansion of the parameters of literary production that new media have brought, Mark Hancock's paper follows on from Martin Rieser's essay on the spatialisation of narratives that ended the previous section. The conversation between sound artist Bill Fontana and Ben Borthwick, Curator at London's Tate Modern, explores a number of issues in relation to the locations that Fonatana has produced his sound art. Artist Janet Vaughan considers the internet as an almost ideal space for theatre-makers, demonstrating key affinities to traditional theatre. Anthony Auerbach examines video as not just an integral feature of the urban environment, but the potentials that this gives to the expansion of art and the Loca group examine the implications and ambiguities of living with locative technologies.

In order to explore the expanded field of literary production, Hancock takes two examples of 'word-art' that differ radically in medium and form, One is in essence a highly conceptual performative piece that is sited on the body (or a number of bodies to be correct) and the other experiments with the immersivity of the text by means of VR technology. What ties the two projects together for Hancock is the mobility of the text – the fact that words are spatialised either through their actual inscription on the living human body, as in artist Shelley Jackson's *Skin* (2003–), or through their three dimensional animation in a virtual environment, as in *Screen* (2003–4), a multi-authored project developed at Brown University, Princeton, Rhode Island. For me, both projects also relate to a larger history of cross-overs between literature and the visual arts which has developed the plasticity of words. On the side of literature, this history would include for instance, Stephan Mallarmé's *Un coup de dés jamais n'abolira le hasard* (1897), André Breton's object poems, and even James Joyce's *Ulysses* (1922) in which the text is made discontinuous and the appearance of words altered into hybrid forms. In the visual arts, it would include Cubist collage, Dada and Futurist typography and, more recently, the work of visual wordsmiths such as Ed Ruscha, Bruce Nauman or Jenny Holzer and experimental typographers such as David Carson.[5]

However, although these earlier attempts at liberating the word from the conventions of the printed page have succeeded in elasticising or plasticising the context in which they are placed (page, picture surface, wall), they have not actually mobilised words or extended their relationship to the body or the three dimensional environment in the different ways that *Skin* and *Screen* do. For Hancock, this move into three dimensions 'thickens' the text, not only because of its spatialisation, but also because of the ways in which the practice of reading is altered through manipulation and interaction. Indeed, Jackson's text becomes at once so dispersed through its breakdown into single words tattooed on single bodies, that may never in actuality ever encounter one another, that it is rendered both obtuse and obscure in its stretching of the play of words beyond the

1   For discussion of 'politics' of technospaces that takes in a range of critical perspectives on space, see Sally Munt, *Technospaces: Inside the New Media* (London and New York: Continuum, 2001), 1–11.

2   Marshall McLuhan, *The Medium is the Massage* (Harmondsworth: Penguin Books, 1967).

3   Ibid. I realise that McLuhan comes close to a position of technological determinism here, although I feel that his claim may be permitted as a generalisation about the influence of technology on the way that we see the world.

4   Peter Lunenfeld, "Unfinished Business," in Peter Lunenfeld, ed. *The Digital Dialectic: New Essays on New Media* (Cambridge, Massachusetts, The MIT Press, 1999), 7–22.

5   I discuss this history in greater detail in, Joan Gibbons, *Art and Advertising* (London and New York: I. B. Tauris Ltd & Co, 2005), 7–28.

limit of comprehensibility. While the words in *Screen* become equally confusing, the more they fly off their virtual walls and rearrange themselves on return, the intention was not to render literature almost entirely conceptual as Jackson does (while paradoxically embodying it) but, as Hancock suggests, to test the notion of readership as a passive mental activity – and explore what might happen when words not only seem to invade the same space as the reader's body but are outside of the control of linear literary conventions (not so far from Tristan Tzara's method for making Dada poems by cutting up words and allowing words to reassemble randomly).[6]

The thickening of the text that Hancock refers to brings to mind the distinction that Roland Barthes has made between the work and the text, which, in its advocacy of intertextuality, seems to prefigure the technological shift into hypertextuality. In *From Work to Text* (1971), Barthes suggests that the time is ripe for a mutation in the idea of the work in relation to what he perceives as a shift towards interdisciplinarity in academia – and this is articulated as a shift from the notion of the work to the notion of the Text (which he capitalises).[7] Unlike the work, which usually abides by literary conventions, the Text is not definable and set meaning cannot be excavated. It is plural, "the activity of associations, contiguities, carryings-over" and it "coincides with a liberation of symbolic energy (without which men would die)."[8] Confronted with a Text, "what the reader perceives is multiple, irreducible, coming from a disconnected, heterogeneous variety of substances and perspectives."[9] It now almost goes without saying how close to the experiences offered by both *Skin* and *Screen* are to Barthes' notion of the Text, and that the expanded field of literature that they separately represent is that of Textual space which has been respectively realised either in the actual bodily navigations of space or in relation to a virtual bodily experience. Moreover, for Barthes, the Text diminishes the distance between reading and writing and "gathers it up as play, activity, production, practice."[10] In other words the reader becomes a producer rather than a consumer – precisely the claim that has been made for the interactivity of internet-based literature. In its flexible and changeable organisation of text, the internet clearly resonates with Jacques Derrida's critique of logocentrism which, as George P. Landow has shown, prefigured the malleability of new media in the production of a textual space.[11] Interestingly, Landow has also made firm connections between hypertext and collage, a hybrid form that can only really qualify as Text. In doing so he itemises the characteristics of what he sees to be the salient features of both: juxtaposition; appropriation; assemblage; concatenation; blurring limits, edges and borders, and blurring distinctions between border and ground – all of which might also be said to characterise the expanded field of literature that Hancock has identified in *Skin* and *Screen*.[12]

Staying momentarily with the theme of narrative, perhaps one of the more overlooked aspects of sound artist Bill Fontana's works is that they often create a form of diegesis by transporting or reconfiguring 'readymade' sounds into sites or places that are already historically 'resonant.' A piece such as *Entfernte Zuge* (1984), for instance, takes the multiple sounds of a contemporary working railway station, Köln Hauptbahnhof, and overlays them onto the ruins of Berlin Railway Station, Anhalter Bahnhof, that is poignantly located, near to Checkpoint Charlie. As Fontana notes, Anhalter Bahnhof had the feel of haunted wasteland that seemed to suggest the sounds of its past.[13] This decontextualisation/recontextualisation, of sound and place again creates a new narrative form, in which potent auditory and visual signifiers are orchestrated to tell a 'story' in an unfamiliar and highly evocative way, and in which narrative is, in effect, spatialised.

In his appropriation of ambient sounds, Fontana situates himself in the tradition of Duchamp's readymades and refers to Duchamp's characterisation of musical sculpture as "sounds lasting and leaving from different places and forming a sounding sculpture which lasts." Unsurprisingly, then, the characteristics of Fontana's work are implicit in this statement.[14] In his original notes, Duchamp corrects what he had first written as "sounds leaving from different places" with the insertion of the word "lasting", which suggests that the sounds, while perhaps disparate, are nevertheless resonant and as such will form sculpture that will have not only duration, but also, paradoxically, a form of durability. In Fontana's works this may be said to be expressed in the fact that they are, at once, monumental in scale and effect and often concerned with the endurance of memory. Furthermore, as Stefan Beyst has noted, the juxtapositions of sound and space that characterise Fontana's work are also of the order of those made by the Surrealists, in which a found object is removed from its original context and acquires new, unexpected meanings in its relocation, extending the significance of the object.[15] The problem with this comparison is that Fontana's work is far more historically grounded and less esoteric than that of the Surrealists, where the juxtaposition of objects was meant to raise the (Freudian) uncanny. Instead, I would argue that Fonatana's redeployment of readymade sounds gains its purchase from the effect of defamiliarisation that Fontana's juxtapositions produce, evoking instead the Russian Formalists who saw the technique of making strange as a way for the avant-garde to make us perceive the world in new ways.[16]

6   In fact, the authors of *Screen* deliberately set out to create three reading experiences, one conventional, one audio visual and one almost hallucinatory. See: ‹www.hyperfiction.org/screen/›.

7   Roland Barthes, "From Work to Text," 1971, in Roland Barthes, *Image, Music, Text* (London: Fontana Press, 1977), 155-164.

8   Ibid. 158.

9   Ibid. 159.

10 Ibid. 162.

11 George P. Landow, "Hypertext and Critical Theory," in David Trend, ed. *Reading Digital Culture* (Oxford: Blackwell Publishers Ltd, 2001),

98-108.

12 George P. Landow, "Hypertext as Collage," in Peter Lunenfeld, ed. *The Digital Dialectic: New Essays on New Media* (Cambridge, Massachusetts: The MIT Press, 1999), 151-170.

13 Bill Fontana, "The Relocation of Ambient Sound: Urban Sound Sculpture", ‹www.resoundings.org/›.

14 Ibid.

15 Marcel Duchamp, *Notes and Projects for the Large Glass*, selected, ordered and with an introduction by Arturo Schwarz (London: Thames and Hudson, 1969), 82.

16 ‹www.d-sites.net/english/fontana.htm›.

The conversation between Fontana and Borthwick took place outside of the seminar series as a complementary event that would contribute to the papers. It was held on 29th June 2005 at the end of Fontana's residency as visiting Senior Research Fellow with BEAST (Birmingham Electro-Acoustic Sound Theatre) at the University of Birmingham. The residency had culminated in a sound piece using the bells of St Martin's Church, situated in the heart of the city in the newly redeveloped Bullring Centre and the resulting sound piece was installed at VIVID's gallery between 30th June and 7th July, 2005. In its careful attention to site and history and its deployment of ambient sound, the piece is typical of Fontana's urban sound sculptures which are, for Fontana, preferably relayed in situ rather than the gallery, according with his belief that "the richness and beauty of ambient sounds come from their interaction with a living situation."[17]

However, the sound sculpture created at St Martin's in the Bullring did not transpose sounds from another context but produced a carillon piece that harnessed the talents of the customary bell-ringers. Fontana's concern here was that the major architectural developments around the church had literally robbed its bells of their resonance, an example of what Fontana sees as a lack of attention to design in the acoustic aspects of the environment.[18] Rather than import readymade sounds, the solution, for Fontana was "to become a composer again" and create big waves or clusters of bell-sounds that would fly off the adjacent buildings and, in doing so, reinstate the sound of bells as a significant component of the environment. Here, Fontana shows characteristic sensitivity towards the identity and history of the site, which as many of Birmingham's long-term residents will confirm has been through too many transformations in the name of commerce and, like most of the city centre, has almost lost the memories that are ingrained in the fabric of its buildings. While the extraordinary bell-ringing event in Birmingham of the 26th June 2005 may be seen as defamiliarising the normal potential and function of the bells, in making us more aware of their presence, Fontana has refamiliarised us with our history and memories – his gift to Birmingham.

The ways in which the experience of net or web art can parallel that of the theatre audience underpins Janet Vaughan's paper, *Are Theatre-Makers Natural Net Artists?* Vaughan is a member of the Coventry-based artist's company, Talking Birds, formed in 1992. Much of the company's work is based in or is about an environment in a way that taps into the identity and history of the site or place in question. This can be about the transformation of a place or building, as with *Wanderlust* (2002), a video and soundscape projection that traces a memory path through a Scarborough car park's former incarnations as aquarium and amusement arcade. Equally, it can be in the virtual linking of two geographically far flung cities as in *twin60* (2004), a piece that commemorates the twinning of Coventry with Stalingrad (now Volgograd) in 1944, through the production of a virtual tablecloth that 'remembers' an actual tablecloth of embroidered names sent by the women of Coventry to the people of Stalingrad in 1944. Talking Birds' project, *The Virtual Fringe* (2004) followed the same principles through a festival of virtual performances, exhibitions and events, nominally programmed to take place around the City of Coventry, and based on an actual building or space. Viewers/participants were able to book tickets for these non-existent events in advance.[19]

By reflecting on web-based audience relations, Vaughan's paper forms an enlightening counterpoint to the above practices and, in making the comparisons to theatre spectatorship, throws up some vital questions concerning the state of net art. As others have done, Vaughan recognises a stage in which net art was preoccupied with the potentials and characteristics of the medium or technology, a route which has led to an emphasis on form over subject matter and produced visually sophisticated abstract works based on data visualisation.[20] Vaughan also notes a complementary tendency to remediate and give old forms and conventions a sense of novelty through the introduction of hyperlinks and the offering of navigational choices in narratives – strategies which open up the nature of the exchanges between 'user' and artwork, but which do not necessarily result in complexity or substance, or even in new narratives.

However, this querying of levels of content is not a criticism of the characteristics of net art, but merely of the superficially seductive nature of participatory engagement, which in the end is controlled by the artist/programmer, and which may often disguise a lack of content. On the contrary, Vaughan is keen to recognise and value salient features of net art such as its potential for instability and its lack of permanency, its accommodation of cross-narratives and ambiguitiy. Indeed, these are the very features that liken net art to theatre, not least the fact that the connection between work and user/audience is similarly immediate and dependent on close engagement. For Vaughan, theatre-makers are well equipped for the sort of complex interconnections that net art allows, able to bring their experience of live performance to the virtual arena in ways that transcend the formulaic navigational procedures of the hyperlink or computer gaming. As Janet H. Murray has similarly noted, it is the mosaic potential of net technology that promises a richer future for narrative and user performativity in cyberspace, although the pieces of the mosaic in the end need to coalesce into meaningful results at some level or in some way, no matter how multiform or improvisational the journey through.[21]

17 Shklovsky's essay, "Art as Technique," is reprinted in Lee T. Lemon and Marion J. Reis eds. *Russian Formalist Criticism* (Nebraska: University of Nebraska Press, 1965).

18 Bill Fontana, "The Environment as a Musical Resource," <www.resoundings.org/>.

19 All of these projects and more are featured on Talking Birds' website, <www.talkingbirds.co.uk>.

20 See Gloria Sutton, "network aesthetics: strategies of participation in net.art," in Andrea Zapp, ed. *networked narrative environments as imaginary spaces of being* (Manchester: Manchester Metropolitan University, 2004), 22-3.

21 Janet H. Murray, *Hamlet on the Holodeck: The Future of Narrative in Cyberspace* (Cambridge, Massachusetts: The MIT Press, 1997), 155-162, 273-284.

What the 'theatre-making' of Talking Birds, brings is the opportunity for creative participation and performativity that is partially orchestrated by the setting up of a scenario that taps into the actuality of a place and the fantasies and desires that are suggested by its history or by the connections that the user/audience makes with it. And, as their project, *Web Demographic* (2003) has demonstrated, this scenario can also be of a more distant nature, setting up a number of hypothetical situations that invite performative and participatory responses though email communication – email as a conduit for psychodrama. As Sean Dixon and his Chameleons 3 company have also proved, cyber-theatre has helped create a more subjective space than conventional television or screen media, "Although the actual physical distance between performers and audience is increased, interactive communication changes the nature of the spatial barrier since the spectators seem as present and often as prominent as the performers within the performance space of the computer monitor proscenium."[22] For Vaughan and co-members of Talking Birds, it is not so much the creation of a new theatrical arena that is at stake for theatre makers embracing net art, but the matter of producing an appropriate balance between audience and artist in the development of new forms and narratives – a challenge that the theatre-maker is already used to facing.

Anthony Auerbach raises a set of issues with regard to the occupation of public space by video technology. The ubiquity of lens-based media in the public realm has been a topic of moral and political concern for cultural theorists for some time – rooted to a large extent in Guy Debord's critique of the society of the spectacle (1967), but also prefigured in earlier criticisms of the stultifying or alienating effects of the mass media, particularly those of the entertainment industries, offered by Theodor Adorno and Max Horkheimer in *The Dialectic of Enlightenment* (1947)[23]. However, it is perhaps French theorist, Jean Baudrillard, who has directed most attention to the domination of lens-based or electronic images in contemporary society in his work on simulacra and simulation. For Baudrillard, the media have formed a self-sufficient, self-governing, self-cannibalising world that no longer has an obligation to the real. This results in a "desert of the real." In Baudrillard's scenario, the image world is caught in a trap where it is impossible to isolate the process of simulation and it is just as impossible to isolate the process of the real, or, that is, to "prove the real," a scenario in which the only hope for recuperation of the real is in iconoclasm.[24] And, as if to put the theory into practice, Auerbach and a number of collaborators have set out not only to explore video as a part of the urban fabric but also to explore ways in which the 'spaces' occupied by urban video can be made the site of critical and reflective practice, and in effect form a basis for iconoclasm.

There are, of course, precedents for this in the outdoor work of several late twentieth century artists such as Barbara Kruger and Jenny Holzer, Felix Gonzales-Torres and even the less overtly political Jeff Koons who appropriated the urban spaces of advertising, subverting the parodying the languages and forms of mass media as the basis for critical practice. Similarly, *Video as Urban Condition* proposes that artists appropriate the spaces, technologies and approaches used in urban video which are diverse and multiform, including home video, independent artist's projects, educational and community initiatives as well as public forms such as those in the service of commerce or surveillance. However, the *Video as Urban Condition* project is not a matter of several artists working separately with similar methodologies, but is the purposeful building of a visual archive that documents critical practice and reflects a shared desire to examine "a medium whose most distinctive characteristics are multiplicity and diversity, a form which is not contained by the norms of art institutions or the exclusive domains of professionals."[25] The artists represented may work independently, but all come under the aegis of a shared vision, which accommodates a range of practices, but which, in the examples given by Auerbach in his paper, seem to priviledge iconoclasm in one form or another. In their separate ways, the projects described by Manu Luksch, Paul O'Connor, Juha Huuskonen and Ole Scheeren at the 2004 *Video as Urban Condition* International Symposium all manage to address the politics of video as part of the urban fabric and rupture what art historian and critic, Hal Foster, regards as the seamlessness of spectacle when he, like Baudrillard, looks for a return to the real through the iconoclasm produced in the practices of contemporary art.[26]

A reality check of a different order also underpins the project described in the paper offered by Drew Hemment, Theo Humphries, John Evans and Mika Raento collaborating on the *Loca* project (location-oriented critical arts). This group seeks to expose the pervasiveness of hidden surveillance and bring an awareness of its insidiousness. The project is purposefully interdisciplinary, sitting within a tradition of challenges to the ivory tower ethos of the artworld that incorporates the everyday, courts low or alternative cultures and shows a disregard of cultural hierarchies. These challenges can be tracked back to the beginning of avant-garde in Courbet's particular brand of realism and the quotidian subject matter of the Impressionists. Following this, the early twentieth century avant-garde also showed an awareness of the importance of lens and screen-based technologies which foretold the advent of a culture that would be dominated by screen-based mass-media, a culture in which the nature and status of both art and artist would change and a culture in which

22 Sean Dixon, "adventures in cyber-theatre (or the actor's fear of the disembodied audience)," in Zapp op. cit.

23 Guy Debord, *Society of the Spectacle*, (1967), (London: Rebel Press, 1992). Theodor Adorno and Max Horkheimer, *The Dialectic of Enlightenment*, (1947), (London and New York: Verso, 1997).

24 Jean Baudrillard, "Simulacra and Simulations," in Mark Poster, ed. *Jean Baudrillard, Selected Writings* (Oxford: Polity Press in association with Basil Blackwell, 1988).

25 <www.vargas.org.uk/projects/video_as/>.

26 Hal Foster, *The Return of the Real* (Cambridge, Massachusetts: The MIT Press, 1996), 127-144.

art would leave the conserves of the museum and gallery. Loca brings together these two related aspects of avant-garde practice (the turn to the everyday and the embrace of state of the art technologies) and also follows another early twentieth century avant-garde principle – that art should be socially and politically engaged.

Loca also takes its place among debates about the potential that networked technologies have brought for the formation of new communities and about the ways in which they might reconfigure the social.[27] Locative media stands in a special position in relation to such debates, as the communities or social situations that are made possible are not only virtual but localised, at the threshold of the virtual and actual life. At their least interactive and potentially most controlling, locative software such as Global Positioning Systems (GPS) or Geographic Information Systems (GIS) provide intricate mapping systems, a safeguard against getting lost in the outdoors, but also in their military origins, capable of surveillance of a quite specific order. In other words, the social structures that GPS/GIS are based on are not those of localised communities, but replicate the regulatory conventions of society at large. But, while the control is largely in the hands of the owners and producers of GPS/GIS, Global Systems for Mobile Communications (GSM) hardware is often literally in the hands of the user in devices that mimic or combine with mobile phone and digital camera technologies. The control that this gives to users can be used as a form of resistance to the ready-made (some would say inherently regulatory) knowledge of commercially or officially/institutionally produced GPS/GIS. Loca's chosen technology is bluetooth, questionable for its powers of insinuous surveillance and thus appropriate to the critique of technological invasiveness at the heart of the project. As these four authors also note, "The intent of *Loca* is to equip people to deal with the ambiguity and to make informed decisions about the networks that they populate." In doing so, the project offers the potential for resistance, the potential for creativity and empowerment and the potential for the development of alternative social networks.[28]

This section of *Hothaus Papers* covers a range of spatial practices using new media both within virtual space and in projects in which new media works inhabit or are produced in the physical environment. The next set of papers addresses similar issues concerning the implications for art of the redeployment and configuration of space through new media, but focuses more specifically on issues of curatorial practice that have emerged with the embrace of new media both by artists and art institutions.

27 See, for instance, the essays in "Searching for Community Online," Part V of David Trend, op. cit., 251-293.
28 For a discussion of the potential for resistance in locative media, see Simon Pope, "The Shape of Locative Media," *Mute Magazine*, issue 19, February 9, 2005.

Expanded Literature: Writing Beyond the Page
Mark Hancock

Much contemporary thinking in the arts has given consideration to the development of the moving image and the development of interactivity and user/viewer engagement. Alongside these developments has been the slow burning of the fuse of writerly concerns of how to engage with the digital and make the reader much more than merely a passive receiver. In the same way that Gene Youngblood coined the phrase 'Expanded Cinema' to emphasise how the moving image might be about so much more than the projector and single screen, so the term 'Expanded Literature' might best summarise how the word is no longer locked into the old paradigm of writer and reader.

So, in what ways has the written word developed? How have writers engaged with the possibilities of new media? One of the developments has been the extra dimensions that they have been able to add to their work. The written word is no longer at the mercy of the flat, two-dimensional page. In the same way that the moving image has expanded out beyond the flat screen of the movie theatre and become so much more, in terms of how we can manipulate and interact with it, so the written word, through its development within media, has become all of these things as well. In short, we have added dimension to our text.

This paper considers the spatial interaction a reader might have with a written work. To consider this interaction and relationship, two works will be considered. The first of these is Shelley Jackson's *Skin* (2003). This project is non-digital in its initial realisation, but considering how it invokes the relationship of the reader to the text, interesting parallels can be drawn between this and *Screen*, a collaborative project at Brown University, Rhode Island.

Around September of 2003 the writer Shelley Jackson posted a request in several art journals and on her website asking for people to take part in her new project. Jackson had previously written works that explored the relationship between hypertext fiction and traditional hard copy fiction, but this project was something new and different. The participants would become words. That is, they would receive one word from a story that had been written by Jackson and have this tattooed on their body. There were stipulations to the tattooing, for instance, if you received the word 'Leg' you would not be able to have that tattooed on your actual leg. In essence the word must not refer to an element of the individual on whom it was written. So instead they become the carrier of the word, and became known as 'Words' themselves. Once the participants had sent in photographs of their tattoo, they would be sent a copy of the complete story as written by Jackson. A further stipulation was that they cannot share the story with anyone else.

The story is contained as individual elements of narrative data, carried by each participant. If we can imagine the story occupying this vast area and the only way to read it might be by viewing the world as a whole, then like a giant kaleidoscope being shaken every time a word moves across the globe, so the story changes as the 'Words' rearrange themselves, continually rewriting the storyline. The work may never be considered as a whole entity, but instead exists as some form of dispersed narrative. The idea of the space in which the novel exists and is accessible, becomes renegotiated, and may in fact never be truly defined. In *Skin*, the 'Words' exist independently of each other and may never come into contact. Further to this point of changing narrative is how it develops as one of the 'Words' passes away and the story becomes something different as there are less 'Words'. It would be interesting to be able to re-read the story every few years to see how much of it had changed! Like an old book that we love and continually find to our annoyance that pages have fallen out of, the *Skin* story becomes something different if we allow this 'decay' to be part of it's development.

Skin destroys the traditional relationship of reader and author. Where, historically, a writer may have attempted to either write for the maximum amount of readers, or, at the very least reach a specific audience, *Skin* seems to care very little for the potential audience. It requires a very active participation of numerous individuals who are the only true readers of the work. All that is left for the rest of us is the documentation of the project as presented on Shelley Jackson's website. We, the non-participants have only our imaginations and a feel for what our relationship to the text might be. This imagined spatial relationship of reader to text is reconsidered and played out along a non-traditional path. One that leads to rather ambiguous feelings about the work for anyone not directly involved in the project itself.

What *Skin* does give us, is a chance to consider how an artwork might occupy a much broader place than the individual elements themselves. An example of the sum of the parts being greater than the whole? Maybe. The 'Words' occupy their space and have a relationship with each other even though they may never actually meet each other. One of the things that intrigues me about this project is in my own relationship to these 'Words'. For instance, there are "approximately 1780 of 2095" 'Words' in existence at the moment (November 2004). A number of these are based in England. It's curious to imagine the proximity of myself to one of the 'Words'. Am I any closer to understanding the overall narrative based on whether or not I personally interact with one of the 'Words'? In some ways I am, because I begin to see the artwork itself, and it moves from the realm of imagination to reality. And this grounding to a particular location dispels the image in my mind of the overall text. After seeing a single 'Word', the imagined web of complete text that I held in my mind's eye, no longer exists as a complete entity.

A project spaced out over such a distance, I suppose may never really be read by anyone. And the story only has one original copy, the one that is tattooed on all of the participants. The electronic copy is only the blueprint of the work. The technical specification? A vibrant harmony links the 'Words' across the world. To quote Jackson when interviewed about the project: "The original story is only the DNA; the real story as living organism is perpetually rearranging and revising itself, and its meaning is the aggregate of a myriad of idiosyncratic personal interpretations that will attach themselves to its words, interpretations I have invited but can't predict or control. This too is true of all stories, in a sense."

For some time my feelings were rather ambivalent about this project. On the one hand I loved it and was envious of the people who had gotten in quickly enough to become 'Words'. On the other hand, it frustrated me. I want to read the story. I feel left out of the project and unable to fully perceive it. But then I realised that this might be an intrinsic part of the whole project. It makes me stop and reconsider what I've taken for granted for most of my life. That any work of art or literature is always right there, both quantifiable and available for me. I can consume and consider (most of the time) and then move on. And in doing so, perhaps don't stop to truly look as hard as maybe I should. So it's odd that a work so intangible, should be the one to make me stop and consider!

A work such as *Skin* presents a paradigm within which we can consider other projects that make use of this spreading out across a network (both physical and virtual.) A quote from Josephine Bosma's essay, *No Ego: Preserving the Exchange Between Artist and Audience* which considers archiving digital works, is equally applicable to this project: "art does make one tend to get stuck, however slightly, in quite rigid ideas about art as a material object of culture"

What reminded me of this quote whilst writing about *Skin*, was the idea of "quite rigid ideas about art as a material object." And of course, *Skin* flaunts this idea of material object. In one way it maps itself directly onto the most precious of objects, the human body, whilst at the same time devaluing itself as a work of art that can be preserved for future generations to enjoy. Eventually, the only things that will exist of the work, are the essays and discussions of it. Like performance art actions, the documentation will be all that remains.

An interesting aspect of this work is how we can use it as a reference point for consideration of the issues facing artists working within the digital, particularly net art. Art created in this environment faces similar concerns of audience relationships and spatial concerns. The idea of spatial relationships within a text translates well into many contemporary interactive works that address the relationship between the flesh and the machine. *Screen* is one such work that sits well between traditional art forms and media arts. *Screen* was developed at Brown University, Providence, Rhode Island in the USA, by a team consisting of Noah Wardrip-Fruin, Josh Carroll, Robert Coover, Shawn Greenlee, and Andrew McClain. The intention of the project was to make a creative work using the University's Cave I facility.

The team were from the University's creative writing department, with many of its members well known within the world of digital literature. *Screen* was developed as a writing exercise and with

Noah Wardrip-Fruin, Sascha Becker, Josh Carroll, Robert Coover, Shawn Greelee, and Andrew McClain, *Screen,* Center for Computation and Visualization, Brown University. Photos: Josh Carroll.

consideration of the textual materiality and engagement being as important as the narrative, but only in as much as the careful consideration of a poem might 'matter.' By this I mean that the words are not merely 'plastered' over the technology, but the technology forms an integral part of the narrative and its reading. By engaging with *Screen*, the reader is caught up into the world of text, just as one might be if one were trying to explain the feeling of becoming deeply engulfed in a spellbinding narrative.

In *Screen* the user dons the headset and glove and steps into the Cave 'room.' Once inside, the text begins to appear in a three-dimensional form across the walls. Initially, the reader stands and enjoys the story. However, after a short period, the text begins to rip away from the screen and move about the reader. At this stage it is possible to engage with the text and knock it back into the blank spaces left on the screen as a result of the departed words. In this way, the story becomes rewritten and neologisms are created.

Reactions to *Screen* have been varied. Apparently one professor who was invited to experience the work, at first thought it was merely three-dimensional text on walls. He sat down in the cave complaining that there was nothing new being done with the technology. Once the text began to rip away from the walls and fly about, he practically fell from his chair in surprise!

Screen reverses what the *Skin* project gives us. Whereas *Skin* is about the text's interaction with the skin and spatial coordinates of the material carrier, *Screen* is about the body's relation to the immateriality of the text: a subtle difference. However, *Screen* and *Skin* have much in common. They are both about how the individual's location and coordinates, in relation to the words, affect how the piece is read. Where hardcopy text remains the same, no matter where we take it, work of this type is altered whenever we move. Constantly shifting and altering its narrative. The traditional idea of a story that is produced by an author and remains in a single form forever, is no longer a given certainty.

The Heisenberg uncertainty principle in physics states that anything we observe is affected by the fact of our viewing it. These narratives are affected in the very same way: the reader makes a difference to the story. This also ties into Barthes' 'death of the author' where authorship ultimately shifts to the reader and away from the writer. And, written within this era of digital literature, we have to accept that it is ourselves, and our bodies, that help shape the new narratives.

> *Skin*: ‹www.ineradicablestain.com/skin.html›.
> *Screen: Bodily Interaction with Text in Immersive VR* (Joshua J Carroll, Robert Coover, Shawn Greenlee, Andrew McClain, Noah Wardrip-Fruin) 2002 ‹www.hyperfiction.org/screen/›
> *TextRain*: ‹www.creativenerve.com/textrain.html›.
> John Gribbin, *In Search of Schrodinger's Cat: Quantum Physics and Reality* (London: Corgi Adult, 1985).
> *Cave* is an "immersive virtual reality lab" developed by six departments at Brown University. The Physics, Geology, Applied Math, Chemistry, Computer Science and Cognitive Science departments were awarded a National Science Foundation grant to develop the eight-foot square cubicle and associated supercomputing facility. Although the equipment was initially developed for these departments, it was made available for University wide use.

In Convesation
Bill Fontana & Ben Borthwick

Ben Borthwick (left) and
Bill Fontana (right) in
converation at VIVID, 29
June 2005

Borthwick

If a conventional definition of sculpture is an object in space, then what
does it mean to have a sound sculpture? For me the key word that links
the sonic with the spatial is volume, which measures both mass and
acoustic phenomena. Within your work, how does the idea of a sound
sculpture actually come together?

Fontana

Well, I began calling my works sound sculptures about thirty years
ago because I read a passage in book by Marcel Duchamp. It was
notes for *The Large Glass* and there's a passage in there that says
musical sculpture sounds lasting and leading, forming and sounding,
a sculpture that lasts. It's sort of ingrained in my memory bank. The
exact quote from Duchamp is "musical sculpture sounds lasting and
leading, forming and sounding, a sculpture that lasts." And so, when I
read that, thirty years ago, and I was thinking about what I was doing
working with what I call the sculptural properties of sound, in the
sense that I had started making multi-track film recordings of sounds
in the environment that were really like sound mapping projects. I
became interested in the fact that if you listen to sounds from different
points in space, each point in space is going to hear the sound a little
bit differently. If you start thinking very literally about a sound that
you are hearing and you think to yourself, 'well what is it?' you kind
of ask yourself a rhetorical question. The rhetorical answer I would
always come up with is that sound is all the possible ways that we
hear. I started to think about mapping sounds in real-time and playing
them out of loud speakers in space. I started thinking about the sounds
as volumes of space that existed in time and I called them sound
sculptures because they dealt with space and volume, but they had a
temporal aspect.

Borthwick

So, you started out as coming more from a musical composition background, and so the field recordings led you to reconstructing these recordings spatially – they were the impetus to move away from the performance environment and into the gallery context.

Fontana

I became interested in my own perception of the world and perception of sound, and composition became a form of listening to the world. If I felt in a musical state of mind, then whatever I was carrying around with me became musical. I started to document these experiences with tape recorders – I carried a recorder around with me wherever I went. Whenever I heard anything interesting, I would record it. Then in the early seventies, I got this amazing job in Australia with the ABC where they asked me to make recordings in Australia of whatever seemed interesting to me – this, for the ABC in Sydney! This gave me access to all of the recording resources that existed at this time I could occasionally check out an outside broadcast truck that had an eight channel recorder in it and I could set off with a technician and set up their crews in the environment and make these real-time recordings. In 1976, it was a pretty unusual thing to be doing – that's really when I read the Duchamp passage and decided that sound is a sculptural material in the way that steel or stone or anything else that we normally think of sculpture as being. The only thing was that it was invisible and it used time. But it seemed that it could be physical and invisible at the same time and I didn't have a problem with that. The advantage of being invisible was that it had the ability to alter your perceptions of the visible, like *Sound Island* (1994), a project in Paris 12 years ago with a famous icon, the Arc de Triomphe, a very visited war monument. I took an invisible sound and wrapped the Arc de Triomphe with the sound of the sea, creating the life of the Normandy coast and that completely altered people's relationship to this visual icon. To me, that was a really interesting moment, especially since half the people that went there were tourists who didn't know anything about what the Ministry of Culture was up to in asking me to do that.

Borthwick

And, also, they maybe didn't know, maybe didn't understand, the specifics of what the Arc de Triomphe meant to the French nation, for instance. So you have this double dislocation, you have the dislocation of the cultural history of the Arc de Triomphe within France – when for many of us, for me anyway, the Arc de Triomphe is a symbol of France but I don't necessarily know what it's historical function is.

Fontana

Well, I think it was built by Napoleon and it is the Tomb of the Unknown Soldier and there's a perpetual flame there, and every day they have some ceremony – about the Tomb of the Unknown Soldier, so it's like *the* war memorial in France.

Borthwick

So wrapping it in the sound of the sea?

Fontana

Well, the sea coming from Normandy on the 50th anniversary of D Day, during the summer of '94.

Borthwick

Ok, so the fact that it's, and this might be a banal, quite literal, point, but the fact that it's a traffic island...

Fontana

Right, it's the noisiest place in Paris.

Borthwick

Maybe we can talk about this idea of nature as white noise. We think of noise as being something imposed on nature by machinery, by industry, but noise is all around us. Something we don't necessarily think about so much is the way that nature is fetishised as an ideal quiet place when, actually, nature is teeming with frequencies.

Fontana

This relates to a project I did in Vienna. It's called *Landscape Soundings* from 1990. It was installed on the facades of these two incredible Neuburg museums, the Kunsthistorisches and the Naturhistorisches museums. Those buildings are 600ft long and they face each other across a park named after Maria Theresia. I did a piece which put live markings on an ancient wetlands forest of the Danube in the eastern part of Austria and transmitted that for a few weeks into that space. It superimposed the natural landscape on the urban landscape and really changed the character of that space. Because the microphones were lurking in this forest by themselves without people holding them, they became like trees, and birds that normally avoid you, especially cuckoos, would happen to sit down next to a microphone. Their voices were kind of echoing through an array of microphones and bigger than life – giant size birds were suddenly sounding off with these parallel sounds in Vienna.

Borthwick

This is the relationship between nature and the built environment that is an ongoing theme in art. I'm thinking that Lothar Baumgarten did a project that had similar motivations where he took photographs of a wetland and then just created a sound track using the sounds of the city, but kind of processing them and tweaking them to invert that relationship between image and sound. That brings us round to the way that in many of your pieces you've transposed the sounds of one environment into the location of another environment – there's the Arc de Triomphe piece, and in Trafalgar Square in London where you did another project with the Maritime Museum that was a live link...

Fontana

...from Trafalgar to Trafalgar square...

Borthwick

So, these works fold in many different elements – you have the
historical, which is memorialised in Trafalgar Square in Nelson's
column, you have the geographical which is this still existing place,
Trafalgar, off the coast of Spain. That link gets lost through time as the
battle of Trafalgar is less and less part of our lives. But maybe let's think
about the temporality of different places and the relationship between
time and place that you've worked with. For some projects where there's
a live link and then others where you've made recordings which are
then installed in a different situation.

Fontana

Very often, the projects have been live transfers of acoustic landscapes
to architectural and public spaces and sometimes to museum spaces.
When I install recordings like I did here at VIVID – this was originally
a live performance – it acquires a second life. A piece from 2004,
Speeds of Time, is an eight-channel installation that is permanently
installed at the Haunch of Venison gallery in London that you can hear
by appointment. It is based on a work that exposes our concepts of
time, exposes speeds of time. It was originally installed as a live piece
inside the Palace of Westminster in which there were microphones and
vibration sensors in the tower of Big Ben, listening to the clockwork
of the bells. Every tick of the clock and gong of the bell went through
eight different time delays that changed over the course of the day.
It was also spatialised in moving through speakers – and this was
installed in a beautiful colonnade under the tower of Big Ben. The work
existed as a temporary installation when it was running in long multi-
track recordings, which now can be repeated as an installation that
runs as an eight-channel recording.

Borthwick

And in that piece, as with the bell composition for St. Martin's church
here in Birmingham, the compositional units that you set up have a
very mathematical, clearly defined, rhythm, which is not unlike the
Speeds of Time. Those rhythms start to fade and depart from their rigid
structure. In their place something much more fluid emerges where
they move out of synch. You have this notion of time but also a notion
of how time is not necessarily fixed, how we have different speeds
of time. *Speeds of Time* relates to a piece you did in Venice, which
elaborates on this and folds different temporalities into a single site.

Fontana

Yes, *Acoustical Visions of Venice* was in the Venice Biennale in '99. It
was installed on the façade of a famous building called the Dogana at
the junction of the Grand Canal and the Giudecca – with these famous
views of the Venice Lagoon. I was interested in creating a work that

described the distance you could see so that when you looked at the Venice skyline you kind of hear the distance. Something pretty magical happened. I had 14 live microphones set up in different areas of Venice and they were transmitting in real time, and so a lot of times what you had were quiet, subtle, ambient collages of Venice sounds: footsteps, water, pigeons, some voices, and if you weren't very sensitive, you might not realise that anything was even happening. Every microphone could hear all the bells in Venice that were ringing within the city centre but because sound travels at about 1,000ft per second each microphone was hearing them at different times. All the transmitted sounds would arrive to the loudspeakers on south of the Dogana at the speed of light because they were being transmitted and because Venice doesn't have traffic islands you would then hear the natural acoustic sounds of the bells arriving there. So whenever these events occurred, suddenly this sort of quiet ambient collage of Venice became multi-dimensional and you would get amazing sensations of acoustic depth.

Borthwick

Essentially, the sound from one side of Venice would be simultaneously transmitted and broadcast in the Dogana, and again as a kind of echo when it reached a microphone on the other side of the city. So there were 14 different interpretations of a single sound that were happening at intervals of up to a few seconds.

Fontana

Actually, it depends a little bit on the weather. Three seconds is about a little more than half a mile and, depending on the wind and temperature conditions, it's possible get a delay. The biggest two bells of Venice, the most audible bells in Venice, are the big clock in Piazza San Marco and opposite at San Giorgio. Those two are the dominant bells that travel the furthest, but there are lots of other churches in Venice.

Borthwick

This idea that you can hear what you can see so the horizon can somehow respond to you in an auditory way is fascinating. There is a time-lapse between the visual and aural modes of perception, and the time those sounds take to travel from one place to another is like a heavily compressed form of memory, another thing that you have worked with in a number of different pieces. For me, sound is a particularly powerful medium through which to transmit memories, whether it's through story telling, through sonic landscapes that become extinct or become so familiar and part of our everyday lives that any challenge or transformation of them becomes a very powerful experience for us. The piece in Berlin that you did on your DAAD Fellowship in 1984 – that's a moment in European history that has a very, very particular place, both because of the non-place that was Berlin during the Cold War, but also that non-place became a very active and fertile environment for a lot of alternative music – Nick Cave and Einsturzende Neubaten were there...

Fontana

Arvo Pärt was there as well...

Borthwick

So in some ways it was like a place out of time and your installation there really excavated that history. Can you talk a little about that?

Fontana

The work was called *Distant Trains* – its German title is *Entfernte Züge*, which is a kind of wordplay in German. Entfernte Züge means distant trains, but entfernen means to remove. It was installed in the room of a famous train station called Anhalter Bahnhof, which was close to Checkpoint Charlie and the Berlin Wall and, in 1984, was this sort of weird forgotten place. People walked their dogs there, it was mostly just an empty field. There's a little bit of the façade of the old station still standing, and it used to be one of the great train stations of Berlin. Imagine how strange it would seem finding King's Cross in London or Grand Central Station in New York was just a vacant lot. To me, this space was haunted with sound and acoustic memories that had such a mixed complicated history because of the war and things that went on there. I wanted to somehow activate it as a space of memory and what I did was I put eight microphones in the main train station of Cologne, which is the busiest contemporary German station, and brought the sounds to Berlin and reconstructed the Cologne station in Berlin at the Ahalter Bahnhof out of loudspeakers that were buried in fields in the positions of the platforms of the original station. And there was something about the acoustic orientation of speakers being buried in the ground: boxes pointing up that reinforced airway frequencies making the sound really present in the space, so you got this mixture of station announcements of trains going to Berlin and you hear the extra sounds of trains, the wheels and the motion. It became a very emotional space because in 1984 there were still a lot of people alive who had memories of the station. Some of those people came there because they were drawn by hearing the sounds of the station in the distance, and one of the partners I had in the project, which was the big public radio station in Cologne did a documentary piece using some of these people. It was quite interesting.

Borthwick

Not only would many of the people remember the train station when it was active, but by inference, that means that they were alive before the war and bore witness to and maybe even were part of the machinery of the war – and it must have been a very powerful and unexpected memory to be resurrected in this way. We have certain mechanisms by which to deal with images and when we see them we somehow know how to situate them within our experience. But when you hear a sound from the past – probably the most familiar is the sound of the voice of a parent who's died or someone close to you who's died, it can really rip you apart emotionally.

Fontana

Well, the thing that was interesting was that it wasn't dealing with sounds from the past, it was taking sounds of the present and putting these in a situation where it activated memories of sounds of the past.

Borthwick

Because of its location. It's again this folding in of the present and the past, these layerings – of representation – basically it's a place and a time...

Fontana

But also it relates to your earlier question about sound as a sculptural medium, because the work is invisible and is very much a sculptural object in that space. It had a physical presence there – and really was very much a sound sculpture.

Borthwick

But on the other hand, without having been there to walk through it, I can imagine that while the material you put in place was invisible, the fact that it was a bombed out shell of one of the greatest Berlin train stations – I'm sure that that carried a poignancy when folded in with the sound...

Fontana

Well, it would have been trivial to do anything visual in that situation – as it would have been trivial in Venice or in Paris or any of these places because the architectural centres are so powerful and so interesting. The thing is, by taking the sound to the edge of vision, the sound is so visual in itself, that it kind of plays with that.

Borthwick

Do you think it's important for people who experience your work to have some kind of understanding of the locations or the sounds that are being referred to?

Fontana

I think that it's always interesting if someone understands something intellectually, but I also believe that the experience, the actual physical acoustic experience has to hit somebody directly so that if you don't have any knowledge of what it is and you just have the experience, it also has to work on that level.

Borthwick

Like a visual experience – you don't need to know what it is you are seeing to have some kind of relationship with it. Just thinking about the history of spaces and sounds, it seems appropriate to think about the changing histories of St Martin's and its current situation where it's enclosed to the point of suffocation by the Bullring. What does that mean culturally and economically? How has it transformed the perception of Birmingham for people who don't live here, as well as its impact on the city's self-image? From the outside, it seems to be a very interesting proposition that the city is going through a process of transformation and shifting the emphasis from an industrial legacy to the Bullring which is the centre piece of Birmingham as a consumer destination. Within that I think there's an analogy or metaphor for St Martin's, which obviously rubs right up against the Bullring, and for bell-ringing in general where there's a cultural history that's on the point of obsolescence. There's a necessity to rethink what that history is – so, in the case of the city, it's the industrial history and in the case of St Martin's, it's bell ringing. The bells no longer mark the time of day for the people who live within the auditory sphere of the Church.

Fontana

Well, the bells now are St Martin's. If you look at its clock faces – at one time in its history it used to actually have a clockwork mechanism and, at a certain level, the tower behind the clock faces in that room is still quote 'the clock' – only there's no clock there to mark the time.

Borthwick

How long ago did you propose the piece?

Fontana

I was invited to Birmingham by the Arts Council of England and BEAST (Birmingham Electro Acoustic Sound Theatre) to do a Research Fellowship to investigate the future of sound issues in this area of Birmingham. Part of this was to think about potential for sound art projects and to get people like architects and urban planners to think about sound quality issues. So, I met a lot of people, walked around, recorded a lot of sounds. St Martin's and the Bullring are actually one side of, part of, Eastside in fact, which is the old industrial part of Birmingham. And I became obsessed with – fascinated with St Martin's because I'd always been interested in change-ringing as a tradition. At St Martin's we have one of the largest collections of bells in England that you literally cannot hear because, when the Bullring was designed and they built Selfridges and the buildings around, it completely blocked off the sound of the bells on that side of Birmingham. St Martin's was built to a 15th century scale (the original St Martin's church was a Norman church). Any building in that part of Birmingham is higher than St Martin's, so the poor bells are just trapped there. It's bad enough that it's surrounded by a lot of buildings, and then you've got traffic noise, so the sound of the bells can't go anywhere. Originally, in pre-industrial Birmingham, St Martin's was the parish church of Birmingham and its bells tended to travel quite far. When change-ringing was first created as a practice in the 17th century, this wasn't an industrial landscape, the heights of buildings weren't very tall. In that environment, sound can go a distance. So it seemed to me an interesting idea to try and be a composer again and get the bell ringers to consider some ideas there were a little bit different from their normal practice – that through distortion they can generate big waves of sound – big clusters of bell sounds that coming out of the tower you'd have flying off the buildings facades and sort of running into the landscape of Birmingham more successfully than older compositions did. At first the bell ringers were very sceptical about this, saying "we don't do this, it's against our tradition" but they gradually kind of came around and feel differently about it now. It was really personal and a very interesting journey for the development of these people.

Borthwick

During the performance it was very hot day and I came dressed totally inappropriately. So I walked from the square in front of the church towards the Bullring to go and buy a pair of shorts to change into. The automatic doors opened and, as soon as they closed, I was in this hermetically sealed climate controlled environment where all I could hear was Kylie Minogue! Every ten yards the 'muzak' would change as you move into a sonic space defined by a different pop song that demarcated a new retail concession. The one time I could hear the bells was when they were all rung together. Only then did they manage to puncture the commodity soundtrack within the Bullring.

Fontana

There's a term for when all the bells ring at the same time, it's called choiring the bells. It's a very difficult thing to do because bells are all different weights when you're pulling them on the rope and its nearly impossible to get them to ring at the same time – the St. Martin's bell ringers are extremely skilled in being able to do that.

Borthwick

Would anyone like to ask any questions?

Audience

You were talking about the socio/historical/political context of some of Bill's previous work. Having been born in Hackney and lived in Harrow, the impact of constantly hearing church bells or, when I lived in India, of hearing Imam's calls or various religious chanting – would you view it as a sonic spread of religion in a way? Bells weren't there just to tell the time for the people, although they were quite a cohesive time telling machine.

Fontana

I guess, maybe because I'm not a religious person myself, to me the religious aspect of the bell is not as interesting as its acoustic aspect, I tend to think of them in a more abstract way.

Audience

I think I can add to that – I presumed that in fact we were talking about this crisis in bell ringing as an actual activity because it is now just done by a particular generation. I also presumed that because most people would associate bell-ringing with religious observance, that would affect how many people came to bell ringing. I was surprised to be told by the chief bell ringer that this was not the case and that bell-ringing in the eighteenth century was considered to be a sport done by the aristocracy. Early in the nineteenth century the Church of England had been so concerned about the anarchistic tendencies within bell ringing that they'd actually brought in and imposed a bell-ringing act, which allied bell-ringing to religious practices whereas it previously hadn't been. Here we get to the really interesting bit – there's a French cultural theorist called Alain Courbin who's written a history of village fairs. He also develops an argument that bells actually serve a lot of social functions outside the religious. This was also the case in Britain, in the eighteenth century, when the aristocracy bell-rang as a sport – they saw it as a physical exercise. So they weren't ringing the hours or bringing people to church services or marriages – they were actually just doing it for fun. Now, how that affected what they would actually play I don't know, I don't know whether any of you knows what that produced as an aesthetic form. But certainly, as a social function, it had to be a sports one, not an aesthetic one at all.

Fontana

It also had the quality of a secret society in a way, because if you look at changing the score there's a lot of mathematics involved and its really kind of remarkable intellectual exercise to create a change in the score. If you think there are seven or eight bells in a tower, and you think of the sequence one to eight, then seven and ten and if you were going to write every permutation for that sequence, how many thousands of permutations could you have? A full peal is supposed to express all the permutations, so there are instances where a re-enactment or change in the composition could take days, continuously – non stop, to perform. If you go into the St Martin's bell tower, you will see plaques on the walls with the names of bell ringers, the date and the tunes that they performed and how long it took, but there's this secular aspect to it that's a kind of secret mathematical society.

Borthwick

Something that's very interesting that Courbin talks about is how, when the church and religion are totally integrated into the fabric of a society, in some ways the church becomes invisible, like a given. Consequently the sounds emitted from the church do not connote religion in a singular way as they do in a more secular society. I always try look for the double meaning in things so that even if something is oppressive, whether it's architecture, sound, law or politics, there's usually some kind of subversive potential or pleasure within those authorities. Whatever seems problematic to outward appearances can also contain potential for misreadings. The piece for St. Martin's takes the harmonies of change ringing and by remapping these sounds onto a different structure it reveals the incredible noise and dissonance contained within bells.

Fontana

But the other thing that's interesting if you think about what kind of bell ringing was taking place in European countries at the time the changing ring was developed, I'm thinking particularly in the Netherlands, they had these Carillon towers that try to mimic the keyboard instrument. You know, you've got stationary valves and somebody's playing keyboard that looks a little bit like some kind of weird organ – and they tried to play tunes, which is very unsophisticated in my opinion, compared to the mathematical extravagance of changing bells.

Borthwick

The other thing that would seem very difficult to play bells on a keyboard is the introduction of mass – and the weight of a bell. If all of the bell ringers want to ring the bell at the same time, presumably the person ringing the big tenor bell, the biggest heaviest one, has to pull on the rope earlier and the people ringing the smaller ones pull later. So the performance to create a single sound is totally broken down into a series of choreographed actions and spread over a short duration of time. For a while on Sunday I was in the bell tower looking into the ante room, which separates the bell ringers from the belfry, where all you can see are the ropes. They appear through a hole in the floor and disappear through a hole in the ceiling. It was incredible, like watching a puppet theatre, but watching the strings instead of the puppets. But, there was always this dislocation between the movement of the string and the sound of the bell it was pulling. It was absolutely fascinating, like inhabiting a piano while it was being played. There you are, I've come back to the keyboard.

Fontana

One thing that's also interesting about English bells is they're on wheels and they rotate, and so the sound is really quite beautiful because it's moving with a little bit of a gallop and shifts the harmonics of the bell.

Audience

Could you talk a little bit about the placing of the microphones when you did the recording. The way we've got surround sound here in the gallery means I can walk up to a particular speaker and experience a particular bell and go to a different loudspeaker and experience a different bell.

Fontana

Well, the recording that I made in the bell tower, I had it on a four channel hard disc recorder, so I set up four microphones that were in close proximity to different bells in parts of the tower. Each microphone heard certain bells more intensely than other ones. There were also microphones in the tower and at recording stations set up outside some distances away. I spent a couple of days editing all these recordings. When I played them in the space that I didn't want to just try to recreate what happened at St Martin's on Sunday, I wanted to make something that was more specific to this place. So I took the recordings and played them through a sort of pan-spatialisation patch that Pete Batchelor from BEAST had produced. This enabled me to take the eight channels of sound and move them in space. I could put in two of those recorded channels that I had made and just have the sounds sort of claim the space, so that at one moment a certain bell's going to be over here and the next time it sounds maybe it's going to be over there. That seemed to me a really interesting aspect – I spent quite a bit of time experimenting with different volumes at which to play it because the real sound of the bell tower is extremely intense and loud. I didn't want to play it that aggressively in here because this is reverberant space and you would get a lot of reflection and it ruins the movement of the sound and you would lose the sound outside. So I basically tried to work the piece specifically for this space out of the recordings.

Audience

Why did you decide to bring a very site-specific work made for St Martin's into a gallery space?

Fontana

Because I was asked to. Also because I wanted it to have some kind of a legacy and because I had put it here it gave me the chance to envisage the problems of organising it and putting it together – and make a kind of public document out of it.

Borthwick

I think there's also the potential for hearing the piece in a way that's very different from being out on Sunday around the Church or around the city. Here, when Bill starts it up, you hear the volume that he's set it at. I had the chance to listen to it at different volumes and when it was louder, it became much more like the experience of being in the bell-tower where it became this very bodily, singlular experience of the sound. The volume that it's at now in the gallery actually allows for a spatialisation of the sound and for a kind of liminal relationship to the outside, where the sounds of the traffic come into the space. Some of the recordings actually have traffic sounds in them as well, so there's this confusion between the inside and the outside – what's live and what's recorded. At a certain moment there's this kind of concentric movement as a single set of harmonies moves from speaker to speaker and kind of creates a slightly nauseous feeling. That's something you can only get with repeated listening, where it becomes more like a story about the thing than the experience of the thing itself.

Fontana

One other idea I wanted to mention about St Martin's relates to the thoughts I had about Eastside. I also was thinking about the audibility of St Martin's as a kind of sound quality indicator for the Eastside area – that the urban planners and architects, as they think of reconfiguring Eastside, take into consideration the acoustic views of St Martins, in that they open not only visual views of St Martin's and Eastside, but allow it some corridors that sound can actually travel through and kind of restore some of its original audibility to the City. I have fantasies now about St Martin's and think of it like friends up there sending the sounds to some other towers (unbuilt towers) in Eastside – I think about putting it in the bell tower – or the tower that looks like a bell tower that has no bells – at the Ikon... so keep going... yes...

Audience

I just wanted to ask quickly about whether you had a fantasy about actually working with urban planners in the future. Do you see a role for a sound artist working with those urban planners and with architects in terms of the design of those urban environments?

Fontana

Well, I think you want to be kind of careful if you're an artist and you don't want to become a consultant. Making art is a lot different from being a consultant or an acoustic designer. But I think the sound artist can really engage in a very important dialogue with the urban planners and developers' sensitivity and I think, by creating an interesting sound work for a public space, that's the best way to actually create a public sensitivity to the space. Personally, I am more interested in making projects in space that cause people to think and ask questions than in writing papers and theories.

Are Theatre-Makers Natural Net Artists?
Janet Vaughan

The instinctive answer to the question 'Are theatre-makers natural net artists?' might conceivably be 'no', since at first glance it is difficult to imagine two more polarised art experiences than those found in the theatre and on the world wide web. The first is a shared experience for a grouped audience in a space populated with live performers, the second, an experience which can be understood as being exclusive to the individual via their computer whilst (potentially unconsciously) simultaneously shared with many geographically disparate audience members. Both theatre and internet art, however, are founded on person to person communication and it could be argued that both are multi-dimensional fictive contexts where truths and realities are played with, questioned and ultimately blurred.

Anecdotal evidence gleaned from discussions with fellow artists suggests that more and more theatre, performance or live art practitioners are making artworks for the web, and that many web artists and designers have crossed over from a theatre design/scenography training or practice. In short, there appears to be a striking number of artists from a background of performative practice (and therefore with a confident three-dimensional, audience-aware sensibility) inhabiting cyber-space, and perhaps beginning to make some of the most interesting work for the web. Companies involved in making devised performance work in the UK in the last ten to twenty years – such as Forced Entertainment, Third Angel, Blast Theory, Desperate Optimists and Talking Birds – tend to write about their work in similar ways, experiment with different combinations of media to explore their ideas and are, in general, making work which could be characterised as being informed by an 'urban' sensibility. All the companies listed have also made artworks for the web, generally as a natural progression from having experimented with film or video.

Although the artworks that these companies make, and the way that audiences experience them, are vastly different, all could loosely be described as making work which is descended from conceptual art and performance practice. They experiment with form, devising fractured or unconventional narratives in the exploration of a central idea or situation; often constructing performance from a series of intuitive connections or combinations of text and images (having confidence in their audience's intelligence and imaginative ability to find (or construct) meaning in, or from, this web of fiction).

Theatre, like all art, relies on sign systems. It works by combining various elements – visuals, sound, text and live performers – with the imagination, knowledge, memories, associations and understanding of the members of the audience, both individually and collectively. The work is incomplete without an audience and so is made very much with the audience in mind. Not least because they will be in the same room and their instant feedback will affect the way the work is performed, received and remembered – each laugh, shuffle or cough has the potential to nudge a performance in a subtly different direction.

Successful design for performance will create atmosphere by capturing the essence of a place rather than illustrating or presenting its appearance in full. It will operate on levels of metaphor and suggestion rather than showing a realistic representation. It leaves gaps, courts ambiguity, creates a world into which it takes the audience and then refuses to give them all the answers on a plate. Such theatre allows, expects and relies on its audience to piece together the fragments they are given, fill the gaps and use their human desire for narrative to piece together an understanding from the fragmentary suggestions that have been put before them. Text is an important part of the piece, but rather than starting from a script, companies devising new work will usually be incorporating the various voices of the artists involved and often combining these with found fragments of text. (In some of these companies, one or more of the performers has evolved over time into a writer and work has become more scripted, but the fragmentary structure and cross-narratives remain).

I would argue that many of these features are also recognisable in online work; and that perhaps these are some of the elements that make web artworks by theatre makers interesting. Perhaps a background in theatre enables a more complex understanding of the three-dimensional nature and possibilities of the internet. Maybe a theatre maker's understanding of an audience's desire to find narratives within a work, and their skill at manipulating content in a live/3D context over a fixed period of time for a captive audience means they have the best possible grounding for making the work which will influence the next phase of development of net-art.

New media – especially those which, like the internet, are adapted rather than invented media – take a while to find their feet, and artworks using such new forms will interrogate these forms themselves as well as using them to explore content. It takes time for those working with a new form to work out what it is, and what its potentials are. The extra dimension of the web is perhaps its organic, evolving, slipperyness. A strength as well as a weakness, no-one can yet pin down whether it is an art form in its own right, a tool to make art, a presentation opportunity for artworks – or all of these things. As artists have evolved their practice into that which moves across and mixes media with scant regard for formal boundaries, so all art has becomes just that – 'stuff' engaged with and made by artists. The very nature of the internet demands experimentation with the form, and the resulting first decade of net art is inevitably weighted towards the self-referential and throwaway – although, where the content of the work is strong and has the ability to engage its audience, the nature of the (web) form becomes less of a focus.

Just as software development can be described as having evolved in three phases: from the technical (programming), to the visual (art/graphics) to the dramatic (where games are structured using the dramatic/theatrical devices of character, perspective, fictional context, narrative, role, and super objective) so net art's progression can be characterised, having mirrored/responded to the world wide web's transition from information exchange mechanism to shop window to immersive leisure environment/activity. Throughout this evolution, online artworks have encompassed and referenced gaming; and the humour and methods of audience interaction used in such works give weight to the web's 'playful' reputation. Perhaps this helps to explain why much web art can be characterised or dismissed as self-referential or throwaway. In a sped-up world we can't believe that anyone will really spend any time looking at our work. As we explore the form, whether dipping in and out of it or making a deeper excavation, the clock is ticking. The web is changing and we are only a click away from losing our audiences. The limitations of dial-up and the instability or unpredictability of a platform with too many variables (service provider/connection/bandwidth/density of traffic) will also have played a part in establishing the throwaway as the prevalent idiom. There's nothing wrong with throwaway net art, or with net artworks which are consciously self-referential, but perhaps net art has reached the point where it's time for something else to develop?

Playfulness and humour don't always have to signal lightweight, throwaway and insubstantial. As in theatre, humour can be the key to exploring darkness, developing depth of content, meaning and audience engagement. As with theatre, there is surely an argument to combine playfulness, seriousness, humour, drama etc. within online artworks for deeper audience engagement and a more meaningful user-experience. Early web artworks by theatre makers tend to juxtapose text and image as if constructing a narrative form, whilst, with a nod to the non-linear/non-directed experience of the audience for web art, building in fluidity and flexibility: constructing a pick and mix order for collecting clues or story-parts and (as with much live work) relying on the audience's desire for narrative to make a sense for themselves out of the information they have been given, informed by the semi-immersive (theatrical) fictive context.

Web art is constantly, perhaps unhelpfully, judged by its freshness and originality, but perversely, it is often also in danger of being appropriated by the gallery or museum; of becoming a commodity artwork that must be conserved. As well as citing the limited success of translating web artworks into a gallery context, I would argue that, like live performance, the essence of web art is actually the audience/user experience rather than what appears on the screen (or stage). Therefore, like theatre, web art is really something temporary/temporal which should be preserved only in the memory – with its ideas, preoccupations, pixels and particles returned in time to the world for recycling through the future work of artists yet to come. Like theatre, it is fleetingness and ephemerality that is part of the attraction for me in the net art experience. Perhaps web art has been misplaced in being appropriated by, or slotted into, the fine art timeline/evolution/frame of reference. Another measure of the success of a work is often how participatory or interactive it is – whether the participation is knowing (eg in the form of email submission) or unknowing (eg in the form of culled data pulled from a third party site into a work, or hyperlinks leading out of it). I would argue that an audience doesn't necessarily need an authoring responsibility in order to be deemed to be participating, since the liveness of their presence as audience is necessary to navigate or complete the web artwork in the same way as it is pointless yet possible to perform theatre without an audience.

Much of the writing about web art observes that projects made collaboratively seem on the whole to have more to them as a user-experience. The number of different sensibilities and specialisms brought to bear on a collaborative project, and the potential for sharing ideas within a critical framework can be an extremely productive and exciting way to make work, whether for theatre, the web or elsewhere. The difference with web work is that it allows not only for collaboration, but for the boundary between collaborator and audience to be usefully and productively blurred.

Talking Birds' web art project *Web Demographic* (2003), for example, was developed through email conversations with about a hundred self-selecting participants who had the option to adopt a fictitious personality and who freely submitted their information, opinions and images. From these we devised ten (potentially contentious) theories about the world.

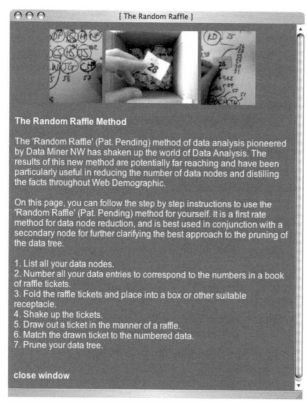

Talking Birds, screengrab from *Web Demographic* 2003

Although Talking Birds remains the author of the work, the audience/ collaborators continually nudged the direction the work took. The participatory nature of the project and the unpredictability and enthusiasm of the participants made it both enjoyable and fascinating for us as artists, but at the point where the theories were channelled into the 'product' part of the artwork, the process became far more difficult. Having got to know the audience/participants far more than we would have got to know our theatre audience – as individuals rather than a more generalised grouping – we now felt obliged to enable them to recognise something of their personal investment reflected in the finished artwork.

The *Web Demographic* process threw up an interesting conundrum for us, in that web art, though ostensibly representing a lower risk engagement for the audience, potentially has a much higher risk engagement for the artist. The geographically distant single audience member has no joint context to inform how s/he responds to the work, as is the case within a geographically near theatre audience and the relationship can become much more personal (despite being remote). Interestingly and surprisingly, the artist/audience relationship assumes a state of flux with the 'power balance' constantly shifting to and fro. Any pre-conception of who is in control is almost always upset. There is arguably more at stake for a theatre audience who have paid for a ticket and are trapped in room for an hour. The web art audience can spend just seconds on a web artwork if they aren't immediately drawn in. This is not, by the way, an argument to provide easily digestible chunks of web art to suit the click-happy browser, but is rather a plea for more experimentation, which stretches the audience, by developing web artworks which invite exploration and have a degree of 'carry-out', something the audience takes away from the experience.

Theatre-makers don't make web art in order to present a straightforward story; a film or a piece of text would be more effective for that. Theatre-makers are interested in using the technology to explore new ways of making juxtapositions and connections, fuelled by the power of suggestion. But we are also interested in it as a new vehicle for ideas, a new formal challenge, a new way to engage with our audience. For theatre artists making work for the web, the challenge is to use our live performance experience to make good use of the things that only the web can do, whilst at the same time experimenting to stretch the form and the expectations of the audience. Either we can continue to treat the web as just one method of communicating a story (utilising legitimate and recognised navigational formulae in order to allow the audience to understand how they may view it) or we can take up the challenge of making work for the internet that treats it in a fundamentally different way.

Audiences can be scared off by complex forms, unclear structures and intuitive navigation, but despite this I would argue strongly for us to persevere with developing complexity of content, aesthetic and navigation – not giving our audience the answers on a plate (and accepting that this will mean some loss of audience) – and continued development of humour as an audience 'hook'. Complexity of content – not the same as complexity of form, which in an online context can be manifest as florid programming masking shallow content – means giving the audience something to get their teeth into, leaving gaps for their imaginations to fill, giving them an experience which lingers in their minds and trusting them not to click off. Essentially creating the conditions where an audience wants to be as engaged in the work as they would want to be in the theatre, and then rewarding them for making that investment. Building complexity, or 'soul', into either medium is key in establishing trust in the audience/artist relationship. Such trust and artist/audience collaboration could transform an audience's ability to engage with our complex future web artworks and be key in countering the inherent difficulties of the non-linear (web) artwork – where an audience feels they might not have clicked on every link; might have missed something important; are having an Emperor's New Clothes experience; or are left with a flat 'Is that it?' Greater trust and complexity might lead to web artworks that engage and move an audience in the way live performance can and might make it possible for an audience to start to care about web artworks.

As the web and the public's relationship with it continue to evolve, the challenges for artists making works for the web continue to shift, but there are fundamental questions remaining about how artists and audiences engage with web artworks. I would argue that the challenges for the next wave of development in web art could be characterised as:

> Finding new ways to attract, develop, grow (and retain) an audience
> Developing the user experience through exploring the artist/ audience relationship
> Finding new ways to communicate meaning to an audience through a complex non-linear, non-directed (web art) experience
> Exploring ways of subverting the throwaway idiom, developing humour as a hook to explore matters of note
> Determining whether a web artwork can be interactive or participatory whilst maintaining a strong coherence of audience experience and audible artist's voice
> Exploring whether, as audience, it is possible to be immersed in and moved by a web work while remaining in control of how you view it
> Experimenting with form, content and complexity to achieve a mutually satisfying balance for artist and audience between enough and too much interactional choice

If some of the factors that are lacking or under-developed in current web art are those that theatre-makers already have detailed knowledge of, maybe it is indeed theatre-makers who are best placed to meet these challenges and perhaps, after all, theatre-makers are the next natural net artists.

Video as Urban Condition
Anthony Auerbach

On 4 December 2004, I attempted to distract the attention of the seminar audience from my presentation by simultaneously showing a series of video clips and a rolling slideshow. My point was that if we are capable holding a conversation while walking down a shopping street, while simultaneously negotiating the multitude of images and messages which accost us through various media, including video, then there would be no special reason why a seminar presentation should be restricted to a single channel. The receptivity of an urban-conditioned subject is hardly diminished when speech, text and moving image, information, narrative, polemic, suggestion and seduction are constantly interrupting one another. Here, in a book, I have to rely on you, the reader, to distract yourself. Or, at least, I do not flatter myself with your undivided attention. I do not know what screens flicker in the corner of your eye, what message alerts vibrate in your pocket, what entertainments beckon, what thoughts or anxieties might reduce your gaze to an empty stare, when appointments or fatigue will interrupt your reading, whether you are channel-hopping and have already skipped to another chapter or whether you are going to fast-forward to see whether I have any conclusion.

Video as Urban Condition is the headline for a project exploring how video shapes urban experience. I am going to describe in broad terms what I mean by that, what I and my collaborators have done about it, and in practical terms how we expect the project to develop in the future.

On the one hand, Video as Urban Condition acknowledges the ways in which video has become part of the urban fabric: that is, the infrastructure of terrestrial, satellite and cable networks; the ubiquity of video equipment in the home, the workplace, commercial and public spaces; the role of video technology in the surveillance and control of urban environments. The photographs that accompany this article document a number of these urban phenomena of video. On the other hand, Video as Urban Condition is about how our knowledge, perception and fantasy of urban environments are mediated by video: for example, through television, Hollywood recycled for the small screen, drama, fiction, documentary, news; through the urban fantasies of SimCity or Grand Theft Auto; through camcorders in the hands of tourists, artists, activists and other amateurs.

Compared with the locative or internet-based media, which other seminar contributors have spoken about, video is 'old technology'. Television has a history dating from the 1920s. It has not lost its place at the forefront of the mass-communications society and consumer culture it helped to create. Video, broadly defined, has continued to absorb and colonise data and transmission technologies from magnetic tape to digital satellite relays. The applications which have brought about perhaps the most remarkable shift in what we could call the relations of representation in recent years are the proliferation of closed-circuit television surveillance systems and the spread of portable video camera-recorders in the mass-market. The accessibility of video technology has encouraged not only the private interests of home video and independent artistic activity, but has also prompted community and educational initiatives putting the medium in the hands of underprivileged or excluded groups in society. Video technology has moreover become established among the tools of communication and witness at the disposal of activists and campaigners who maintain a position beyond the mainstream. At the same time, the power of video as a means of controlling desire and space continues to grow.

As an artist, such a condition represents a challenge because video fails to provide what most artists want from their medium, namely, the security of the work being framed and recognised as art and its ability to produce the particular kinds of subjectivity and receptivity associated with art. Crudely contrasted, an oil painting in a frame instructs the viewer that what you are looking at is an artwork and that you should be appropriately reverent and attentive to the surface in front of you (even if in practice we are not). But video does not do that. To be sure, the video screen captures eyeballs, but does not by itself dictate a particular mode of viewing. We are capable, indeed trained, to adjust our subjectivity, perception and receptivity instantaneously, almost continuously, as quickly as we flip the channels with a remote control.

We are accustomed to the idea that video images assert a multitude of different claims, that the same video screens, tubes or projectors convey a multitude of different messages and will ambush us in almost any location. This condition seemed to me to present a more exciting set of possibilities than the battle for artistic credibility. What strategies would emerge if we could create the opportunity for artists to make use of the existing video infrastructure? In other words, not to offer a TV set on a plinth in a white cube or a projection in a black box, but instead to remove the protection of such institutions, expose the work in urban space and accept this less reliable frame; to accept that video will not support an artist's claim to exceptional status or of itself command respect.

That seemed like a good idea and I began to investigate the practical possibilities. It will come as no surprise that in probing the structures that regulate public space and artistic production, I soon discovered the naivety of my proposition. To ground the project better, it was necessary to devise a means of gathering more information and mobilising critical reflection. The first outing of *Video as Urban Condition* therefore consisted of a presentation of what we called the *Video-pool Archive* and an international symposium (Austrian Cultural Forum, London 2 July 2004). The emphasis in this first phase was on the diversity and complexity which could be hidden behind a title like *Video as Urban Condition* and on understanding both aspects of the topic, video and the city, as interdisciplinary and public. The

contributors to the symposium, who drew on experiences, from architecture to activism, touching on a wide range of practices, interests and locations within the field, reflected the diversity of approaches we wanted to bring together.

Anna McCarthy, a media historian based at New York University, interprets the urban geographies of television at the crossroads of visual and material culture. She spoke about the origins of television as an urban phenomenon, how TV assembled people for communal viewing before TV sets could be found in nearly every home and the fascination exerted by live broadcasting before videotape. She considered the ways in which video is a tool for the production of knowledge: how 'site-specific' commercial television networks, for example, channels directed at airport lounges or doctors' waiting rooms, commodify their captive audiences and how mainstream news reporting, documentary and reality-TV (in the US) identify and objectify specific urban populations and urban geographies. She also considered the ways in which this knowledge is contested.

Manu Luksch founded ambientTV.NET, a collaborative platform which, as the name indicates, combines television (seeing over distance) and network architectures with a mise en scène which does not recognise a definite entrance or exit, beginning or end. She spoke about works which appropriate video images from existing urban networks: for example, *Broadbandit Highway* (2001), an endless road movie which hijacks the streams from traffic webcams posted on the internet; or a project for a movie shot on location not by a camera crew, but by the surveillance cameras already in place. Footage is recovered by the protagonist herself as a citizen under the provision of the UK Data Protection Act.

Paul O'Connor is co-founder of Undercurrents News Network, one of the organisations for whom the term 'video activism' was coined. In addition to producing and distributing programmes in support of a variety of local and global campaigns and supplying broadcasters with video images from its unique archive, Undercurrents has helped to bring camcorders on to the street to confront the police and mainstream media. Paul mentioned an incident when activists came to a demonstration armed with remote controls that they used to switch off the police surveillance officers' camcorders (the same consumer products as everyone else uses). In more ways than this, video activists have played an important role in protecting non-violent protesters and opening alternative channels of information, although it has to be said the scope of this work is severely limited outside of affluent liberal western democracies. However, a measure of the potential power of video would be suggested by imagining the risks an activist would run in filming popular protest or police action in a country where the mainstream media are under the strict control, for example, of a military government, occupying forces or a one-party state.

Juha Huuskonen is a founding member and chairman of Katastro.fi media art collective and is also the director of Pixelache electronic art festival based in Helsinki. He described the do-it-yourself, collective-competitive approach to the creative misuse of new media technology, which is behind the emergence of the VJ. VJing is creating and mixing video material in a live situation in connection with the music. In the hands of a VJ, video appears unrecorded and unrepeatable, uninhibited by traditional content (as we might expect, for example, from TV or from art, however abstract), but is embedded in a specific social situation both in its mode of production and of display.

Ole Scheeren is Director of the Office for Metropolitan Architecture (OMA) Rotterdam office. As an architect he is one of a minority to have taken video seriously and to have attempted to integrate it in the process of interpreting urban situations and design. He has also been involved independently in various art projects and exhibitions, such as *Cities on the Move,* London and Bangkok (1999) and *Media City*, Seoul (2002). I persuaded him to speak about OMA's biggest project to date: China Central Television Headquarters (CCTV) and Television Cultural Centre (TVCC) of which he is partner in charge (with Rem Koolhaas). In many ways at the opposite end of the scale from what Paul and Juha were talking about, this project makes the presence one of the world's most powerful broadcasters spectacularly felt in a city now undergoing extraordinary development and change. A huge building with an equally daunting technical and cultural programme, the project has to negotiate the future of television amidst the upheaval of rapid economic and social change, under a still repressive communist regime ambitious for capitalist development. Nonetheless, the structure of the building seems to anticipate the kind of undercurrents that emerge as portable video and communications technologies escape the control of centralised authorities.

The aim of the symposium was to open the field of enquiry by examining the implications and applications of video against the background of the myriad forms in which it appears in urban spaces. The speakers' contributions and the discussion they provoked helped to bring into focus the challenge of video I mentioned at the beginning of this article.

Curating video is still a problem even though conventions such as I mentioned earlier have evolved in an effort to contain this slippery medium within the norms of art institutions. These conventions attempt to assimilate video with sculpture (TV on a plinth) or a cross between monumental painting and cinema (big screen but no comfortable chairs), in any case to resist the ways in which gallery or museum-goers ordinarily encounter and use video in daily life, or indeed in other parts the same building on information screens, CCTV monitors, in the cafe, shop or lobby. These conventions moreover have influenced and been supported by artists. Nam June Paik's irreverent incorporation of TV into sculpture with the watchword, 'I make technology ridiculous' seems isolated. At the other extreme, Bill Viola provides his videos with all the paraphernalia of serious art: monumentality, authority, fear, suffering, nudity etc. Jeff Koons's work would have been a much more troubling and difficult to interpret had he chosen television sets instead of vacuum cleaners.

The *Video-pool Archive* is an attempt to step away from the kind of anxieties a museum curator might have had. We wanted an interpretative method that would, in the first place, be informative for us. A definition of the meaning of *Video as Urban Condition* was neither the starting point nor the goal. We needed a networked approach to gathering a collection of works and a more flexible way of presenting them. An open archive of video and other documentation, the *Video-pool* comprises compilations put together by artists and curators, informed by individual interpretations of 'video as urban condition' and based on particular areas of interest, experience and expertise. The *Video-pool Archive* therefore represents a variety of approaches and methods, forming a constellation of points of reference. It includes works by Blast Theory, Martin Bruch, Ursula Damm, Tomislav Gotovac, Juha Huuskonenen/Pixelache, Klub Zwei, Kristina Leko, Manu Luksch/ ambientTV.NET, Anna McCarthy, Isa Rosenberger, Carlo Sansolo, Ran Slavin, Hito Steyerl, Axel Stockburger, Superflex, Surveillance Camera Players, Milica Tomic, Undercurrents News Network. The aim is to maintain the anti-reductive approach, welcoming diversity as the collection expands.

The Video-pool installation functions as a self-service videotheque. Users are able to select tapes from the archive and view them using a group of players and monitors. The equipment (as far as possible cheap, reliable and easy-to-use: monitors, TVs, VCRs, cameras, DVD players of various shapes and sizes together with a library of VHS tapes and DVDs) is arranged in a way which suggests a miniature model of a city, an urban configuration hinting at aspects of video as an urban experience such as shifts in scale, duration and attention, networks and closed circuits.

The project is now developing on parallel lines:

> Working towards a presentation of the *Video-pool Archive* which could be distributed via National Touring Exhibitions as a growing, migratory resource. The difference between this project and most NTE products is that it is designed to encourage local input, with participating venues contributing collections to the archive reflecting local or specific thematic interests and concerns.
> Developing more informal international contacts with a view to presenting *Video as Urban Condition* events in cooperation with artist-led and independent organisations (from Bratislava to Tokyo) including screenings and discussions.

I have also been invited to develop the project for a museum in Austria. An exciting aspect of this project is the possibility of presenting a video installation using an outdoor space at the museum, simultaneously giving this space an identity as a public space within the city and generating an urban model within the museum. This installation would be the location for presenting a range of video works we have explored in the project.

Consumer culture is often blamed for the homogenisation of urban experience, through the domination of global brands and the insidious effects of the entertainment industry and media corporations. Video is at the heart of this process and is perhaps the pre-eminent means of propagating norms. Video has also produced the subjective hybrids that we know as infotainment, docudrama and reality TV, as well as diverse, unnamed alterations of perception and behaviour that are mediated by the video screen. Such alterations certainly influence, but do not necessarily bind the ever-growing number of people who are video makers. The distribution of video technology suggests the possibility of engendering as many approaches as there are users. Among them, perhaps, are ways of contesting the conventions and habits that video persuades us are second nature, as well as means of making the specificities of urban experience perceptible.

LOCA: Location Oriented Critical Arts
Drew Hemment, Theo Humphries, John Evans & Mika Raento

Loca is an interdisciplinary project on mobile media and surveillance. Loca explores the shifting boundaries between art practice, the event, and data systems. Loca is grass-roots, pervasive surveillance – tracking digital bodies in physical space.

A person walking through the city centre glances at the screen on their phone. Instead of an SMS alert they see a message reading: "We are currently experiencing difficulties monitoring your position: please wave your network device in the air."

The project foregrounds secondary characteristics of mobile communications, such as the ability to locate consumer mobile devices in real-time and near-real-time, and the kinds of peer-to-peer pervasive surveillance that is possible as a result. Loca explores the shifting nature of surveillance as it ceases to be the preserve of governmental or commercial bureaucracies. What happens when it is easy for everyone to track everyone else, when surveillance can be affected by consumer level technology within peer-to-peer networks without being routed through a central point?

Loca aims to lightly touch large numbers of people. The aim is not complex interaction, but subtle affect, and only a minority of people will be affected by it, let alone give it any more than a passing thought. It is like a picture glanced at sideways, a message caught in the corner of the eye, or a mosquito swatted on the arm. Like a mosquito it will not always be welcome, but can be expected to infuriate, annoy and provoke.

The Loca project has involved the iterative development of several strongly integrated component projects, each one evolving according to knowledge and experience gained from the others. A major component of Loca is the deployment of a cluster of interconnected, self-sufficient bluetooth nodes within inner city urban environments. Loca observes people's movements by tracking the position of the bluetooth enabled devices that they carry. Each node runs a modified version of ContextPhone software, gathering data and then uploading it to a modified version of the Aware platform. This enables Loca to track anyone with any device that has bluetooth set to 'discoverable'. New nodes can be added or old nodes removed to create a surveillance swarm. Inferences based on analysis of the data (server-side) guides communication with bluetooth users, via 'bluejacking' (unsolicited messages sent to devices), or through interaction with performers. The purpose of these messages is to make the presence of the Loca network known, and to illustrate the types of data that can be gathered and the inferences that can be drawn from it. These messages could highlight people's daily routines 'You have been here for an hour', reveal the 'others' within the network 'You can be seen by 4 other devices', or even be used to control people's behaviour 'Please wave your phone in the air'. The messages also make the Loca project accountable for what it is doing, and provide channels for feedback and further enquiry.

Other components include personalised maps that illustrate people's habits as inferred by actual data collected by the Loca network, strap-on devices that alert users to otherwise anonymous bluetooth scans, stickers that allow people to record the presence of digital identities they themselves detect in physical spaces, and surveillance (or counter-surveillance) 'Loca packs' which inform people about pervasive surveillance and provide tools to intervene in this process in several ways.

Loca seeks active engagement with people in every day contexts, face-to-face, to enable them to explore the positive and negative impacts that pervasive surveillance could have for them. Public reaction ranges from shock or fear, through blasé dismissiveness to excitement. As a result of these discussions some people are eager to engage with the network; turning bluetooth on in order to do so. However others are trepid; turning bluetooth off in order to avoid participation.

An aim for Loca is to make people aware that they have agency, that they can avoid being tracked by turning off their device or switching their bluetooth device to 'invisible'. But Loca also sets out to reveal the limit of this agency. With all technologies that are susceptible to pervasive surveillance techniques, the only way to opt-out of the surveillance is to switch off altogether, which is often impractical, and means losing the benefits of that technology. This was not inevitable, and we need to ask why these technologies are not privacy preserving: why, for example, do all network technologies use permanent unique IDs, who made those decisions, on what agenda, who has it benefited? Equally, computers that are invisible are bad for privacy: do you want the things that are tracking you to be hidden? Loca advocates the development of countermeasures and of better privacy management provisions in policies and protocols. An issue with bluetooth is that bluetooth scanning is anonymous. Should not the person or device doing the scanning have to provide their identity *before* they obtain the identity of the devices that they are scanning? Many such measures will involve a cost, so unless an argument is made and demand exists, then it will not happen.

Loca examines the surveillance potential of different consumer platforms. It currently focuses on bluetooth for a number of reasons: because bluetooth has been designed in a way that is problematic for privacy management; working with bluetooth rather than GSM makes possible some independence from the mobile phone companies; and because bluetooth is the first 'everyday' network technology that enables people to be tracked, and to track each other, within the physical environment. The privacy trade-off found in many contemporary forms of surveillance (you need to incrementally give up every more privacy in order to access new services) is common to all network technologies, but here it is not just data but also bodies in space that are being tracked. (WLAN is similar, but is not always on and is less mobile; GSM tracking remains largely the preserve of the mobile phone companies; RFID (at this time) is still not established in the consumer domain.)

Loca works independently from the mobile phone companies and other service providers so that it is clear to participants that Loca is not swayed by commercial interests in technology and also to show that the project can be done in a low-cost way. Each node is built using readily available, cheap parts, and is encased in concrete in order to be deployed in the urban environment. Loca does not need any special privileges nor to break the law – nothing stops one from bluetooth scanning, in fact it is part of the protocol, whereas GSM is prohibited. All you need to participate – to watch or be watched – is a bluetooth device.

Loca explores peer-to-peer surveillance, and yet, like many such projects, it is peer-to-peer only to a point. Surveillance data is generated independently on each node, but then that data is relayed between the nodes and a server via the GSM network. This does not compromise the principle, however. The surveillance is independent, a server is only used for convenience within this project as it simplifies implementation, and the data could be relayed between nodes in alternative ways, but with less mobility, or higher cost. This would lead to a new set of parameters, alternative questions, and a change in the nature of the project.

Loca is an anticipated accident. The project was initiated in 2003, out of an interest in how surveillance and social control emerge as a residue or unforeseen effect of otherwise virtuous information systems and network technologies. Then it sat in waiting for the accident to happen.

The accident was when the Aware <www.aware.uiah.fi>/ ContextPhone <www.cs.helsinki.fi/group/context/> collaboration started generating surveillance data that was unforeseen by its designers. When users published media to Aware directly from their phone, using software called ContextPhone, it automatically annotated this media with contextual information derived from the phones actual surroundings, e.g. time, GSM cell-ID (an approximate geographical locator), and the bluetooth environment, i.e. a list of the bluetooth devices around at the time. The premise of Aware and ContextPhone (themselves developed by Loca participants), is that the social context of the media can be used both to situate the media and to help organise it. The bluetooth information would allow queries like 'show me all the pictures captured when I was in the vicinity of that person', which would be useful in a wide variety of contexts – if, for example, someone wished to gain an overview on an event at which they were present. This contextual information leads to unforeseen consequences, such as the 'accidental' tracking of people present during the media arts festival ISEA2004 in Helsinki. If someone wanted to reproduce what Aware/ContextPhone had done, but for commercial gain or unethical ends, how hard would it be to implement technically and legally?

Projects and debates surrounding surveillance have yet to properly address locative media. Likewise locative media has yet to fully address its own critical context. Loca seeks to make a contribution to these debates, while at the same time critically assessing its own methodology and the risks of its approach. How can creative work with surveillance technologies add to or distract from traditional campaigning strategies? Does it risk getting the public used to a new control technology prior to its deployment in a coercive way? How may both positive and troubling sides of a new technology be simultaneously explored?

Loca does not ask people in advance; it does not want their permission. Then it would not be surveillance, but a performance by people for Loca. One principle of the project is that people should be able to participate through their own mobile phone without their device needing to be modified in any way, either through installing Loca software or by altering settings. Working under the banner of 'art' offers license that could not otherwise be obtained. But equally an art project is easier to write off and disregard. Art is a frame to be used sparingly.

Loca asks 'How do people respond to being tracked and observed? How ready are people to observe others? Who is the user, and how? What does it mean to participate in this project? Do we fear surveillance, disinterest, scopophobia or scopophilia? What kinds of behaviour is this technique suited to mapping, and what behaviours is it not suited to? What kinds of behaviour can evade this form of surveillance? How does the contextual information we can detect (such as location, time spent in one place, etc) relate to people's everyday experiences of the environment? What happens in-between physical, embodied space and the digital space of abstract data? What is the relationship between the embodiment of the mobile user and the abstraction of the data we capture?'

Pervasive surveillance has the potential to be both sinister and positive, at the same time. The intent of Loca is to equip people to deal with the ambiguity and to make informed decisions about the networks that they populate.

Curation

Introduction
Joan Gibbons

The etymology of word curate goes back to the Latin word for care, cura, which in the Middle Ages developed a particularly religious inflection as curatus, referring to the care of the soul.[1] Although the activities of curating have since expanded to include the care of artefacts of one form or another, traditionally in libraries and museum collections, it is a definition that still carries a lot of relevance – after all, what is the care of our cultural products, if not essentially the care of our souls? And, in a highly secularised age, it might be argued that art is one of the principle means in which we attend to the soul and are able to see some promise of consolation or even redemption. However, if the curating of art is framed in this way, it puts a heavy responsibility on curators who act as intermediaries between artist, work and audience. This is neither an easy nor a straightforward matter for the curator. As Lawrence Alloway has shown, there are traditionally a number of factors that may compromise the integrity of the curator's work – negotiating with and pleasing the artist and his/her dealer (who is always going to have an eye to the commercial potential of the work), meeting the expectations of the institutional powers that be, meeting the expectations of his/her peer group and, although Alloway omits this, increasingly working with/around the expectations of the audience.[2]

Yet while these might still be dominant factors when working with the most established (and by that token, perhaps the most conservative) artists, museums and galleries, there have been many developments before and since Alloway wrote his article for *Artforum* in 1975 that have expanded the scope and contexts of curatorial practice. Take, for instance, the tendency for making large anti-institutional gestures that emerged in from the late 50s to the late 60s that Brian O'Doherty has mapped out with characteristic eloquence in his much cited seminal essays on the ideology of the gallery space. The landmark subversions of the gallery that he cites include works such as Yves Klein's empty gallery space, *Vide* (1958), Daniel Buren's *Sealed Gallery* (1968), where entrance to gallery space was prohibited by the gluing down of his characteristic striped canvases onto the door, and Christos' *Wrapped Museum* (1969), in which the gallery was rendered *informe* by the act of wrapping it, inside and out.

Such gestures not only challenged audience expectations, but also demanded an unprecedented relinquishment of institutional controls and conventions. Producing his essays between 1976 and 1986 in an economic climate that fostered the commodification of the artwork and a conspicuous return to painting, O'Doherty laments the short life (approximately a decade) of this period of anti-gallery gesture, but perhaps unnecessarily so, as the late 1970s and 1980s also saw the emergence of alternative artist-run spaces such as Fashion Moda,

1978, and Group Material, 1980, in New York's East Village as well as individual practitioners that took the public realm as a preferred venue for their work, Barbara Kruger and Jenny Holzer, for example. In the UK, Artangel have achieved an impressive record of projects that have materialised in contexts beyond the gallery, including Jem Finer's, *Longplayer*, featured earlier in this publication. In addition, the ICA started off as a space run by practitioners and theorists rather than gallery professionals that provided a model of sorts for the development of artist-run spaces in the UK, such as the now well-established Transmission Gallery in Glasgow.

Alongside this artist-led emancipation of exhibition spaces came changes in the role of the curator, who in many instances began to acquire the status of *auteur* – a position not dissimilar to that of the artist as procedural author that I have already referred to in the discussion of narrative in my introductory essay in *Progression*. In both cases, there is a lead person, who orchestrates a team of people around their central concept, and in doing so can claim credit for the authorship of the work/exhibition in the way that the film director gets overall credit for a film.[4] The figure of curator as auteur is also closely related to the development of the artist-curator – a figure that has precedents at least as far back as Courbet with his 1855 Pavilion of Realism and a figure that survived in the exhibition-based innovations of prominent leaders of the early 20th century avant-garde, exemplified by Duchamp with his gallery takeovers, *1,200 Bags of Coal* (1938) and *Mile of String* (1942).[5] Moreover, the practices of curator as auteur or those of artist-curator are not necessarily beholden to the gallery. Both have extended the field of curatorial practices to develop independent initiatives that relate to and take place in broader contexts. In particular, artist-curators such as Gavin Wade, currently Curatorial Research Fellow at UCE, have raised important questions concerning the boundaries of curatorial practice, such as "What should the role of the curator be in the future? Where should the impetus for curatorial development originate? (When is it time to be a curator and when to be an artist?) Also how far can curatorship or art head towards being integrated with life's routines beyond the gallery, before it is no longer differentiated as art and is this a problem anyway?"[6]

These questions are not only pertinent to the wide range of curatorial practices that exist in this first decade of the new century, but apply quite specifically to the curating of new media art. New

----

1   See the Merriam-Webster Online Dictionary, <www.m_w.com>.
2   Lawrence Alloway, "The Great Curatorial Dim-Out," reprinted in Reesa Greenberg, Bruce W. Ferguson and Sandy Nairne, eds. *Thinking About Exhibitions* (London and New York: Routledge, 1996), 221-230.
3   Brian O'Doherty, *Inside the White Cube: The Ideology of the Gallery Space*, (1986), (Berkley and Los Angeles: University of California Press, 1999), 87-10.
4   Natalie Heinich and Michael Pollak, "From Museum Curator to Exhibition Auteur," in Greenberg, op. cit, 231-250.
5   O'Doherty, op. cit. 65-86.
6   Gavin Wade, "QRU Proposal," in Gavin Wade, ed. *Curating in the 21st Century* (The New Art Gallery, Walsall and the University of Wolverhampton, 2000), 19.

media, from video to digital and net-based art represent the biggest shift in artistic forms, production and reception since the move into the expanded field in the 1970s that included, minimalism, land art, performance art, installation art and conceptual art – and, as Martijn Stevens suggests in the first paper in this section, somehow encompasses aspects of all of these. As the debates that dominated Baltic's *Curating New Media* seminar (May 2001) testify, the advent of new media has meant that major art museums and galleries have had to adjust their terms of reference with regard not only to the problematics of introducing new technologies to the exhibition space, but also with regard to the status and nature of the art object.[7] This has proved particularly the case with the representation of internet art in the museum or gallery, in which differences exist, as Sarah Cook notes in her paper on re-enactment, between the experience and expectations of their respective audiences. A potentially diverse cyber audience experiences works created to exist online in a mutable set of relations, while the conventional gallery visitor has expectations and experience of the exhibition space as a specifically located repository (however temporary) of ideas, objects and images.

The first of this set of papers, by Martijn Stevens, provides a valuable resumé of these issues and reminds us that they have by no means been resolved. The second paper, by Caitlin Jones, concentrates on the practical, legal and theoretical concerns of curating variable media, which are not to be confined to the realm of the digital, but to be considered in relation to the wider problematics of curating contemporary art. Sarah Cook's paper tracks similar issues but places the focus of her discussion specifically on the difficulties and rewards of transferring real-time projects to the gallery space. The remaining two papers speak to location or context-specific new media curatorial practices and initiatives. Jon Bird and Andy Webster concentrate on their experiments in open ended curation in an urban context, which share similar issues of representation to Anthony Auerbach's *Video as Urban Condition*, in the previous set of papers. Last but by no means least, Chris Byrne relates his experience as commissioner of a number of digital art projects in Scotland that have been developed in relation to specific localities that pose a particular set of problems for the curating of new media projects.

Tying the rhizomatic structure of the internet to Nicolas Bourriaud's notion of relational aesthetics, Stevens calls for museums, rather than galleries, to adapt the ways in which they conceive and present artwork. In this, Stevens is recognising the fluidity of form and knowledge that characterises contemporary culture that new technologies have made such a contribution to and that is not as yet firmly embedded in conventional museum or gallery practices. However, as Jones notes, the dilemma for curators in this state of instability, while exacerbated by the demands of digital and internet art, is not confined to the issues and practicalities that these forms, media or technologies have brought. Rather, it is one that sits within the wider compass of museum or gallery practices and infrastructures, many of which have already been challenged. I have already touched on the long history of alternative curatorial practices that O'Doherty maps in his renowned essays, a more extensive, if not so detailed, chronology of which has been compiled by Alison Green in Wade's (ed.) *Curating in the 21st Century*.[8] Yet, while this alternative history of exhibition organisation and exhibiting strategies demonstrates the existence of other models, most would agree with Stevens in his general assessment of museum practices as largely conservative.

Several of the exhibitions that Green charts were staged within major institutions and museums, signalling their sometimes willingness to accommodate and experiment with alternative practices. Moreover, many museums have already embraced new technologies and present their collection on line in a way that gives the virtual visitor much more freedom in their navigation of the collection. It may be, however, that beyond the attitudes of museums, it is the architecture itself that is a major factor in prohibiting a more radical revision of practices of display. For obvious reasons changes in the architectural structures of museums are going to be more slow moving, but again they are not without a history and not without an ongoing development. Notable examples of high profile galleries that eschew the white cube include Frank Lloyd Wright's Guggenheim in New York, with its curved walls and spiral ramp, Hans Hollein's Municipal Museum in Abteiberg Mönchengladbach, Austria and Richard Meier's Museum of Decorative Art in Frankfurt, both of which in the words of Rosalind Krauss, "can be said to transcend the obstacle of wall or floor. For the reigning idea in both museums is the vista: the sudden opening of in the wall of a given gallery to allow a glimpse of a far away object, and thereby to interject within the collection of these objects a reference to the order of another"[9] Such museum spaces provide a circulation which is "as much visual as physical" and which decentres "through the continuous pull of something else."[10]

To me, the description that Krauss gives of these two museums is more than reminiscent of the rhizomatic structures that Stevens invokes. Another architect to think in this way is Rem Koolhaas, who according to Hans-Ulrich Obrist combined "a kind of topology of museums" in his project for a Museum of Contemporary Art in Rome.[11] Relatedly, Koolhaas' interior design for the Prada shop on Broadway, New York, has been singled out by Lev Manovich as exemplifying the sort of augmented space that the combinations of new visual technologies with innovative interior architecture have produced.[12] The most recent example of designing the fabric of the

---

7   Sarah Cook, Beryl Graham and Sarah Martin, eds. *Curating New Media* (Gateshead: Baltic, 2002).

8   Alison Green, "A Short Chronology of Curatorial Incidents in the 20th Century," in Wade op. cit, 157-165.

9   Rosalind Krauss, "Postmodernism's Museum Without Walls," in Greenberg, op. cit, 347.

10 Ibid.

11 Hans-Ulrich Obrist, "Kraftwerk, Time Storage, Laboratory" in Wade, op. cit, 45.

12 <www.manovich.net/DOCS/augmented_space.doc>.

building to accommodate alternative ways of experiencing the gallery, still under construction at the time of writing, is Will Alsop's building for community arts organisation The Public in West Bromwich. The design of the exhibition spaces in this new complex is founded on the firmly held tenets of the then Director of The Public, Sylvia King, who is insistent on an architectural space which is inclusive and participatory. The walk towards the entrance to the exhibition spaces is to be flanked by steel 'trees' in order to deinstitutionalise the approach. The experience of the visit is then further enhanced by the marriage of new technologies and architecture – a clear move in the direction that Stevens is calling for. Before entry, visitors are to be issued with wireless devices into which they can input personal details. This will form the basis of customised interactivity at various hot-spots along the ramp that spirals around and through the exhibition spaces. Alongside this there are participatory installations such as Paul Sermon's *Telematic Embrace*, a version of his earlier piece, this time using a sofa instead of a bed and giving the opportunity to (virtually) embrace someone unseen and unknown at the opposite end of the exhibition suite. The idea is to make the experience more of a journey or even an adventure and to build a digital record of the visit that can be stored or transformed in whatever form the visitor might chose.[13]

Caitlin Jones' paper returns us to the issue of curatorial integrity that I flagged at the start of this introduction. Jones gives an illuminating account of the problems that face a curator dealing with new media and especially with technologies that have a limited life before being replaced by newer, more sophisticated, more convenient technologies. The problems here are ethical – to do with faithfulness to the original and producing as authentic a version of the work as possible. Such considerations disclose an idealism that subscribes to an auratic view of the work – a respect for its original singularity of form, medium and intent, despite the fact that the work is, as Jones demonstrates, more than convincingly emulatable by varying the technologies, including the emulation of some of the technical hitches of the original technology.

While this concern for the authenticity of the work is a fine example of ethical curatorial practice, it also establishes a marker in the polemics that surround the viewing of works of art in an age of technological reproduction, to paraphrase Walter Benjamin's famous essay title. The re-presentation of Grahame Weinbren and Roberta Friedman's *The Erl King* inherently avoids the sense of decontextualised 'exhibition value' that Walter Benjamin saw as the result of the transference of works to the museum – its interactivity serving to preserve its original intention or usage, or in Benjamin's terms, its 'cult-value,' the fact that it is essentially a participatory activity rather than contemplative.[14] The issue of authenticity also brings to mind an exhibition that László Moholy-Nagy staged in 1930 in the Landesmuseum, Hanover, which in itself is famous for the modernisation of methods of display that pioneering curator, Alexander Dorner, brought to the permanent collection. Dorner commissioned Moholy-Nagy to design an installation, *Room of Our Time*, which represented the most recent developments in the visual arts. Extraordinarily, rather than include any original work, except for a *Light Space Modulator* (1928–30), by Moholy Nagy the exhibition made use of the reproductive technologies of the time for the representation of these developments.[15] The complete absence of any original work of art, with the exception of the *Light Space Modulator*, puts this exhibition at the opposite pole of museum practices to those employed in the Variable Media Initiative and perhaps suggests a yet another factor to add to the equation, that of fitness for purpose.

Thus, in opposition to the authenticity that Jones and her colleagues at the Guggenheim cultivate is the fact that art can be and is constantly consumed vicariously through reproductions, rather than first-hand.[16] Implicit in this discussion about the 'value' of the reproduction is André Malraux' notion of a museum without walls, which seems be an appropriate term for the internet as a host for art – a medium, that like the art books that Malraux discusses, enables virtual access to works that might, due to a variety of practicalities, be ordinarily too remote.

All of this leads me to the important question that Sarah Cook poses at the end of her paper on re-enactment, which concerns the relevance of the gallery in a society of endless duplication and redistribution. One answer would be that the gallery is but one element in this vast circulation of culture that also now includes the internet and that it demonstrates the easy survival of existing methods alongside new approaches to representation and curating. It may be said that the gallery is an arena inherently devoted to the staging or restaging of art, and not infrequently to the actual performance of art. In other words, the art object is re-enacted by its display and similar issues of authenticity arise in respect of this as in the performance-based re-enactments that Cook discusses. When Walter Benjamin spoke of the 'exhibition value' that the museum confers, he implicitly recognised that the (re)presentation of the artwork in the museum was a form re-enactment or a restaging at least, and not in his time one which respected the integrity of the object in the way that the Variable Media Initiative does. But, Cook has also importantly put her finger on a significant aspect of the production and reception of all art – that of the "shrinking distance between the event (and I would add the art object) and the mediation of it that we experience in everyday life." In this, her paper raises issues concerning both the ordering of representation and the ordering of knowledge through representation.

----

13 Based on a UCE visit to the building to see work in progress, hosted by Sylvia King, 13 January 2006.

14 Walter Benjamin, "The Work of Art in the Age of Mechanical Reproduction," Hannah Arendt (ed.) *Illuminations* (London: Fontana, 1992), 221-220.

15 Mary Anne Staniszewski, *The Power of Display: A History of Exhibitions at the Museum of Modern Art* (Cambridge, Massachusetts: The MIT Press, 1998), 21-22.

16 See John Walker, *Art in the Age of Mass Media* (London: Pluto Press, 1983), 15-18, 67-75.

Indeed, the endless duplication and redistribution that Cook speaks of testifies to the constant hold of the symbolic in our lives and the need, in a culture of complex and plural forms of mediation and representation, for many points or means of access to this realm of knowledge. The re-enactments that Cook discusses are replays of historical events, and in this respect belong to Baudrillard's second and third orders of simulation, where an original is copied with greater or lesser degree of faith – the same difference that can be identified between Jeremy Deller's reconstruction of the Battle of Orgeave which attempts to 'copy' the original event and the documentation of that reconstruction in film, which is a copy of a copy.[17] However, while Baudrillard is apprehensive about the masking of the real that simulation entails – that we are cut off from the reality of War, for instance, by its media representations, it could equally be argued that re-enactments, such as *The Battle of Orgreave*, return us to the reality of the event, as does Rod Dickenson's re-enactment of Milgram's experiments in *Obedience to Authority*. History has been notoriously susceptible to misrepresentation and revisionism according to the ideology of whoever is making the representation. This is as true of art as of the mass-media, although the message of political correctness can be said have been well absorbed by many contemporary artists and influences their themes and approaches. The projects that Cook singles out not only give insight into the representation of representations, but are revisions of history that allow for subjective engagement – the sense of 'being there' while leaving room for critical reflection because we know simultaneously, in our postmodern media awareness, that they are revisitings as much as re-enactments.

In his writing on the orders of representation, Baudrillard speaks of the evil demon of images in the precession of simulacra that relentlessly permeate our environments – something that Jon Bird, Andy Webster and Garrett Monaghan situate themselves both against and within in their publicly-sited curatorial experiments. In projecting video art onto buildings in the centre of Croydon, Bird, Webster and Monaghan insert a series of artworks into what Marc Augé has termed the non-places of supermodernity – places that are experienced as part of the mobility and transience of contemporary life.[18] Mike Featherstone has argued that such places are the privileged arenas of postmodern society, symptomatic of the collapse of old social hierarchies embodied in traditional architecture and monuments and symptomatic of the way that consumer signs have emerged as a site for social values.[19] Moreover, the insertion of video works that Bird, Webster and Monaghan's *Tabula Rasa* admits into such spaces represents the sort of appropriation of public space that Henri Lefebvre refers to as situational, in which the environment can be subverted to make people more critically aware of their 'situation' or situatedness.[20]

Bird, Webster and Monaghan also provide an impressive example of representational strategies that, for Cook, shrink the distance between the event and its mediation in everyday life. This again has resonance in the work of Lefebvre, particularly in his theories of the everyday as something with the potential to become, as Ben Highmore puts it, "something other (something more) than bureaucratic and commodified culture allowed."[21] The insertion of video art into the urban environment introduces the element of play and creativity that Lefebvre thought would undercut the routines of the everyday and the homogeneity of mass culture.[22] It also, as Bird, Webster and Monaghan claim, introduces new vantage points for the passer-by, which is why they opted for an open submission of works and the minimisation of curatorial influence and avoided any determining master plan. While Lefebvre's ideal would be for the person in the street to initiate his or her own acts of subversion or creativity, this is difficult to imagine without the sort of catalyst that *Tabula Rasa* offers, and much to their credit the curators are sensitive to this issue and strive to remain as open-ended in their practice as possible and to maximise the 'vantage points' of the passer-by.

Also to their credit is the transference of this open-ended approach into the gallery. In the case of *Sixty Second Art*, for instance, in which curatorial decisions are transferred to the gallery visitor, who selects the material to be viewed and determines the running order of the footage. *Blip@Newlyn* took this principle of audience participation or the ordering and reordering of the material on view by the visitor even further by providing multiple points of reference for the audience as well as varied forms of interaction. In both of these gallery based curatorial projects, Bird, Webster and Monaghan can be seen to follow up their intention to strip curatorial practice down as near to degree zero as the situation and parameters of the project allowed. In this, they can be seen to have successfully pushed some boundaries, tested the limits of curatorial controls and relinquished some of the authority of the curator in the interest not only of opening the vistas and perspectives of the visitor in experiencing art, but also in understanding that art is not a timeless and unchangeable entity, but something that is reconfigurable according to its presentation and context.

The issue of location is at the heart of the curatorial projects that Chris Byrne describes in his paper, *Space, Place, Interface: Location in New Media Art*. Byrne is acutely aware that access to new technologies assists in the privileging of one locality over another and of the way

17 Jean Baudrillard, "The Evil Demon of Images and the Precession of Simulacra", Thomas Docherty, ed., *Postmodernism: A Reader* (New York: Columbia Univ. Press, 1993), 194.

18 Marc Augé, *Non-Places: An Introduction to the Anthropology of Supermodernity* (London and New York: Verso, 1995).

19 Mike Featherstone, *Consumer Culture and Postmodernism* (London, Newbury Park and New Delhi: Sage Publications, 1991), 95-111.

20 Henri Lefebvre, *The Production of Space* (1974), (Oxford: Basil Blackwell, 1984).

21 Ben Highmore, *Everyday Life and Cultural Theory* (London and New York: Routledge, 2002), 113.

22 Ibid. 119.

that media art has often tended towards an internationalism that neglects the issue of location, both in its themes and choice of venue. So, the curatorial challenge for Byrne has been to commission and curate media artworks for locations in Scotland that, in either in their remoteness or their lack of cosmopolitan kudos, are not especially favoured by media artists. In meeting this challenge, Byrne facilitated a number of non-mainstream venues that fit the category of Michel Foucault's heterotopias – places of otherness or difference that are exist outside or on the margins of the mainstream, and which provide alternatives or oppositions to that mainstream (the mainstream in this case being the gallery or media arts festival circuit that Byrne speaks of – utopias rather than an heterotopias, according to Foucault's scheme of things).[23] The locations used in the projects that Byrne curated varied according to the artists' concerns and included four haunted houses, an offshore safety training pool in the industrial fishing port of Aberdeen, and the Highlands wilderness.

Beverly Hood's *trans-locale* is the exception, as it is a virtual intervention into online video conferencing. But, even here, the work is characterised by a placelessness that offeres an alternative to location and at the same time invokes Deleuze and Guattari's celebration of 'nomadic' space, a space that is characterised by a free ranging journey between any number of localities.[24] In their various ways, the location-specific projects that Byrne describes, (Colin Andrew's *Geist*, Ann Bevan's video installation, Thomson and Craighead's *The Price of Freedom*, Cavan Convery's *A History of the Interpretive Panel*, r a d i o q u a l i a's residency with MAKROLAB and Simon Fildes and Katrina McPherson's *If I follow you, do we make a path?*) create what Deleuze and Guattari have termed 'smooth' spaces, whether real or virtual. These are spaces in which transformations and new experiences can take place, as opposed to 'striated' spaces that are socially ordered and regulated. These 'smooth' spaces allow "room for vagabondage, for wandering between regions, instead of moving straight ahead between fixed points."[25] And, of course, connect directly with the model of the rhizome that Deleuze and Guattari have famously offered in opposition to hierachical and linear forms of understanding and experience, exemplified by their own *A Thousand Plateaus*, and the paradigm for the changes that Stevens has wished on museum practices in his earlier paper.

All of this also applies to Byrne's online project, *Host*, a curatorial initiative that allowed artists to experiment with computer systems and servers – the technologies that play 'host' to the data that is entered into and allow for its circulation. Here it is not only the ways in which space is experienced that is at stake, but the ways in which the infrastructures of online technology and the cultural forms that it has produced can be used to activate the space. The works produced by Claude Closky, Jorn Ebner and Luci Eyers are all part of a growing history of software art, exemplified by the works shown in the *CODeDOC* exhibition at Whitney Artport in 2002, and add to a growing critique of the ideological role of codes, programs servers and their use

in the creation or, indeed, ratification, of cultural forms and values.[26]
The parallel experience of the online and location-specific curating
of new media has led Byrne to reflect on the relationship of space to
location and that of site to medium. As he notes, the curating of new
media is still a matter of emerging practices and experimentation and,
I am certain he would agree, a matter of shared knowledge and debate
that all of the papers in this section have contributed to.

23 Michel Foucault, "Of Other Spaces,"
    1967, in *Diachronics*, Spring 1986,
    See also, Edward. S Casey, *The Fate
    of Place: A Philosophical History*
    (Berkeley, Los Angeles, London:
    University of California Press, 1997),
    297-301.

24 Gilles Deleuze and Félix Guattari,
    A Thousand Plateaus (Minneapolis:
    University of Minneapolis Press,
    1987).

25 Casey, op. cit., 304.

26 *CODeDOC* was curated by Christiane
    Paul who commissioned 12 artists to
    produce pieces of code to connect
    three points in space - the work
    being the code rather than its end
    product. See Rachel Green, *Internet
    Art* (London: Thames and Hudson,
    2004), 156-160.

Museums: Cemeteries! The Relational Aesthetics of Internet Art
Martijn Stevens

"We will destroy the museums, academies, libraries of every kind"
Filippo Tomasso Marinetti in *Manifesto of Futurism* (1909)

Focusing on changing notions of authorship, authenticity and audience, in this paper I will explore some of the challenges internet art brings upon the concept of the museum, suggesting that conventional museological notions are informed by 'relational aesthetics'.

New media art
Internet art is often viewed as electronic or new media art. Like other forms of media art, its history is closely intertwined with the history of technology. Directed by developments outside the art world, the arts have entered the domain of engineers and technicians.[1] However, by thinking about internet art in merely technical terms we may neglect the social, cultural and aesthetic aspects of artistic practices that reflect the influence of digital technologies on our contemporary society. Internet art is part of what Christian Andersen and Søren Pold denominate as a software and interface culture which goes beyond the more functional uses of computers.[2]

When approaching internet art as a cultural and aesthetic, rather than a technological phenomenon, it can be useful to examine the so-called avant-garde movements of the 1960s (which did not necessarily use electronic media), such as Minimalism, conceptual art and performance art. Although often referred to as new media art, internet art shares many characteristics with these trends, such as their event-like, participatory character and their variability. Furthermore, these movements also challenged the institutions of art, among which the art museum – the so-called white cube – predominates.

White cubes
Stemming from early Modernism and replacing the tradition of the Salon from the late 19th century onwards, the white cube met the needs of a new art.[3] Gradually institutionalised, it has shaped the way we think about art and its functioning in contemporary society. In *Inside the White Cube*, Brian O'Doherty elaborates on the ideology of the white cube as an exhibition space.[4] He argues that the museum isolates the work of art from society by placing it in a space that is constructed as a closed system of values and conventions. The white cube strives for eternity and universality, where art is concealed from the chaos and variability of the outside world, untouched by time. In this context, art is considered to be an autonomous, closed system, having an everlasting, knowable meaning.[5] However, such beliefs about knowledge, the arts and our culture as a whole have been rejected rigorously in the postmodern era. Postmodern thinking has heralded

the end of history, which has put the historicity of art and museological objects in a different perspective. The narrative structure that used to find (historical) connections between objects has lost its value and has been replaced by a more dynamic structure that makes room for many, often conflicting, histories.[6] In this view, art history becomes a non-linear process in which various interests, goals and assumptions foster (or vie) each other. It is against this background that internet art can be better understood. As a new artistic practice, it undermines the dominant exhibition style, the same way that early Modernist art did in opposition to the Salon.

Rhizomes and networks

The white cube embodies a solid linear meta-narrative in which everything has its own place and meaning and, as such, it may not be the appropriate place for internet art. As a metaphor to describe the hierarchical structure of the museum we can use the tree of knowledge, which is exemplary for the way traditional institutions of heritage and knowledge are organised – not only the white cube, but also libraries, universities, archives et cetera. The tree of knowledge implies a solid and rigid view on classifying our heritage. Opposed to the tree of knowledge is the rhizome, another term with a botanical flavour. The concept was introduced by Gilles Deleuze and Félix Guattari in the introduction of their book *A Thousand Plateaus: Capitalism and Schizophrenia*.[7] In contrast with the tree, which stratifies and fixes an order or unity, the rhizome – literally a root – is characterized by principles of connection, heterogeneity and multiplicity. As part of a complex network, single elements do not have any intrinsic meaning or value, but are merely nodes within a whole, deriving their meaning from the relationships with their surrounding elements. Each element relates to many other elements in many different ways. Since these relationships are ever changing, meaning is not stable, but variable.

1   Michael Rush, *New Media in Late 20th-Century Art* (London and New York: Thames & Hudson, 1999).

2   Christian U. Andersen and Søren Pold, "Software Art and Cultures - People Doing Strange Things with Software", Olga Goriunova and Alexei Shulgin, eds. *read_me. Software Art and Cultures Edition* (Århus: Digital Aesthetics Research Centre, University of Aarhus, 2004), 11-15.

3   Aislinn Race, "Context becomes Content, through Concept: A Brief Look at Modern Gallery Space", in: *Contrapposto,* Vol. XVI. Online, 2001 ‹www.csuchico.edu/art/contrapposto/ contrapposto01/theme/race.html› (29 November 2005).

4   Brian O'Doherty, *Inside the White Cube. The Ideology of the Gallery Space* (Berkeley, CA: University of California Press, 1999).

5   Joke Brouwer and Arjen Mulder,

"Feelings are Always Local", in: Joke Brouwer et al. eds. *Feelings are Always Local* (Rotterdam: V2_Publishing/NAi Publishers, 2004), 4-5.

6   Throughout his work, Jean-François Lyotard elaborates on this idea as the end of the 'Grand Narratives'. See Jean Francois Lyotard, *The Postmodern Condition*, (Manchester: Manchester University Press, 1984).

7   Gilles Deleuze and Félix Guattari, *A Thousand Plateaus: Capitalism and Schizophrenia* (London and New York: Continuum, 1987).

A textbook example of a non-hierarchical rhizomatic network is the internet, which is constituted by a relational, variable structure.[8] In fact, the internet is a huge database of text, images and sounds which are connected via hyperlinks, transforming separate media into hypermedia. Websites are hypermedial assemblages, very much depending on their context. Surfing the internet we notice that this chain of related elements is practically endless and has numerous entrances. For example, _readme.html (Own, Be Owned or Remain Invisible) by Heath Bunting (1998) consists of a text in which almost every word is a hyperlink to its corresponding domain (the word 'mission' for instance links to www.mission.com), thus connecting the project website to many other websites. Non-linear and opening up in every direction, websites and art projects using the internet are hardly delimited, if at all. This means that the closed systems that are complete in themselves as (re)presented in the white cube are replaced by non-linear networks that consist of a multiplicity of nodes and connections.

Shifting relationships

We could say that 'relational aesthetics' underlie contemporary artistic practices, a term with which art critic Nicolas Bourriaud refers to art using performative and interactive elements. These types of practice establish relationships between people, thus turning art into a social event or an encounter.[9] According to Bourriaud, ideas that were introduced conceptually by Minimalism several decades ago, such as the relationship between works of art and their audience, were brought into practice during the 1990s.[10] Instead of just looking at a work of art that was presented as a fixed, closed system, the audience was included in the process of constructing it. The changing role of the audience coincides with other developments in the arts during the 1960s and 1970s, when artists began to challenge the art institutions and their obsession with unique, authentic objects. By introducing new forms of art and new ways of relating to the artwork, such as happenings, performance and conceptual art, the avant-garde challenged the fetishisation of the material object and the cult surrounding it. Bringing aspects of the performing arts into the domain of the visual and plastic arts they turned art into an event, often taking place outside the museum space, in which the audience was invited to participate. In contrast to the more contemplative atmosphere of the white cube, art as an event became a participatory experience, in which the boundaries between artists and audience became blurred. These practices have brought forth art forms that challenge the assumed autonomy of both artist and audience. Emphasis has shifted from object to process and from introspection to context. Meaning is always contingent according to different factors, such as the art work, the artist and the audience. All these elements are merely nodes in a networked and interconnected rhizomatic whole.

Dematerialised art

Since the 1960s the conventional categories that formed the basis of the white cube have shifted. Digital media have reinforced this shift away from the classical museological model. One of the striking features of internet art – one that it shares with conceptual art for instance – is its retreat from the material. Internet art can be seen as the culmination of the dematerialisation of the art object that started in the early 20th century, for it is not only immaterial, but it also exists in a completely virtual realm that challenges the materiality of museums and galleries. The digitisation of the arts creates exhibition spaces online, stretching and extending the boundaries of the white cube. We no longer have to visit the museum, because an internet art project can be distributed over several locations, both online and offline, that are connected via telecommunication networks. Tied to this immateriality is another characteristic that internet art shares with conceptual art and other avant-garde movements, namely its temporality. Constituted as an event, art has become a flow, a process in time instead of an object in space. Change and intervention are inherent to this process-based art. The internet challenges the materiality of the museum, both its own physical appearance and that of the objects it collects and displays, by transforming space-time into 'timeless times' and 'spaces of flows'.[11]

The inter

When the object disappears from the art museum and becomes virtual, the physical presence of both audience and art at a certain time in a certain space is no longer required for them to interact.[12] As we have seen, during the 20th century artists have increasingly turned their art into participatory or even collaborative events by expressly inviting the audience to take part in their projects. Art thus became more of an interactive process. In the age of computers and the internet, interaction is a frequently used hyped-up word, however, it remains a useful term to describe the effects of internet art.

To explain its usefulness I would like to divide the word into the prefix 'inter' and the noun 'action'. Inter is Latin for 'the between'. In the complex networked structure of the rhizome, the inter is the in-

---

8   Actually, the internet can be seen as rhizomatic in a number of ways, but it does not always operate according to the principles of a rhizome. Quoting Matthew Fuller, Julian Stallabrass points out that the net has a physical basis which is in fact a hierarchical structure. See also Julian Stallabrass, *Internet Art: The Online Clash of Culture and Commerce* (London: Tate Publishing, 2003).

9   Nicolas Bourriaud, *Relational Aesthetics* (Dijon: Les presses de réel, 2002).

10 Bennett Simpson, *Public Relations*. An interview with Nicolas Bourriaud for *ArtForum*, 2001, <www.findarticles.com/p/articles/mi_m0268/is_8_39/ai_75830815> (29 November 2005).

11 Manuell Castells *The Information Age: Economy, Society and Culture. Vol. I: The Rise of the Network Society* (Cambridge, Massachusetts: Blackwell, 1996).

12 I use the verb 'interact' here, because art always evokes a reaction in its audience, be it disgust, euphoria or indifference.

between, resting between two nodes or actors, or, in this case, between an artwork and a user. The inter is about reciprocal feedback. It effects change and produces meaning – be it temporary. In a rhizomatic structure, interactivity is the relationships between art projects and their users, a process in which all actors affect each other, a process that starts off transformation.[13] Action, on the other hand, implies activity, an event, a process, indicating that looking at art has changed into experiencing art. This requires involvement of the audience, which is no longer is solely spectator, but a participant, a co-creator, a user.

Authorship and artistry

When art is interactive and audiences become participants, users or creators, not only the white cube loses its significance, but also the romantic ideal of the artistic genius, originating from the 19th century, does no longer have as much value as it used to. A work that illustrates the shifting relationships between artist and audience is *communimage*, calc & Johannes Gees (1999–). *communimage* is an online project that consists of a collage of images. These images are added by the audience (i.e. people who visit the project website), who can attribute certain values to them, such as a title, a date or an emotion. Subsequently, they can assign this new image a place among the already uploaded images, thus changing and expanding the collage. *communimage* is not a stable or static piece of art, but work in progress and therefore never completed. Participation by an audience is a condition for the project to work. In contributing to the collage, users define the development of communimage. Authorship is actually shared and distributed between the artists and a multiplicity of users. We can even extend the notion of authorship and contribution, for the images that are used to create the collage are often copied and pasted from other websites. After all, creativity in the digital age does not necessarily mean creating a unique work from scratch; it also means combining existing material in countless new variations. Contexts are not fixed, but continuously changing.

The use and re-use of old material does not mean that no new art is being made. As Fredric Jameson puts it, by re-using and re-contextualizing the known, we create new insights and we constantly rewrite our histories.[14] Copy-and-paste has become an artistic tool in the dynamics of contemporary historicism.

Another test for conventional authorship is Sawad Brooks, *Global City* (2002) which consists of a piece of software crawling the internet and searching certain news sites, recombining their elements in a collage of texts and images. In this project, instead of an artist or an audience creating the collages, software searches the web. We could say that authorship is automated. As an online project using input from other websites, *Global City* never looks the same. Not because of the uploading of images by an audience, but because the news sites that are used to create the collages are updated regularly. Every time we visit the *Global City* website its appearance has changed. Again we see that artworks in the digital age are not closed systems, but interdependent processes. There is not one unique version of the work.

Temporary manifestations

The variability of internet art is often considered a problem, for it makes it hard to identify the original of an artwork. Yet, is authenticity really an issue? In the age of digital re/production, myriad copies can circulate without a distinct source or original. As early as 1936, Walter Benjamin concluded that reproductive media outdate traditional artistic notions, such as creativity and authenticity, thus changing the way we experience art.[15] Moreover, the constant external input causes art projects to have no unequivocal appearance or fixed state. Being an event, it is rather a range or composite of differentiated manifestations over time that all are equally 'original' or 'authentic'. This means that we no longer have to wonder what exactly defines a work of art, for there is no essence. Again, it is the processes that matter, instead of exhaustive definitions. Artworks are the mobilisation and re/assembling of relationships.

Contesting the institutions

As noted above, the position of the artist is also moving away from exact definitions. Not only can users or software create art, but artists reconsider their own status too. No longer necessarily skilled craftsmen, they present themselves as facilitators, directors, researchers or engineers, disseminating parts of the creation process over the context in which the art project functions.[16] As a result, formerly 'autonomous' art projects merge with the environment in which the artist operates. Another noticeable manifestation of the relational aesthetics of internet art is the number of collectives that have emerged. The many, often temporary, collaborations between artists reinforce the idea of the end of art-history as a procession of the names of great individuals.[17] Artistic processes no longer centre around artists as autonomous subjects, but form part of collective processes. Artists operate in networks, as nodes in a rhizomatic structure.

New non-institutional ways of organization within the field of the arts were fostered by the boom of the internet in the 1990s. Digital media not only offer new ways of artistic expression and experiment, but they also contribute to the rise of a digitally networked art scene,

---

13 These ideas about the 'inter' are based on Dutch philosopher Henk Oosterling's theories. In the context of this paper, elaborating on his work would lead me too far afield.

14 Fredric Jameson, "Postmodernism and Consumer Society", Hal Foster (ed.), *Postmodern Culture* (London: Pluto Press, 1985), 111-125.

15 Walter Benjamin, "The Work of Art in the Age of Mechanical Reproduction," Hannah Arendt (ed.) *Illuminations*

(London: Fontana, 1992).

16 Taco Stolk, "Introduction to SonicActsX", in: Arie Altena (ed.), *Unsorted, THOUGHTS ON THE INFORMATION ARTS, An AtoZ for SonicActsX* (Amsterdam: Sonic Acts/De Balie, 2004), 54-56.

17 Arie Altena, "Collectives and art, a few remarks", in: Arie Altena (ed.), Ibid. 26-32.

as fluid and ephemeral as the net itself. Email and online mailing lists bring artists, curators and scholars together to discuss theories and practices of internet art, a context to contest the establishment.[18] Raising the tension in the debate is the clash of conventional ideologies about art with the commercial colonisation of the web.[19] Artists can curate their own exhibitions online without the interference of museums and galleries, independent from conventional curatorial practices that are often criticised as confirming discourses of power, creating meta-narratives and canonising the arts. Like authorship, curating can even be automated, as shown by Jon Bird and Andy Webster's project *Tabula Rasa* (2002) an art project presenting self-generating curation from a bottom-up, artist-led point of view and taking art out of its institutional context.

Cemeteries?

The rhizomorphic structure of internet art is difficult to capture into stable regime-like contexts, and it challenges persistent ideas about authorship, authenticity and spectatorship. These transformations have contributed to a rethinking of the museum. The white cube does not seem to suffice anymore for the new forms of cultural expression of our digital age. Operating in the field of tension between their familiar identity and their changing role within a larger network, art museums need to reassess their expertise and modus operandi. They should no longer be merely terminals for the arts, but rather a hub where new insights are constantly produced and dispersed. The concept of the museum should be reconsidered to allow for the idea that it can be rhizomatic re/arrangements of events. Or are museums indeed cemeteries and does internet art call for the post-museum society, as Marinetti called for?

18 Rachel Greene, *Internet Art* (London and New York: Thames & Hudson, 2004).

19 Christiane Paul, *Digital Art* (London and New York: Thames & Hudson, 2003).

Object and Behavior: Variable Media Preservation
Caitlin Jones

There is a great concern to directly address the challenges new media art poses to its curators, conservators and producers. These challenges however are not unique to the digital realm. Much of contemporary artistic practice shares the same practical, legal and theoretical concerns as 'new' media and nowhere is this parallel more evident than in the work of the American artist Dan Flavin. The delicate relationship between object and meaning, and social context and meaning are in serious jeopardy as the hardware becomes obsolete and collectors and museums become fixated on the idea of 'the original.' *[G]old, pink and red, red* (1964) is an installation of unadorned fluorescent lights which reflects this predicament. As Flavin was deliberate in his choice of off-the-shelf fixtures and tubes, conservators in museums around the world are facing major challenges as the red tubes are no longer available and the fixtures wear out. This situation has led to special orders (often at great expense), infrequent exhibition, and the general fetishization of objects that were chosen by the artist for their commonplace qualities. This focus on the physical object as the sole object to be preserved rather than how that object produces meaning often becomes a stumbling block for media art conservation.

How does a fluorescent light installation relate to a work of computer programming and how can that relationship guide preservation practice? The answer does not lie in the physical materials, but in the medium independent qualities. The way an artwork behaves, rather than a simple medium line on a gallery wall label and list of physical components, offers curators and conservators a broader framework from which to approach the preservation of these ephemeral works. At the core of the Variable Media paradigm is the belief that we should look to artists to offer creative solutions and help us define acceptable limits of an artwork's inevitable change. A group of curators, conservators, and technicians at the Guggenheim Museum developed guidelines designed to elicit information directly from artists regarding the behavior and variability of their work, drawing on artist's creativity and vision, in combination with traditional conservation practice, to help preserve the original intention once the current form is no longer viable. The behaviors as defined by the Variable Media Initiative are not permanent or fixed, but they give us guidelines for discussing the more ephemeral qualities of a work of art – exploring media art as part of a continuum rather than a discreet occurrence in the artistic landscape.

To say that an artwork must be *installed* implies that its physical installation is more complex than simply hanging it on a nail. Are its dimensions fixed? Should it occupy the space alone? These questions cannot simply be recorded by a set of dimensions (unless of course it has set dimensions that can never change) or simply 'dimensions variable' in a collections management system. Does the work have a *performative* element – not simply in the traditional notion of dance, music, theatre and performance art, but also for a work in which the process of creation is as important as the product? A medium is *reproduced* if any copy of the original master of the artwork results in a loss of quality – such media include analog photography, film, audio and video. Alternately, if a work is *duplicated* it is implied that a copy could not be distinguished from the original by an independent observer – applying not only to artifacts that can be perfectly cloned, as in digital media, but also to artifacts comprising readymade, industrially fabricated, or mass produced components including computer hardware or playback devices.

Behaviors commonly, although not exclusively, applied to electronic media such as computer driven installations and websites, are *interactive, encoded* and *networked. Interactivity* describes installations that allow visitors to manipulate or take home components of a physical artwork. To say that a work is *encoded* implies that part or all of it is written in computer code or some other language that requires interpretation (eg. dance notation, or by extension a musical score). A *networked* artwork is designed to be viewed on an electronic communication system whether a Local Area Network or the internet. It could also, however, be applied to a piece of mail art or the output of a Surrealist 'exquisite corpse' game. Lastly, even paintings and sculptures can provoke prickly questions when some aspect of their construction alters or requires an intervention. For example, the style of frame a painting is presented in could considerably alter its reception. Such works are *contained* within their materials or a protective framework that encloses or supports the artistic material to be viewed.[1]

For the purposes of this paper, I would like to focus on works in which the *duplicable* components (in these cases consumer electronics) shape its other behaviors and how too much or too little reverence to the original hardware can affect the future of an artwork. A singular focus on the hardware (the object) can jeopardize the less quantifiable attributes of that work (how the viewer interacts with and perceives the object). Often the root of new media conservation's concerns, hardware is subject to much wear and tear and a shocking rate of change dictated by the electronics industry. A promising strategy to replicate obsolete materials and hardware is *emulation*. To emulate a work is to imitate the original look and feel of the piece through completely different means. The term can be applied generally to any refabrication of an artwork's components, but it also has a specific meaning in the context of digital media, where emulation offers a powerful technique for running a program from an out-of-date computer on a contemporary one.

Grahame Weinbren and Roberta Friedman's *The Erl King* (1982–1985) is a work of interactive cinema. As it is also a combination of obsolete hardware, artist-written software and custom made components, it was chosen by the Guggenheim and the Daniel Langlois Foundation to be a case study for this preservation strategy. Heralded as one of the first works of interactive video art, *The Erl King* invites the viewer to control the work's narrative structure through the use of a touch-screen monitor. *The Erl King* explores the relationship between two nineteenth century texts: Freud's *The Burning Child* dream, and Goethe's *Erlkönig*. Accompanied by Schubert's music of Goethe's poem, the viewer is invited to discover their own connection between the two texts. The viewer, or in this case 'editor' is able to control the narrative flow and create their own cinematic experience with the possibility of unlimited connections. A medium dependent description details that the work is constructed through an aggregate of off-the-shelf and custom built hardware – a 1982 SMC-70 computer (z80 processor running at 8mhz, 64K of RAM with 250K dynamic (cache) storage cp/m operating system), custom built video switcher, three laser disc players, Carroll touch screen, CRT monitors and laser discs – all on the verge of major malfunction. A medium independent study of the work would indicate to future curators and conservators that the most salient features of this work lie in the interactive qualities, and how these duplicable components contribute to the viewers experience of the artwork.

For over a year, in tandem with the artist, we partook in numerous discussions with technicians, conservators, and computer programmers to identify the components, and their functional relationship to the work of art itself. As stated by Grahame Weinbren himself, "physical limitation of the components of the early 80s was embedded in the program of *The Erl King* to such an extent that they became determinants of the way it produced meaning."[2] Although the physical equipment itself held no particular importance to the artists, its limitations needed to be clearly understood. In addition, the original code was written by the artists and their collaborators and was therefore deemed critical to preserve the authenticity the work. The necessity of preserving these two elements of *The Erl King* drove the decision to emulate this artwork rather than migrate it to newer components. A program was written to interpret the original source code, the video and audio files were all digitized and all other hardware devices (excluding monitors and touch screen) were emulated.[3]

During this process, many times a line had to be drawn at where to modify the original systems behavior and where to replicate the system 'warts and all.' For instance, the original system had errors that would cause it to crash. Is this something that is necessary to emulate? Would it compromise the authenticity of the work if we eliminated potential system failure? In other cases improvements to

1   A more complete discussion of the behaviors and strategies can be located in Alain Depocas, Jon Ippolito and Caitlin Jones Eds. *Permanence Through Change: The Variable Media Approach* (Montreal: Solomon R. Guggenheim Museum and Daniel Langlois Foundation for Art, Science and Technology, 2003). Also available in PDF format at <www.variablemedia.net>.

2   Grahame Weinbren, *Navigating the Ocean of Streams of Story.* (forthcoming), earlier versions appear in *Millenium Film Journal.* No. 28, 1995, and *Future Cinema.*

3   A detailed outline of the process written by programmer Isaac Dimitrovsky is available online at <www.variablemedia.net>.

the system were unacceptable. For example, the new system had a considerably faster response time from when the viewer touched the screen and the cut in the film was made. According to the artist "it was so fast that one could not believe that one's action had had an effect on the system, and the power and complexity of the piece dissolved into an arbitrary porridge with no distinction between the viewer-caused changes and those built in."[4] The artist advised that the speed degraded the viewer's experience, so the system was slowed to match the original speed, replicating the right balance of delays and waits and "distinguishing between those caused by disc search time and the time required for the computer to communicate with the laser disc players and the touch screen." Another example was a "simple RGB overlay system in the SMC-70 that enabled text and simple graphics to appear on the input screen and not the public viewing screen."[5] This simple output function of the SMC-70 was not possible on the new system. As a peculiarity of the original hardware had developed into an integral part of the artwork, two separate streams of video had to be run out of the new system to accurately emulate the original.

Both versions of *The Erl King* were presented side-by-side in the Guggenheim exhibition *Seeing Double: Emulation in Theory and Practice* (2004). With *The Erl King* as the focus, seven other works from the 1960s through 2004 were paired with versions of what that work could look like in the future if its original hardware was no longer available. Supported by the Daniel Langlois Foundation for Art, Science and Technology, works by Cory Arcangel/BEIGE, Mary Flannagan, Jodi.org, Robert Morris, Nam June Paik, and John F. Simon Jr., were displayed with their emulated versions – allowing media and preservation experts, as well as the general public to compare both versions directly and test the relative success of this preservation strategy.

Grahame Weinbren and Roberta Friedman *The Erl King* 1982-85. Left: 1982-85 version, right: 2004 version. Solomon R. Guggenheim Museum. Preservation made possible by the Daniel Langlois Foundation for Art, Science and Technology.

Two other works in the show presented us with further unorthodox preservation options. Cory Arcangel and members of the programming ensemble BEIGE create works by hacking old Nintendo game cartridges. The work *I Shot Andy Warhol* (2002), a hacked *Hogan's Alley* game, was included in *Seeing Double* without an emulated partner. Although created with the use of a Nintendo emulator on a Macintosh, Arcangel felt that in his case the replacement of the original NES with new hardware would remove the work so far from its context that it would be rendered meaningless in a gallery context. Arcangel states "because the public doesn't necessarily understand an emulator, the reason I make works based on game consoles is that all you have to do is see the cartridge to understand what happened... In 30 years a laptop running that game is going to mean nothing to the public. So I want *I Shot Andy Warhol* to be exhibited with a real light gun, the Nintendo and preferably a period TV."[6] Simple storage (and buying up old equipment on eBay) is therefore, for the time being, considered the strategy for preservation of this incarnation.

Arcangel gives us a complimentary strategy for his Nintendo work's preservation however – in essence opening multiple streams of preservation for the same work. He releases his code on the Internet and invites users to build their own games, alter the code, and engage in an open source dialogue. For Arcangel, "Other people have already been porting my work to other versions. Somebody wrote me and was like, hey, I got it to work on a Gameboy emulating the Nintendo... Because I also participate in behind-the-scenes emulation culture. Everything I learned about programming comes from the homebrew culture, and it's important to me to give the code away so someone else could learn from it." Placing a NES in a crate in a warehouse may save the installation attributes of the work, but releasing it over the network insures an equally important attribute of it, which is its place in a network context – preserving the artwork beyond its object value.

An additional form of emulation is evidenced in Jodi's, *All Wrongs Reversed* (2004), a recording of a Spectrum computer based installation, *10 Programs Written in Basic ©1984* (2004). *10 Programs* consisted of eight vintage ZX Spectrum computers in a gallery space where the public was invited to take on the task of programming in BASIC – an obsolete computer language on archaic machines. The artists have offered numerous interpretations of this work, one is that *All Wrongs Reversed* captures the behavioral qualities of the ZX Spectrum, without capturing the physical ZX Spectrum. The noise generated when a program is loaded via cassette tape, the texture, the interference would be lost if we were to migrate to newer equipment or emulate the Spectrum on a Pentium machine. As an alternative to stockpiling old equipment and having *10 Programs* tied to this specific

4   Weinbren, op. cit.
5   Ibid.
6   Cory Arcangel, didactic material
     for *Seeing Double: Emulation in*

Theory and Practice (Solomon R. Guggenheim Museum), available at <www.variablemedia.net>.

jodi.org *All Wrongs Reversed* 1984 (Recording of *10 Programs Written in BASIC* 1984) 2004, video, courtesy of the artists

hardware, the artists made the decision to document the process of writing in BASIC and all its inherent by-products: "...of course you don't see the cassette or the TV or the computer – you see someone coding and typing and having a simple result. But making a DVD was a way to record the original action."[7] It was not just the physical hardware, but the display qualities that hardware produced which was deemed worthy of preservation – thus documenting them independently of their original hardware environment. In this example, the object itself is not preserved in a physical sense, but what the artist deemed important about the object is.

There is no single approach for dealing with new media preservation – there never has been for the conservation of more traditional art objects either. The Variable Media paradigm provides just one strategy, and one that we hope will allow artworks of an ephemeral nature to exist beyond anecdote or document. There is an inherent conflict when an institution is charged by the mandate of history to keep something inherently dynamic in a static form. *The Erl King, I Shot Andy Warhol,* and *10 Programs Written in BASIC ©1984* are all interactive artworks with a computer at their core. The relationship between hardware and meaning varies in all three, and therefore the treatment of them is equally varied. To the artists of *The Erl King* the hardware was just a means to create a cinematic experience, to Arcangel, without the hardware the experience is totally degraded. In no way are these conventional methods of preservation and some will argue that it is not preservation at all. Flexibility and ephemerality are often at the root of new media works and collecting institutions need to adapt and embrace these elements within more traditional models of collecting and conservation if they are to preserve any essence of the work, outside of its object value.

7   Joan Heemskerk and Dirk Paesmans (jodi.org), didactic material for *Seeing Double: Emulation in Theory and Practice*. Solomon R. Guggenheim Museum. Available at <www.variablemedia.net>.

The Art of Re-enactment: Curating Real Time Presence
Sarah Cook

Introduction

As part of my work with CRUMB, I investigate the presentation
of networked art in gallery spaces.[1] One challenge of exhibiting
networked art – art made using computer technology that draws on a
digital networks and invites interaction from the viewer – is how much
a curator might change the format of the work in order to make it
stable in a gallery environment and accessible to an audience member.
New media art is by definition dynamic and interconnected; gallery
spaces are by tradition static contemplative spaces. And yet many
works of new media art change through the viewer's interaction; if the
work reads differently each time it is accessed how does the curator
ascertain the right context for its presentation?

In my curatorial practice I strive to be led by the artists rather than
led by the technology. In the shifting field of new media art, it is often
the case that artists are savvy about their tools of production (video,
software, coding, telecommunications networks), more so than the
producers/gatekeepers of the institutions in which those artists are
showing their work. Furthermore, with new media, tool and method,
process and product are the same, or much closer than one would
think. The internet might be both the means of the work's production
and the site of its distribution.

In this paper I argue that re-enactment is an exciting area of practice
that suggests some of the challenges of curating technology-based
work for a gallery context. I have chosen to focus on a subjective
selection of artists' projects, interwoven with a discussion of the form
and method of re-enactment practice.[2]

Curating real-time presence

What do I mean by real-time work? And what do I mean by real-time
presence? On June 17, 2001, artist Jeremy Deller collaborated with
historical re-enactment groups to re-stage a clash that took place
between striking coal miners and police on June 18, 1984 in South
Yorkshire, England. Jeremy Deller's work involves collaboration,
community groups and popular culture. His practice ranges from live
events (concerts) to audio records (the project *Acid Brass* has brass
bands playing interpretations of acid house anthems), to drawings and

1   CRUMB is the Curatorial Resource
    for Upstart Media Bliss, an
    international website and mailing
    list for curators of media arts. <www.
    crumbweb.org> .
2   Thank you to VIVID and UCE, The
    Banff Centre's New Media Institute
    and Sara Diamond, the artists, and

the University of Sunderland for
supporting this research. Thanks
especially to curator Vivienne
Gaskin for commissioning much of
the work discussed here and to Tom
McCarthy for his excellent writing on
the topic.

collections (*The Folk Archive* (2000–) is an ongoing investigation into contemporary folk art in the UK).

The clash, known as *The Battle of Orgreave* (2001), between the National Union of Mineworkers and the police was a turning point in a dispute that lasted over a year and changed government-industry relations in the UK. The artist enlisted the help of dozens of re-enactment groups, local villagers, as well as ex-miners and a few members of the constabulary who had participated in the original incident. The event (attended by the general public and produced by Artangel) was documented by film director Mike Figgis, whose resulting documentary *The Battle of Orgreave* (co-commissioned by Channel 4), serves not only as a record of Deller's artwork, but also as an alternative to the media portrayal of the event 17 years earlier. It entails footage of the re-enactment, press images of the original event, as well as recent interviews with former miners, policemen, politicians, supporters and Deller himself about how the event affected them.

The Battle of Orgreave suggests how re-enactment-based projects each have a unique approach to technology and its use as a tool or method. In some cases the representation of the actual event (the representation of a 'real-time') hinges on its documentation through media technologies (television, for instance). In other cases the technology adds a completely new (mediated) layer to the 'real-time' of the event. The projects are experienced both over time in a looped/repeated linear fashion (the time it takes to watch the event and its subsequent documentation) at the same time as they as they make evident the time that has passed between the event and its re-presentation/re-mediation. In both instances the reality of time passing is inescapable. This breaks down further in a questioning of both the form and method of re-enactment art projects.

Nina Pope and Karen Guthrie *Living with Tudors* 2005

Form and characteristics

The technology of re-enactment can include costumes, actors, blogs, live web-streaming, webcams, photography and broadcast video, and other documentary devices and methods that facilitate representations of the past in order to make them experiential. As these varied technologies are used in part to facilitate the audience's experience of an artwork that is entirely sited in the actual or metaphorical re-enactment of a past or other event, the work also exhibits the unique characteristics of its technological medium. For instance, re-enacting and documenting an event using digital video streamed live over the internet lends it a vastly different aesthetic and experience than documenting it using pinhole cameras and displaying the resulting photographic print in a gallery, as Nina Pope and Karen Guthrie have done in their re-enactments of Tudor life.[3]

Some of the key characteristics of new media technologies that are exploited by artists working in the field of re-enactment include:

> Non-linearity – the use of hypertext on the web has proven that narratives no longer have to be linear. Stories can be told in such a way that the audience member can decide at what point to enter the 'text', where and when in the story to connect one piece to another, and when to exit the story.
> Simultaneity – with broadcast and networked technologies such as radio, television and the Internet, numerous audience members can engage with the same story at the same time from disparate locations.
> Virtuality and 'being there' – with computer programming, computer generated images and techniques of simulation, it is possible for a project to suggest the inhabitation of an unreal space. With the creation of virtual space comes a sense of un-real time also as the programme might allow the construction of a past to be relived or a future as yet unknown.
> Connectedness and interaction – virtual simulations are often used in science to play out hypotheses and visualise abstract data sets. These are unlike the simulations and re-enactments artists are creating in that artists working with performance might set up a situation in order to be in it (or let other people be in it); as opposed to setting it up just to watch it unfold.

Art projects using re-enactment seek to explode the notion of the linearity of media and technology, explode time and our perception of it – in part through performance and installation, but using fundamentally different methodologies. These characteristics of the art of re-enactment help to think about how the presentation of the work might be affected by its placement within a gallery context.

---

3   Nina Pope and Karen Guthrie are featured earlier in this volume. At the time of this original presentation I presented some of the pinhole camera images and diaristic video footage of their *Living with Tudors* project.

Method and aesthetics

Artists are increasingly using simulation as the concept, form and also methodology of their work. If we are to take re-enactment practices as art, then what are their methods that make them art?[4] As collaborator Kris Cohen writes, "Artists can play with reality, intimacy, and experiences of otherness, which arise in the process of the work. In a sense, this work represents a reclaiming of past events, a way of deterritorialising them, unseating them from embedded meanings and cliché, and representing them as unfamiliar, as phenomena to be re-engaged with anew. It allows the artist to choose the level at which their work is perceived as art, to control and play with the relationship with the audience, to relate directly to a non-gallery based audiences. It allows the artist to literally be present in the work."[5]

Re-enactment based projects also disturb our notion of 'real world experience' and hence question the idea implicit in simulation that experience has to map on to the simulated event in order to learn something from it. This is in dispute from one re-enactment project to another. As Iain Aitch writes in response to *The Battle of Orgreave* "After all, re-enactments are not about creating a new event, but rather attempting to understand a past one. 'I was interested in expanding that definition of heritage to include something that happened quite recently and that is not a particularly proud moment in our history, but was a very important moment,' says Deller. '[The work] was originally called *The English Civil War*. I saw that dispute as feeding into history and being part of history.'"[6]

Whether new knowledge is an explicit goal or not, art projects which employ the tactic of re-enactment have in common that they are in part designed to expose or show systems of knowledge. As a result, I have noted that there are three possible models (or subcategories) of simulation and re-enactment, which are:

> The hypothesis or experiment model – adopted from scientific practices and where new knowledge is deliberately sought
> The ritual model – where "re-enactment is not about finally laying that moment to rest – rather, it is more about our need for custom and ceremony"[7]
> The documentary model – where the project takes on the characteristics of social or living history practices, often in a 'mockumentary' style

With all works of art in which the technology serves not simply as the tool of making but also as the tool of distribution of the work, the method becomes the medium. Methodological choices influence the resulting aesthetic of the work. The work of UK-based artists Jeremy Deller, Nina Pope and Karen Guthrie and Rod Dickinson draws on these models. However, each project demonstrates a particular aesthetic borne of the decision about method taken at the outset.

Seeing if it can be done

"I wanted to know what it was like, without doing it."[8] A number of contemporary art projects which use re-enactment originate from an analysis of textual accounts of journeys or events. This is certainly the case with Ben Coode-Adams, Marcus Coates and Bow Boys School's project *The Man Who Ate His Boots* (2002), based on John Franklin's first voyage to the Polar Sea. The resulting video – a work-in-progress – is comprised of footage and still photography shot by Coates and Coode-Adams as they attempted to re-enact in real-time the journey by canoe (but transplanted to many small rivers in the UK) that Franklin undertook in 1818 in his search to claim territory and find the Northwest Passage.

Ben Coode-Adams & Marcus Coates *The Man That Ate His Boots* 2002

In the case of Coode-Adams' project with Kris Cohen, *Is Someone Coming to Get Me?* numerous accounts of the Everest disaster were pieced together and the ascent was performed on a scale model of the mountain, in real-time, with paper figures standing in for the ascent parties.[9] The artists kept both a text-blog and a photo-blog on an accompanying website allowing viewers not present at the re-enactment event itself to either experience it in real-time from a distance, or as documentation after the fact. The artists were primarily concerned with modelling an unseen space and learning from the discrepancies in the different accounts of the original participants' experiences.

4   The keywords I've hung on to in my investigation of this area of practice include: performance; camouflage; disembodiment; collaboration; self-effacement; technology.

5   Kris Cohen in correspondence with the author.

6   Iain Aich, "Doing it Again" published online by *Eyestorm*, 2003, <www.eyestorm.com/feature/ED2n_article.asp?article_id=363>.

7   Robert Longo, quoted by Iain Aitch, op. cit.

8   Ben Coode-Adams in correspondence with the author.

9   *Is Someone Coming to get me* was first performed at The Banff Centre and later at Hastings Gallery, UK, and was discussed by the artists in their presentation at the *Summit on Simulation and Other Re-enactments* at the Banff Centre on the morning of Saturday 1 May 2004 at 10.45am, audio archive of online at <www.banffcentre.ca/bnmi>.

The project thus demonstrates the importance of the script in re-enactment based work – the practice of writing out everything you know about the event and then performing it. How does the re-enacted event relate to what the documentation of the original event tells us? This could also be seen to be the case with the project *File Under Sacred Music* (2003) by Iain Forsyth and Jane Pollard, wherein they meticulously recreated a bootleg videotape of a concert by the rock band The Cramps.[10] Forsyth and Pollard began with a copy of the tape (23 minutes long, black and white) purchased from eBay, and from a close 'reading' of it, wrote a script for how it could be re-made, shot-by-shot, in a staged performance event with re-enactors and a live audience at the Institute for Contemporary Art in London. They write, "Our interest and investigation is concerned with... cultural perceptions of live performance and the nature of liveness itself – reflected back through the gaze of a mediatised culture, the quest for authenticity through the 'live-like' experience of something like 'MTV unplugged' – history and memory, nostalgia, illusion and myth, participation and communication, reproduction and interpretation.... Part of our strategic approach to the dissemination of our practice is through techniques learnt and borrowed/stolen from the music and entertainment industries."[11]

In this, certain technological characteristics of the media used (scratched three-quarter inch video tape versus sharp digital video, which carries a time-stamp) were closely considered in the realisation of the aesthetic authenticity of the work. Forsyth and Pollard later exhibited the script itself, along with the video projected, in the exhibition *This Much is Certain* at the Royal College of Art.[12]

Verisimilitude

Re-enactment projects generate obvious comparisons to lived experience, especially where they are set up with the intent of learning something from them. This process invites the question, what do you have to get right for it to count as re-enactment?

Rod Dickinson's practice demonstrates his continuing interest in belief systems. He is known for his collaboration with a group of people who make crop circles in British landscapes. Dickinson admits that he began working with re-enactment because he was looking for something similar to crop circles (be it a model or methodology) that was in effect an undeclared form of representation. In this he sees re-enactment as a form of covert folk art: as it is a hobby, the participants in most cultural re-enactments don't think of them as representational. Rather they think of them as an activity, not as an authored event. Dickinson has previously worked on restaging elements of the 1978 Jonestown Massacre, the mass-suicide (or murder depending on your viewpoint) in Guyana of over 900 members of a cult led by the Reverend Jim Jones, through a fire and brimstone 'living history' preaching session by Jones, complete with miracle healing – also staged at London's ICA in 2000. Dickinson writes: "I make very carefully researched live reconstructions of historical events. The events I select to reconstruct have often had a conflict or misunderstanding of beliefs at their centre. The projects attempt to examine and repeat the social mechanisms that underpin extreme actions that are generated by beliefs."[13]

Dickinson's film *Obedience to Authority* (2002) presents a re-enactment of Stanley Milgram's infamous electroshock experiments at Yale University Laboratory in 1960.[14] Milgram found, surprisingly, that 65% of his subjects, ordinary residents of New Haven, were willing to give apparently harmful electric shocks – up to 450 volts – to a pitifully protesting victim, simply because a scientific authority commanded them to. The victim was, in reality, an actor who did not actually receive shocks, and this fact was revealed to the subjects at the end of the experiment. But, during the experiment itself, the experience was a powerfully real and gripping one for most participants. Dickinson orchestrated the re-enactment at Centre for Contemporary Art in Glasgow in 2002 using actors performing in a to-scale, purpose-built reconstruction of the original rooms in which the experiment took place. "The replica contained many of the original features of the room. Copies of the furniture, architectural detail and most importantly the electro shock equipment that Milgram used."[15] The performance also attempted to recreate the necessary endurance test in its observers as it had created in its participants. The audience was instructed that they could not leave and a guard was stationed at the door."

As Tom McCarthy observed, "The 'scientist' and 'subject' of Milgram's experiments were already actors; Jones's 'miracle healings' were already fake – pieces of tawdry theatre, sleights of hand. On top of that, both were already re-enactments, reiterations of previous versions of themselves."[16]

Where are we when we are in it?
In this paper I have presented a number of re-enactment-based projects as examples of what I call real-time work, where the experience of the performed event is mediated through a possibly simultaneous experience of the documentation and dissemination of the event. I have

----

10 The projects of Iain Forsyth and Jane Pollard are integral to any discussion of re-enactment based work. In the original presentation at VIVID I screened their project *File Under Sacred Music*. Information about this work and their others can be found online <www.iainandjane.com>.

11 Iain Forsyth and Jane Pollard in correspondence with the author.

12 *This Much is Certain* RCA Curating Course exhibition, 2004. London. There is an excellent accompanying catalogue with an article by Tom McCarthy on the work.

13 Rod Dickinson. In his recent project for the ICA, Dickinson reconstructed the audio and light psychological warfare (sensory deprivation) programme used by the FBI during a well-documented siege against a small non-denominational religious group based in Waco, Texas in March and April 1993 (the Branch Davidians, lead by David Koresh).

14 For more information, see The Milgram Re-enactment project website <www.milgramreenactment.org>.

15 Ibid.

16 Tom McCarthy, *Invoking the Invocation*. Published online, available from <www.milgramreenactment.org/pages/tom.xml?location=4&page=5&text=5>.

suggested that the methodological choices that the artists made in the set-up of their re-enactments has determined, in part through choice of technology, the aesthetic characteristics of the work.

The Battle of Orgreave in particular but many of these projects also raise the question of self-effacement and embodiment, and the politics and ethics of re-enactment (Who is it for? Who is in it?). People often ask Rod Dickinson, not just 'why do it?' but 'what is your relationship to the original?' And 'what is your relationship to the people involved in the original?'

It appears that scientific simulation (as a method) differs from re-enactment (as form/medium) in that artistic re-enactment is about the experiential access to a situation or event, to allow an audience to be present in the work, not just in watching it. This invites the question, is re-enactment in art simply just 'experiments with an audience'?

In a gallery context, audience behaviour is determined by the passive consumption (watching and observation) of works of art. The varied characteristics of new media art – its interactivity and possibility for simulating other spaces and places – combined with the performative elements of re-enactment work lead to a completely different kind of audience engagement.

In re-enactment works like those described above, artists appear to be undertaking the controlled manipulation of participants who appear (in the mediated event) as an audience and, in that, create the actual audience for the work. This is achieved through mostly technological means, such as video documents, photographs, and blogs. In some cases, the technology is the work of art; in all cases, the work cannot exist outside or without technology. Technology has never been a simple 'tool' which the artist can possess, but rather a process and a methodology.

The practice of re-enactment suggests the shrinking distance between the event and the mediation of it that we experience in everyday life, as well as the impossible task of the archive to document every facet of lived experience. Are we committed to live in a technological future where we have to do everything twice – once for real and once for the record? With networked digital technologies we find ourselves living in the society of a different kind of spectacle – that of endless duplication and redistribution. If media is itself a distribution network (as evidenced in the project *Is Someone Coming to Get Me*), then what use is the gallery?

Experiments in Open-Ended Curation
Andy Webster, Jon Bird & Garrett Monaghan

Introduction

"Classical exhibition history emphasized order and stability. Nowadays, what we are seeing is fluctuation and instability: the unpredictable... Combining incertitude and unpredictability with organization is an important issue here. In the place of certitude, the exhibition expresses connective possibilities: evolutional displays, exhibitions with an ongoing life, exhibitions as dynamic learning systems with feedback loops, a concerted effort to revoke the unclosed, paralysing homogeneity of the exhibition master-plan, and thus question the obsolete idea of the curator as the mastermind."[1]

In all of our projects we eschew any notion of a paralysing master-plan. Our approach involves setting up minimal conditions that allow unpredictable forces, outside of our control, to influence the structure and content of our work. We want to be surprised by the results; our goal is always to 'get more out than we put in' by setting up open-ended projects. For the purposes of this paper we delineate four strategies that we have employed in our approach to curation: minimising curatorial influence; collaborative decision making; responding to site; and maximising vantage points. None of these strategies is particularly novel and nor do they constitute a written recipe that we follow step-by-step: in each of our curatorial projects we have adapted them as appropriate given the ingredients to hand. In this essay we describe three of our recent curatorial experiments, indicating how our open-ended approach to curation resonates with some of the more general issues in contemporary curating.

Minimising curatorial influence

"When curators seize the conceptual ground usually occupied by artists, this places artists – often in vast numbers – in the subservient role of interpreting and delivering the curator's a priori, overarching premise."[2]

We have consciously attempted to minimise our curatorial influence and not subsume artists' work under any overarching premises. *Tabula Rasa* took place during two weeks in December 2002. Fifty-eight artists' films were projected onto four buildings in the centre of Croydon each evening from dusk to midnight, and also shown each day in the Parfitt Gallery at Croydon College's Higher Education Centre.[3] The project was

1 Hans Ulrich Obrist, "Evolutional Exhibitions, The Happy Face of Globalization," Biennale of Ceramics in Contemporary Art, Albisola, Liguria, 2001. ‹www.attese.it/attese1/article13/›.

2 Alex Farqhuarson, "Curator and Artist", *Art Monthly*, 270, 2003, 15.

3 ‹www.skylineprojections.co.uk›.

supported by Croydon College, Croydon Skyline Project and University College Falmouth. The content and structure of the show was shaped by the films that were submitted and the context in which they were displayed, rather than any *a priori* theme. The use of artists' films developed from a desire to appropriate and use formats consistent with the commercial modes of display used in the centre of Croydon and not from any personal aesthetic considerations. In our open call for submissions we specified four pragmatic constraints: the work had to be submitted on mini DV tape; each film had to be less than 20 minutes long; we had to be able to legally display the films in public; and no accompanying sound tracks could be played (where could we place speakers when a film could be seen from a multitude of vantage points in a mile radius?).

Tabula Rasa Croydon, December 2002

We employed two strategies to minimise our curatorial influence. Firstly, we decided to include *all* of the submitted work that met the criteria specified in the call for submissions and to display every film at each of the sites over the duration of the project. Secondly, we developed software for producing show reels for each projection site that was not dependent on our own aesthetic judgment. Artists were asked to send five keywords to describe their work and an automatic curation system, implemented with a genetic algorithm, used these keywords to cluster the submissions into four distinct groups for display on each of the buildings.[4] Our software resulted in show reels that self-organised in unforeseen and unexpected ways.

Collaborative decision making

"Collaboration in art is fundamentally a question of cultural form. By this, I mean that the decision to teamwork with other artists and/or with non-artists directly involves shaping the ways in which art finds its sensuous and intellectual place in the world. In this it draws into view the very nature of how, and under what conditions, art might appear in the world."[5]

We see collaboration as a means of promoting differences and diversity and therefore as a powerful tool for exploding restricting hierarchies and their associated master-plans. Our decision making process emphasises the importance of allowing imperfection, mutation, and heterogeneity over more prescriptive practices. *Tabula Rasa* was developed in collaboration with computer scientist/philosopher Joe Faith.[6] In another project, the generative curation system for Sixty Second Film Festival was created in collaboration with the festival directors, Garrett Monaghan and Karen Savage. Similarly *Blip@Newlyn* involved collaborating with Blip, a number of artists, and the Interact Lab, a research group at the University of Sussex.[7] Successful collaboration requires a commitment to dialogue and an acceptance that the final structure of a project will be shaped by a number of different perspectives. As Roberts points out in the quotation that introduces this section, working collaboratively shifts the focus of projects onto process and dialogue and away from any individual's conception of the end result. We are not interested in presenting a definitive set of results. Rather, we agree with Bourriaud that "[t]he artwork is no longer an end point but a simple moment in an infinite chain of contributions" – we view exhibitions and other events as a catalyst for dialogue and the further development of a project, which consequently remains open-ended.[8]

Responding to site

"For only when an organism shares in the ordered relations of its environment does it secure the stability essential to living. And when the participation comes after a phase of disruption and conflict, it bears within itself the germs of a consummation akin to the esthetic."[9]

In some of our theoretical work we have considered how one might construct interactive artworks which have the potential to display novel behaviour.[10] We identified two of the fundamental properties of artificial devices that display strong forms of emergent behaviour:

4   For a detailed description of the automatic curation system see the technical paper that we presented with Joe Faith at EvoMUSART: Jon Bird, Joe Faith and Andy Webster, *Tabula Rasa: A Case Study in Evolutionary Curation* (EvoWorkshops, 2003), 479-489.

5   John Roberts, "Collaboration as a Problem of Art's Cultural Form", *Third Text*, 18(6), 2004, 557.

6   <www.computing.unn.ac.uk/staff/CGJF1/>.

7   <www.informatics.sussex.ac.uk/interact/>.

8   Nicolas Bourriaud, *Postproduction* (Lukas and Sternberg, 2002), 14.

9   John Dewey, *Art as Experience* (Balch, 1934), 14-15.

10 See for example: Jon Bird, Paul Layzell, Andy Webster and Phil Husbands, "Towards Epistemically Autonomous Robots: Exploiting the Potential of Physical Systems," *Leonardo*, 36(2), 2003, 109-114.

they consist of functionally-open components (that is, their material substrate can potentially play a large number of different roles); and they can autonomously change their structure independently of any human designer. We focused on two devices that exhibited these properties and which enabled them to construct their own sensors: that is, autonomously determine how they interact with their environment. This research informed our approach to collaborative work, and we became interested in how we could adapt and apply insights from cybernetics and artificial life in our art projects.

In *Tabula Rasa* the goal was to collaboratively develop a project that was both functionally and structurally open – so that it could respond to its context and be shaped, to some extent, by environmental contingencies. The centre of Croydon was the starting point for *Tabula Rasa* and a brief inventory of this environment presented us with the excesses of consumerism: shopping is what makes sense in and of this space. Almost every surface is inscribed with the logic of the market, evident in the branded and controlled space of daytime trading and the illumination of corporate headquarters each evening. Importantly, the centre of Croydon is a space that shoppers and commuters experience on the move. We were interested in how we could use this context to develop projects that would allow the place and its everyday situations to influence their structure. A key aspect was to identify what the role of the artist working in this site might be, and to develop strategies that enabled artistic interventions into this shopping space.

The format of *Tabula Rasa* took shape once we had negotiated the hire of four projection sites from Croydon Skyline Project, an arm of Croydon Borough Council which coordinates large-scale projections on buildings in the centre of Croydon throughout the winter months. This provided us with an existing distributional channel through which we could intervene in the site by replacing the daily broadcast of messages from local businesses with artists' films. *Tabula Rasa* was not a large-scale 'art event' but more a clandestine activity that subtly infiltrated, for a short time, the corporate forms that normally occupy the centre of Croydon. The way that art is positioned and ultimately received in this context requires a wholly different strategy to that of gallery-based shows. Although the content of the projections was different from the normal material shown, the project's coherence with the usual modes of display would, we felt, allow the work to blur into, rather than rupture, the everyday activities and 'ordered relations' of the space.

Maximising vantage points
"Autonomous movement is what defines the proper place of a multitude. Multitude fights the homogenisation of globalisation; actually it constructs new temporalities, immanent processes of constitution."[11]

One of our constant aims is to maximise the ways that an audience can engage with a project. A 'vantage point' is a perspective from which somebody can interact with an art work. It has a spatial implication, referring to how people can move relative to the piece. The term also relates to the connective possibilities resulting from presenting work in multiple formats which "open up non-linear, multi-directional paths where viewers are expected, over and over again, to find their own crossings".[12] The format of our projects is dynamic and our aim is that they generate an ongoing, open-ended dialogue. For example, we have presented our work in the form of academic papers, public discussions, work-in-progress situations, documentation of laboratory experiments, simulations, maquettes, performances, and multi-layered events at experimental sites and traditional locations.[13]

The internet is an example of a dynamic open-ended system which is encountered by huge numbers of visitors, possibly thousands of miles apart, who autonomously explore an evolving, emergent space. Net-based art projects can be received at multiple locations across the globe at any time of the day and as part of ongoing everyday activities, reading email, listening to music, downloading software, checking train timetables, chatting etc. The unchoreographed nature of the audience's engagement with net-art is a real source of power in this work: there is the potential for meaning being generated through the chance encounter, at unexpected times and in diverse contexts. Placing net-art into an institutional setting is highly problematic as it lifts the works out of the rich context of the web where they were originally realised and reduces the vantage points from which they can be experienced.

In *Tabula Rasa* we moved artists' work out of the gallery and into the public context of the centre of Croydon. We hoped that this shift of context, unlike the institutionalisation of net-art, would enrich the art films. The typically clean, white settings of galleries were replaced by dirty, noisy streets, which are subject to the vagaries of the weather and other changing environmental conditions. In contrast to gallery spaces there were no entry points or exits, no clear beginnings or endings. For passersby there was no invitation to experience the work, nor would the public have expected or necessarily even wanted to see 'art'. The individual works in *Tabula Rasa* were seen casually, often accidentally and over time, not necessarily wholly or in a single viewing or at a single site. The projects formed the backdrop to many activities being played out on the streets and vice versa.

We did not know how the work would be received. One can only try and imagine what rush hour commuters stuck in four lane jams made of a 60 ft by 40 ft text simply stating 'Fields'.[14] Similarly what would passersby taking shelter in bus stops from driving horizontal snow storms have made of Rosie Hinrichsen's film *Watching Dust Motes Glinting in the Sunlight* which captures the gentle thermodynamics of dust movement? The points of reception were endless, the relationships always fleeting, potentially meaningful, possibly meaningless but importantly open.

11 Hans Ulrich Obrist, op.cit.
12 Hans Ulrich Obrist, op.cit
13 See ‹www.andywebster.info› for examples.

14 Jonathan Allen, *Voluntary Experiential,* ‹www.discogroup.co.uk/ jonportfolio.htm›.

How does our approach translate to the gallery?
After *Tabula Rasa*, for us, gallery-based projects have the potential
to feel constrained and over-determined. A clear example of this was
when the *Tabula Rasa* was showcased at the Royal College of Art.[15]
Here the four external sites were replaced by a single monitor display
which, akin to institutional net-art shows, removed the all important
dynamic context of the centre of Croydon. We are therefore particularly
interested in enabling gallery visitors to dynamically generate the
structure of projects and maximising the vantage points available to
them in a gallery context.

Collaborating with Sixty Second Film Festival gave us the
opportunity to use touch screen, network and database technologies
to provide the public with a participatory experience where their
choices were decisive in shaping the event.[16] In October 2004 thirty
four short films from regional and international artists were shown
in an open-plan gallery and adjoining theatre at the Third Floor Arts
Centre in Portsmouth. The project was set up by Karen Savage and
Garrett Monaghan as part of a broader initiative by Sixty Second Art to
open up the traditional presentation of artists' moving-image projects.[17]
The goal was to create an experimental environment that would engage
the general public by placing aspects of the curation process in their
hands. It was supported by Arts Council England, OTV, Portsmouth
City Council and the University of Portsmouth. Established artists were
invited to present work alongside selected open submissions. Final
curatorial decisions were handed over to the public as an experiment
in generative curation.

The system used a very simple mechanism. Stills taken from the
beginning of each of the films were presented on four touch screens
(ten of the films on one screen, eight on each of the others) with the
title and artist's name positioned below each image. Touching a still
resulted in a larger image and film synopsis being displayed on the
screen. The visitor could then touch a 'Play' button and watch the
film full screen on the monitor; pressing a 'Stop' button returned
the visitor to the initial screen showing all of the films available for
viewing. The darkened theatre space contained banked seating and a
large screen typical for showing a film festival programme. However,
the sequence of projected films was determined entirely by the way
visitors viewed the films on the touch screens in the gallery space.
Custom software logged and interpreted the selection behaviour of the
public to ascertain the most popular films. If a film was viewed from
start to finish, it was given a score of +1; if it was viewed for more than
20 seconds, but not the whole way through, it was assigned a score of
−1; if it was viewed for less than 20 seconds then that selection did not
contribute to the viewing statistics. A database logged the cumulative
scores of all the films throughout the day and the ten most popular
choices were projected on the theatre screen in a looping sequence.
This sequence was updated every hour in order to respond to changes
in the film popularity data.

The strength of the project lay in the fact that the nature of the event was wholly reliant on audience participation for the generation of a constantly shifting and unpredictable running order. It also raised important questions about how an audience might engage with an arts project and from what vantage points they might access and receive the project.

Blip@Newlyn at Newlyn Art Gallery in October 2004 was an attempt to enable the audience to engage with a project from multiple points of reference. Blip is a Brighton-based forum that organises public events where the focus is on both artistic and scientific work that explores generative and procedural processes, interaction, emergence and artificial life.[18] These events take the forms of presentations, exhibitions, gigs, workshops, talks, screenings and the *Big Blip* festival. For each event Blip develops and coordinates a network of individuals (artists, scientists and technologists), institutions and other organisations. Blip generally uses venues such as bars, clubs, theatres and cinemas in order to facilitate public access by presenting art and science outside of their normal institutional contexts. *Blip@Newlyn* was the first Blip event in a gallery context, and was organised so that several activities occurred simultaneously, ranging from exhibits, workshops and demonstrations to a public forum on the relationship between art, science and technology. It was supported by Arts Council England, University College Falmouth and Digital Peninsula Network. Much of the work invited the audience to play and interact and we purposely made the event child friendly. The environment encouraged exploration and offered opportunities to engage with art, science and technology at different levels ranging from building and racing Lego robots to publicly debating the relationships between art and science. The diverse audience that came to the show and the length of time that they stayed in the gallery, actively participating in the event, demonstrated the value of maximising vantage points.

Conclusion

"If a flexible framework with the barest limits is established by selecting, for example, only five elements out of an infinity of possibilities, almost anything can happen. And something always does, even things that are unpleasant."[19]

In order to achieve open-endedness, we aim to under, rather than over, determine our projects. We insist that chance and contingency become significant factors in a project's development. For us, artworks are not inert or fixed but unpredictable and wholly undomesticated and in our approach to curation we aim to set up minimal conditions

15 Royal College of Art, The Lux Open, 2003, London, UK.
16 <www.sixtysecondfilm.com/>.
17 <www.sixtysecondart.com/>.
18 <www.blip.me.uk>.

19 Allan Kaprow, "Happenings in the New York Scene" In Jeff Kelly (ed) *The Blurring of Art and Life* (University of California Press, 1993), 20.

that allow them to thrive in an open-ended way. In *Tabula Rasa* we had no particular end in mind, except to project a diverse population of artists' projects in the centre of Croydon. Some people questioned our policy of showing all of the submissions and not applying some set of selection criteria. Our inclusion policy was motivated by a belief that any aesthetic judgements motivated by gallery-based criteria would have limited validity given the dynamic, public context of the event. *Tabula Rasa* was an experiment where we observed the effects of placing artists' films in an urban space rich with connective possibilities; the outcome was unknown and out of our control and failure was a real possibility. We found it significant that some submissions, which seemed weak when we first viewed them on a monitor, became powerful pieces when they were projected on buildings and glimpsed around a corner or viewed on the move.

It is important to emphasise that we have adapted our approach to gallery contexts and that in our collaborations with Sixty Second Film Festival and Blip we worked with art that had been selected by panels. Our goal has not been to describe a blueprint, or master-plan, for open-ended curation: none of our strategies is particularly novel, nor are they the only way that a project can be made open-ended. Rather, this essay is a snapshot of our evolving practice and, we hope, a small contribution to the ongoing dialogue about issues in curation.

Space, Place, Interface: Location in New Media Art
Chris Byrne

In film-maker Richard Fenwick's short *RND#91: 51st State* an anonymous caller enquires of numerous technical support specialists where exactly the internet is, and whether he can buy a piece.[1] Fenwick responds to the entrepreneurial spirit of dot-com, satirising the culture of venture capitalism and 24/7 help lines. He also raises the question of the borderlessness of the internet. The expansive, 'everywhere' rhetoric of the technocrats contrasts sharply with the reality and the restricted ownership of the networks. The work questions our assumptions about the supposedly liberating potential of computer networks.

There's a mythology of networks as ubiquitous and universal, yet in reality the internet is still restricted to a small percentage of the world's population.[2] Across much of the southern hemisphere, fixed line internet hardly exists, because fixed line telephony is scarce. To an extent, the same overblown hyperbole is applied to technological art forms. The artworks which tour the media art festival circuits are internationalist and location neutral, rather than site-specific – we're asked to engage with the concepts and methodologies inherent to the medium, rather than to a specific geographical context. Just as the internet was and is largely confined to the wealthy urban elite globally, so the media art scene is concentrated in metropolitan centres – Amsterdam, New York, London, Berlin. As an artist/curator living in Scotland, it often seemed like I was practising on the periphery of the media art world. It was partly in response to this sense of the limits of the nascent digital art scene that I became involved in planning a series of commissions for artists using digital technologies based at locations around Scotland.[3]

Embarking upon such a project necessitated some thinking through of the respective roles of the artists and of the curator. Based on the model of open submissions around a theme, what I dubbed 'open source' curating recognised the importance of the artists independent research, and the need to broaden horizons beyond normal curatorial research in order to bring about possibly unanticipated, perhaps

1   <www.richardfenwick.com>.
2   A breakdown of the global population of Internet users by nation state is provided at: <www.clickz.com/stats/web_worldwide>.
3   The digital art commissions were organised between 1999 and 2001, comprising projects by artists at sites across Scotland. Artists were Colin Andrews, Trevor Avery, Anne Bevan, Jorn Ebner, Alistair Gentry, Catriona Grant, Beverley Hood, Roshini Kempadoo, Nigel Mullan, Chris Rowland, Euan Sutherland. Hosting organisations were Peacock Visual Arts, Aberdeen; Visual Research Centre, Dundee; Stills, Edinburgh; CCA, Glasgow; Collins Gallery, Glasgow; National Review of Live Art, Glasgow; Streetlevel Gallery, Glasgow; art.tm, Inverness; Changing Room, Stirling; Pier Arts Centre, Stromness.

interesting proposals from artists. The task was to set the conditions, define parameters within which the artist would work: location, organisation, budget, equipment access. So a framework was built for artists to respond to. Within an open system another necessity is to encourage artists to apply. Therefore the pre-selection activity is more a networking exercise in itself, the curator acting as a catalyst or node which distorts the flow of information (and hence proposals) away from the potentially arbitrary.

It was necessary to address the nature of a temporary transformation of a space or area. How to square the apparent contradiction between information flows in a network, and the fixity of locale? There is of course a history of artists working with the tensions and paradoxes of physical space, site, and context. The writings of artists such as Robert Smithson and Robert Irwin were useful pointers towards a way forward. Irwin's categories for artworks and their relationship with place were site determined, site dominant, pre-existing work placed on a site, site adjusted, and site specific.[4] We might adapt these categories for media art as technology determined, technology dominant, pre-existing work placed within a technological context, technology adjusted, and technology specific. Somewhere in between these typologies lay the artistic approaches it seemed useful to investigate. Awareness of blurrings and fine distinctions between different types and methods of working became central to the process of selecting artists to create works in specific locales. One example was Colin Andrews' work *Geist* (2000), designed for the specific architecture of the Pier Arts Centre, situated in Stromness, Orkney and also referenced the social and historical traditions of Scotland. The spaces of the 'haunted' houses interacted through the telephone network with the library of the Pier Arts Centre.

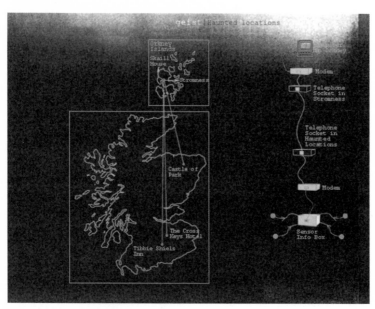

Colin Andrews *Geist* 2000

Four traditionally 'haunted locations' across Scotland were networked. These remote locations acted as nodes, gathering data such as changes in temperature and fluctuations in electromagnetic radiation. This information was then relayed via electronic networks to the library at the Pier Arts Centre where it was used to 'feed' an audio installation. The work was experienced as a four channel audio installation, with each of the channels representing one of the remote 'haunted' locations. The audio was derived from traces of 'voices' extracted from recordings made at each location at an earlier time. Andrews used so-called Electronic Voice Phenomena (EVP) techniques used by researchers from the late 1950s onwards to make audio recordings at the haunted sites. One of the issues which arose during the production of this work was the difficulty and unreliability associated with connecting to the internet in rural Scotland at the time. Customised modems and special software were created to make automatically dialled telephone calls to network the separate components of the installation due to the lack of dependable internet connections in the remote locations where the haunted houses were situated.

Anne Bevan's installations and interactive work combined sculptural processes and techniques with moving images. Her commissioned work *level* (2002) explored the physical effects of weightlessness, weight and buoyancy, through the movement of objects through air and water. The work existed in two forms: as an installation of video projection, sound and sculpture, and as a limited edition CD-ROM. The artist sought to present the processes and experiences of experiments with volumes of air underwater. Sculpture became process and performance. The location for this research was Aberdeen, ideal for its connections with the oil and fishing industries. Most of the video work was undertaken with the assistance of sub aqua divers at a safety training pool for offshore oil workers. The work involved 'experiments' with, for example, shipping floats, cast aluminium forms, balloons, weights, bubbles, oxygen and helium. The movement of these hollow forms through air or water was a central image.

Another work attempted to question notions of place entirely, whether real or virtual. Beverley Hood's *trans-locale* (2001) explored the transitory nature of interaction and examined the potential of movement as a physical and virtual activity. The work was an intervention within the environment of online video conferencing, comprised of a vast network of users. Within this still relatively new technology, visual conventions had evolved, particularly in how users present themselves, generally staring blankly at the screen. In stark contrast to this, *trans-locale* threw into this virtual environment an inherently physical, passionate and intimate activity, the Tango. The work broadcast two dancers from a live performance space into

4   Irwin, Robert. *Being and Circumstance: Notes toward a*   *Conditional Art* (California: Larkspur Landing, 1985).

the online conferences. The dancers' movement around the internet was automated, connecting to a conference for a set period before disconnecting and connecting to the next. In this way the dancers leapt from server to server, country to country, temporarily visible to those connected to each conference. Perceptions of place and physicality began to blur into the online realm.

Beverley Hood *trans-locale* 2001

A subsequent project, *Remote* built upon the experience of commissioning work in situ.[5] Again the impetus for the project was to respond to a particular context: in this case, an area of the Scottish Highlands around the Cairngorms range of mountains. A residency model seemed appropriate to allow artists to experience and respond to the environment they were working in. The residencies facilitated the production of online projects which were also prepared for gallery exhibition at the Iona gallery, a converted schoolhouse in Kingussie, just South of Aviemore. The artists involved were Thomson & Craighead, r a d i o q u a l i a, Simon Fildes & Katrina McPherson and Cavan Convery.

The Cairngorns in the Scottish Highlands formed the location for the *Remote* residencies in 2002

One of the issues we faced immediately was again the scarcity of internet connectivity and bandwidth in the local area. The solutions found were prone to disruption: for the exhibition we hired in satellite broadband, however the satellite uplink that was on such a shallow incline to the earth's surface that if someone parked their car in front of the dish, the internet connection was cut off.

Thomson & Craighead had to change the nature of their planned work in response to the conditions. They had intended to take forward their *template cinema* series with an online film using live web cams situated in the Highlands. Instead the lack of fast internet connections meant they devised a low-bandwidth strategy for their exhibits. *The Price of Freedom* points to four lines from John Barbour's epic poem, *The Bruce,* and re-presents them as a series of domain names parked for re-sale.[6] The poem was found in a second hand volume in a local shop, creating a link from an earlier form of storytelling to the current environment of late capitalism, where everything can be commodified. The second work entitled, *Making a Case for the Twinning of Newtonmore and Las Vegas* was an online open letter alluding to the Highland settlement's history as a purpose-built Victorian resort.

Cavan Convery's project was also transformed by the experience of working in the Highlands. The artist attempted to immerse himself in the natural landscape of one of the last wilderness areas in the UK, hiking and camping in the Cairngorms. His aim had been to experiment with GPS and other mapping technologies. However he quickly realised that the land was rapidly being colonised by signs, plaques and textual information, designed to help visitors. These phenomena were so prevalent it began to annoy him. Convery made a work specifically in response, *A History of the Interpretative Panel.*[7] The artist draws attention to the increasing branding, labelling and systems management of the countryside by non-governmental organisations, some of the largest employers in rural Scotland.

r a d i o q u a l i a were resident at MAKROLAB, conducting research into a number of artistic applications of remote technologies.[8] MAKROLAB, the brainchild of artist Marko Peljhan, was a temporary media lab which coincidentally landed in nearby Blair Atholl the same summer as the *Remote* residencies took place.[9] The r a d i o q u a l i a project, *listening_stations*, was the first phase of an ongoing project entitled *radio astronomy. listening_stations* was an interactive net-radio service consisting of three discrete channels. Each channel presented

5   *Remote* took place during the Summer and Autumn of 2002 in Newtonmore, Kingussie, Dalwhinnie, Blair Atholl, and the area of the Cairngorms national park.

6   <www.thomson-craighead.net/freedom/>.

7   The artwork can be downloaded in PDF format: <www.a-r-c.org.uk/remote/convery>.

8   r a d i o q u a l i a are Honor Harger and Adam Hyde. They have experimented with net.radio since the mid-1990s. <www.radioqualia.net>.

9   MAKROLAB was a global project which landed in Scotland during the Summer of 2002. Artist Marko Peljhan started the project in 1994. <www.makrolab.ljudmila.org/>.

live and prerecorded audio material captured from nearby objects in our solar system, including the planet Jupiter and the Sun. The cosmic and internationalist nature of this project fitted well with MAKROLAB's situation. An admirable undertaking in many ways, MAKROLAB's sojourn in Scotland alas took little account of the social or historical context of the landscape within which it was located.

r a d i o q u a l i a's listening station for the *Remote* residency was based in Marko Peljhan's MAKROLAB, Blair Atholl, Scotland, 2002

Sited in the Atholl sporting estates, the wilderness where artists and scientists experimented with technology was entirely man-made. Within sight of the futuristic sleeping pods lay the ruins of settlements whose residents had been cleared from the land by the Duke of Atholl a century before. It was unfortunate that the significance of their location was largely lost on the many creative people who visited the area because of MAKROLAB's presence. This seems indicative of the disconnection which sometimes occurs between international media art practitioners and the places where they carry out their research.

My collaborators on this project, artists Simon Fildes and Katrina McPherson, lived in the area. Their work for the project was thus informed by an in-depth knowledge of the social context. Their project was based around the winding road from Dalwhinnie to Laggan, 'the most dangerous road in Britain'. The web-based work *If I follow you, do we make a path?* (2002) comprised a slow motion composite journey in which the road takes centre screen and all other obvious traces of human activity have been edited out or altered, recreating a kind of false wilderness.[10] The artists' conscious appreciation of the ways in which visitors or tourists idealise the rural landscape stood in contrast to the romanticism of the MAKROLAB premise.

In parallel with these activities at disparate physical locations, I initiated and curated the online project space, *Host* (2002).[11] In computer jargon, the host is a computer system that is accessed by a user working at a remote location. The system that contains the data is the host, while the computer at which the user sits is the remote terminal. Following the advent of the world wide web, the term host is commonly used to describe a web server, or the act of providing such a server. In wider language, apart from religious connotations, the host is the person who welcomes guests to the home. *Host* began partly as a response to the nomadic, distributed nature in which new media artists operate. There was a feeling that artists needed space for experimentation. This was particularly acutely felt in Scotland, as compared to other countries there had been a relatively low profile for new media art practice. The sense of a 'place' dedicated to artists projects on the website seemed important. It had its own identity, separate from other, often geographically dispersed activities and was promoted accordingly.

Artists' activities often come about through building partnerships with others, who provide physical spaces, equipment or resources. With *Host*, the 'place' was constructed through a different set of conventions and limits – those of HTTP protocols, data storage, domain names, scripting languages and browser technologies. When artists focused on these issues in the building of a 'space' some interesting work was the result. The idea of the 'project' from visual arts or performance traditions was important too. It felt freer than 'exhibition', 'show', or 'gallery': lending the possibility to try something new. Several of the projects presented in some way explored notions of space, and attempted to articulate the position of the viewer in relation to the space constructed by the artist. But dealing with these issues was not a prerequisite. *Host* projects explored a variety of different concerns, notably popular culture, artist's software, politics, and cultural identity. My original intention with *Host* was to present projects only temporarily. But it soon transpired that artists were keen to keep their work in view for as long as possible. So the emphasis moved from temporary to semi-permanent artworks in public space. This shift influenced the presentation of web-specific works, which did not proscribe time-based or performative elements to *Host* projects, but meant the artist had to consider what would remain after a specific event or time-span ended.

10 Detailed documentation of this project and the work itself: <www.left-luggage.co.uk/a889.html>.

11 The *Host* online project space was active from 2000-2004, featuring 18 artists' works over that period. At the time of writing, the works are still online at <www.mediascot.org/host>.

One of the early commissions for *Host* was by Claude Closky, who uses a variety of media – drawing, photography, sound, video and the internet to create subtle distortions of mass media. In *Going for the High Score* (2000) he took the computer game *Tetris* as his starting point. He positioned the screen as a space for play, but also voyeurism. The viewer's expectations were subverted as the work allowed no user interaction, only the observation of Closky's gamesmanship as he pursued the ultimate high score. Closky made a wry comment on the nature of interactive media, whilst examining the tensions between the artefacts of popular culture and the contemplative realm of art.

Artist Jorn Ebner's work is concerned with situations such as migration, settling down, creating environments. In his performances and drawings, he uses objects as playful tools to create visual narratives. In *Life Measure Constructions* (2000–1), the viewer was invited to create their own worlds on the web. An interactive electronic drawing, *Life Measure Constructions* allowed the user to make decisions as to how the online environment would develop. The project attempted to adopt a very personal symbolic order of objects from Ebner's performance works, in order to create an interface for a virtual three dimensional space. This was realised through a graphic style which derived from Ebner's delicate line drawings, giving a visual quality which was quite unlike those commonly associated with online 3-D worlds.

Luci Eyers participates in art projects focused on independent mediation and distribution systems. She is a member of the low-fi collective, an artist/curatorial practice working with net art.[12] Her website *cyberskiving* was a collection of favourite non-work related sites visited by employees during work hours. *cyberskiving* was searchable either by topic or occupation. The project was an open, generative system which developed as cyberskivers submitted information on this covert activity. The artist addressed the context within which many people experience the internet, and how that influences perceptions of what the network is for and people's choices of sites to visit. Eyers looks slightly askance at the internet as a place to while away spare moments through small acts of defiance.

To conclude, my involvement has been with artworks which interrogate our interactions with space and place. This has led naturally to an interest in so-called 'locative' practices and in current forms of collaborative authorship. There is not the room here to explore these in detail, but some final observations may point to some of the principle issues for these emerging practices.[13] The problematic interrelationships between technology and site referred to at the start of this text come into play in new and interesting ways. 'Location aware' projects can share characteristics with site-specific work, but in many instances invert the nature of specific sites by mediating our experience of real space. Locative media tend to be more concerned with process than specific locales. The systematisation and mediatisation of urban or rural space becomes the primary focus in creating and disseminating the artwork. The contrast is between making an artefact for a locale, with making one from/within a locale. The audience experience is different, in that a 'location aware' work is a hybrid of performance and artefact. The viewers/users are very often participants in a networked relationship with each other, annotating or tagging electronic and physical space. What is the role of curating in this new environment? Perhaps not so different from other site-specific artworks or the networked practices. The curator is involved in setting parameters for the creation of the work and the audience experience, and the relationship to the site where it occurs.

12 <www.low-fi.org.uk>.
13 Some recent locative projects are discussed in my essay "Mobile realism?" published in *Reclaiming Cultural Territory in New Media* (Ed. Mare Tralla) (Tallinn, Estonia, 2005); and also online at <www.a-r-c.org.uk/weblog/?p=17>.

Biographies

Joan Gibbons is a Senior Lecturer at the University of Central England and Programme Director of an MA in Contemporary Curatorial Practice. Her interests lie in the interconnectivity and fluidity of contemporary cultural practices, particularly in the way that contemporary art has become an expanded field, moving towards a norm of interrelated practices and interrelated contexts. She has recently published, *Art and Advertising* (I. B. Tauris, 2005), which addresses the complexities of the relationships between these two fields of contemporary practice. Her next book (forthcoming 2007), for the same publisher, is on memory as a major thematic in contemporary art. Her essays for *Hothaus Papers* are intended to frame and contextualise the wide diversity of knowledge offered in the papers.

Kaye Winwood joined VIVID as Projects Manager in 2002. Since this time she has worked toward an interdisciplinary programme of activity including practice-led research, residencies, commissions, talks and performance. This programme has included Heather and Ivan Morison, Brian Duffy and Layla Curtis. She also works as a freelance curator and in 2003 established Capital Art Projects with colleague Alli Beddoes. In 2004-5 they curated *the distance between us*, a programme of site-specific interventions exploring the regeneration of Birmingham's Digbeth and the Jewellery Quarter. In 2005-6 they produced *Charade* with artist Simon Pope which will be touring nationally and internationally during 2006-7. Kaye previously worked at Ikon Gallery as Exhibitions Coordinator, where she worked in all aspects of organising gallery exhibitions, coordinating national and international tours and producing publications, including Ceal Floyer, Graham Gussin and On Kawara.

Reinvention, 25 October 2003
Emma Posey is an artist and writer focusing on the effects of technology on place. She is founding Director of Bloc. She has lectured and written widely on art and technology. She is an editor and consultant on visual arts publications and projects. Her work incorporates photography, video, electronics and microprocessors.

Progression, 2 October 2004
Sadie Plant is a writer and cultural theorist based in Birmingham. She has a PhD in Philosophy from the University of Manchester, and has taught in the Department of Cultural Studies at the University of Birmingham and the Department of Philosophy at the University of Warwick. Her publications include *The Most Radical Gesture*, *Zeros and Ones*, and *Writing on Drugs*.

Space, 4 December 2004
Professor Martin Rieser is co-editor of *New Screen Media; Cinema, Art, Narrative* (BFI/ZKM, 2002). He currently works at Bath Spa University College at Bath School of Art and Design as Professor in Digital Arts. He was Principal Lecturer in Digital Media at Napier University in Edinburgh at the Department of Photography, Film, and Television 1997-2000 and was in post as Senior Lecturer in Electronic Media at UWE Bristol 1986-1998. As Senior Lecturer in Graphic Arts he set up one of the first post-graduate courses in the country in Digital Art and Imaging at the City of London Polytechnic 1980-85. Martin was shortlisted for TRACE new media writing fellowship and Clark's Digital Bursary in 2003. In 2004 he was awarded the Arts Council England's United Artists Senior Research Fellowship and Residency at Coventry University and received an AHRB research grant to write a book on Mobile artworks and to create a new interactive work *Hosts* for Bath Abbey, shown in February 2006. He has exhibited and presented papers widely, including ISEA (1994,5,6,7,2002), Siggraph (2004) and Plan, ICA (2004) and has curated various exhibitions, including *Electronic Print* the first international exhibition of its kind (Arnolfini, Bristol, 1989).

Curation, 29 January 2005
Helen Cadwallader is currently Visual Arts Officer: Media Arts, based in the Visual Arts department of Arts Council England, national office with national lead responsibility for the strategic development of digital/new media and photography. She writes about contemporary practice and time-based media and is published in a wide range of books and publications including, *Locus Solus* (Locus +), *Mute*, *Hybrid*, *Women's Art Magazine* and *Performance*. She initiated and co-edited *New Media Art: Practice and Context in the UK 1994-2004* (ACE/Cornerhouse Publications, 2004). She was the first to manage and develop the BAA Art Programme, a strategy to commission contemporary art in BAA airports including Heathrow and published *Art in the Airports* which operated from 1994 to 1999.

Anthony Auerbach PhD is Project Director of Video as Urban Condition. His work as artist, organiser and researcher revolves around the critique of knowledge and representation, with a special interest in practices such as drawing and video, which cannot be claimed exclusively by art. ‹www.vargas.org.uk/aa› / ‹www.video-as.org›

Jon Bird and Andy Webster have worked together over the last five years collaborating with other individuals and organisations on a range of projects which include live performances, films, interactive and relational installations, texts (fictional and scientific) and curatorial projects. Consistent across their collaborative work has been the employment of an open-ended approach where the structure and outcomes are, to some extent, emergent. Jon Bird is a Research Fellow in the Centre for Computational Neuroscience and Robotics at the University of Sussex. He researches artificial life that focuses on the modelling of adaptive behaviour using computer simulations and robots. He is currently working on the multi-disciplinary *Drawbots* project which explores creativity by building robots that can draw. Applying his research across disciplines he has published several papers that simultaneously consider both the artistic and scientific potential of emergent and evolutionary systems. He is a co-founder of Blip, a Brighton-based arts-science forum. Andy Webster is currently a research student in the Art, Nature, Environment research group at University College Falmouth, Cornwall. He is interested in arts practices that foreground process and method as the main constituents and materials for artworks. He is currently researching how such process-led work can engage with ideas from the field of complexity theory to contribute to the development of an ecological model of arts thinking.

~~~~~~

Contributors

~~~~~~

Ben Borthwick is an Assistant Curator at Tate Modern, London. He is curating a sound work by Bill Fontana based on the Millenium Bridge (June-July 2006), a collaborative project with Platform for Art. He has worked on large-scale exhibitions such as *Martin Kippenberger*, *Open Systems*, *The Unilever Series: Bruce Nauman*, and *Constantin Brancusi* as well as the upcoming Gilbert & George retrospective. Before joining Tate Modern, he was involved with a number of offsite projects at Artangel, the Henry Moore Contemporary Projects at the 2002 Liverpool Biennial and the alternative space Milch. He has written extensively about sound and spatial issues, and since 1998 has been a regular contributor to music magazine *The Wire*.

Chris Byrne is the co-director of Art Research Communication, an Edinburgh based company working nationally and internationally with artists, exhibitions, projects and critical context. He also lectures in Contemporary Media Theory at the University of Dundee. He has long experience in the field of media arts as a curator, producer and artist. His main practice as a curator and researcher over the past nine years has been focused on internet art, networked art practices, sound, performance, and more recently mobile and locative media arts. He has also continued his long standing interest in moving image media, in particular video art and experimental film.

Dr. Sarah Cook is an independent curator and post-doctoral research fellow at the University of Sunderland, where she is the co-founder of CRUMB - an online resource for curators of new media art <www.crumbweb.org>). Since 2000 Sarah has split her time between the UK and Canada, curating exhibitions (*Database Imaginary*, 2004; *The Art Formerly Known As New Media*, 2005; *Package Holiday*, 2005), organising educational projects, editing publications and managing artists' residencies in conjunction with BALTIC, The Centre for Contemporary Art, Gateshead, the New Media Institute and The Walter Phillips Gallery at The Banff Centre. She has lectured and published widely on art, new media and curatorial practice.

Brian Duffy is a conceptual artist, whose work involves live performance, installations, original music composition and the creation of new musical instruments. He has performed and presented internationally. His central themes explore the limits of human sense data and the notion of perceptual habit in an attempt to reveal the hidden world around us, by utilising modified and self built apparatus. Brian was recently awarded a three-year fellowship from NESTA (National Endowment for Science Technology and Art). He is using the Fellowship to expand the themes and concerns of his work: investigating the harmonic structure of the universe - by focusing on the rotational frequencies of pulsars. As well as looking into other possible uses for the Japanese art of paper folding - origami.

Jem Finer is an artist and musician working in a diverse range of fields, including music, film, performance, sculpture, installation and photography. Between October 2003-July 2005 he worked as artist in residence at the Astrophysics Department in Oxford, concluding in the construction of two sculptural observatories, *Landscope*, on the banks of, and in, Lough Neagh, Northern Ireland, and *The Centre of the Universe* in University Parks Oxford <www.cosmology.org.uk>. Ongoing work includes *Longplayer* <www.longplayer.org>, a 1000 year long composition which started to play on the 1st January 2000. As winner of the PRS Foundation New Music Award, he is currently working on a new project, *Score for a Hole in the Ground*, with Stour Valley Arts (in Kings Wood, Kent) to be completed in the autumn of 2006.

Contributors

Bill Fontana was born in USA in 1947 and is internationally known for his pioneering experiments in sound. Fontana is interested in transforming the aural environment, and uses the physical environment as a living source of musical information whose aesthetic and evocative qualities can conjure visual imagery in the mind of the listener. Since his breakthrough work, *Kirribilli Wharf* (1976) Fontana has developed a practice based in real time recordings of natural and man-made events presented in site-specific sound installations. Fontana has presented sound sculptures at the Venice Biennale, the Reina Sofia in Madrid, the Whitney Museum of American Art, the Museum Ludwig in Cologne, and the San Fransisco Museum of Art. In 2004 *Primal Soundings*, a permanent installation, was unveiled at Leeds City Art Gallery. Fontana is currently working toward a new sound work based on the Millenium Bridge, London (June-July 2006), commissioned by Tate Modern with Platform for Art.

Paul Granjon has been interested in mechanics and electricity from an early age. He founded his company Z Productions in 1988. In 1995 he was offered a lectureship at Cardiff and it was at this time that he began an intensive period of research in electronics and robotics. Paul was awarded a NESTA (National Endowment for Science Technology and the Arts) Fellowship in 2004. He was one of the artists representing Wales in the Venice Biennale 2005, where he exhibited a Robotarium. In February 2006 he premiered a new performance that includes Sexed Robots and primitive technology in the Arnolfini, Bristol. More information on Paul Granjon and Z Productions at <www.zprod.org>

Mark Hancock is interested in exploring the intersections between Media Art and Literature. The new forms of writing that present themselves to us are as much a means of exploration of process as they are of final product. Mediating this hybrid through a theoretical framework of political and cultural tension laid down by the Situationist Internationale allows for a reconsideration of digital literature projects and our relationship to them, as much as it is about their relationship to us. Mark works as a writer and publisher and is also contributing writer and co-editor of *furtherfield.org*. He is currently a PhD candidate at DeMontfort University and a member of the Narrative Lab and Institute of Creative Technologies.

Caitlin Jones has recently jumped into the commercial gallery world and taken a position as the Director of Programming at the Bryce Wolkowitz Gallery in New York. From 2001-2006 Jones held a combined curatorial and conservation position at the Solomon R. Guggenheim Museum. She co-curated the groundbreaking exhibition *Seeing Double: Emulation in Theory and Practice* (2004) and coordinated the Deutsche Guggenheim exhibition, *Nam June Paik: Global Groove* (2004). As one of the lead researchers and organisers of the international Variable Media Network, Caitlin has been uniquely responsible for developing important tools and policy for the preservation of electronic and ephemeral artworks. Her writings on new media art presentation and preservation have appeared in a wide range of catalogues and international publications.

Michelle Kasprzak is an artist, writer and curator. Since winning the InterAccess Electronic Media Arts Centre 'Emerging Electronic Artist' award in her early career, Michelle has proceeded to exhibit her work across North America and Europe. Her work has been featured in numerous publications and on radio and television broadcasts syndicated worldwide. As a writer, Michelle has been published in magazines such as *Mute*, *Spacing*, *Broken Pencil*, and *Public*. Her recent curatorial projects include an online exhibition produced with Virtual Museums of Canada/Gallery TPW, and a year programme of video art on a public video billboard in Toronto, Canada. She was awarded a Master's degree in Visual and Media Arts from the Université du Québec à Montréal in 2006. She is currently based in Edinburgh, UK, and is the Programmes Director of New Media Scotland. She maintains a web presence at <www.michelle.kasprzak.ca>.

The Loca group consists of Drew Hemment (Future Everything/UK), Concept co-author, artistic development; John Evans (3eyes/UK/FI), Concept co-author, interaction design; Theo Humphries (3eyes/UK), Concept co-author, interaction design; Mika Raento (ContextPhone/University of Helsinki/FI), Concept co-author, software development. The interdisciplinary Loca project was initiated in 2003, out of an interest in forms of horizontal surveillance using mobile media. Then it sat in waiting for the accident to happen. The accident was when the Aware/ContextPhone collaboration started generating surveillance data that was unforeseen by its designers. *Loca: Set To Discoverable* has been accepted for 'Interactive Cities' at ISEA2006 and ZeroOne San Jose; included in an online gallery curated by A. Paterson (FI), A. On Ni Wan (Hong Kong) and S. Hur (Korea) for Leonardo Electronic Almanac; proof-of-concept installations have been presented at PixelACHE, Kiasma, Helsinki (2005) and RCA, London (2005).

Garrett Monaghan is Associate Senior Lecturer in the School of Creative Arts, Film and Media at the University of Portsmouth. He also works as an independent Arts Management Consultant with an extensive portfolio that includes curation, training, organisational development and project management. His clients have largely come from the grant-aided, business, education and government sectors. As a practising artist his work focuses on place and abstract form. He has a PhD in Culture and Communications from the University of Sussex and lives in Brighton.

Nina Pope is an artist / film-maker who works collaboratively with Karen Guthrie. Pope and Guthrie live and work in London and Cumbria respectively. After studying together at Edinburgh College of Art they completed their studies in London before beginning their career as collaborative artists in 1995. They launched their multi-disciplinary company Somewhere in 2002, and have since led diverse creative projects with an emphasis on new audiences and innovative technology. They have been commissioned by and exhibited at many high profile venues including Tate Modern and the ICA (where they received a 1999 Imaginaria Digital Art Prize). Most recently they have completed their first feature film, *Bata-ville: We are not afraid of the future,* which was selected for the prestigious Edinburgh International Film Festival and then premiered in the US at the noted SXSW festival in Austin, Texas. This summer they will be shooting their next film documenting one of the UK's largest Tudor re-enactments at Kentwell Hall in Suffolk. Nina Pope and Karen Guthrie are co-directors of <www.somewhere.org.uk>, where details of all their projects can be found.

Paul Ramírez Jonas lives and works in New York. Solo exhibitions include a survey at Ikon Gallery (UK) and Cornerhouse (UK); LFL Gallery (NYC); Roger Björkholmen (Sweden); and Postmasters Gallery (NYC). Group exhibitions in the Gallery for Contemporary Art Leipzig (Germany); P.S.1 (NYC); Seoul Biennial (Korea); The Whitechapel (UK); Irish Museum of Modern Art (Ireland); Künstlerhaus (Austria); Johannesburg Biennale (South Africa); Exit Art (NYC); The New Museum (NYC). Paul has taught at R.I.S.D, Cal Arts, Columbia Universtiy, New York Universtiy, and the School of the Museum of Fine Arts Boston. He has been profiled in ArtForum, Zing, ARTnews, New York Times, Art in America and others. (2003-) Assistant Professor of Studio Arts, Bard College

Robert Sharl is currently a Lecturer at UCE Birmingham within the Birmingham Institute of Art & Design, and a researcher affiliated with the Visualisation Research Unit. He is also the founder of Futurilla, a network for new ideas around technology, community, design and education and a voracious blogger whose work can be found at Usergland <www.usergland.blogspot.com/>. He has recently given papers on transformative technology and digital learning environments.

Dr. Gregory Sporton is Director of the Visualisation Research Unit at the Department of Art, University of Central England (UCE) in Birmingham. His background is in performance, and he was a dancer for many years prior to joining higher education. He trained at the Victorian College of the Arts in Melbourne, Australia before working around the world in a variety of projects in dance and performance art. His postgraduate study was at Warwick University and University of Sheffield where he was awarded his PhD in the cultural studies of dance. Previously Head of Research at Laban, he is currently working at UCE on the use of technology in performance and visualisation. The work of the lab can be seen at <www.biad.uce.ac.uk/vru>.

Martijn Stevens is a PhD student at the department of Comparative Arts and Cultural Studies at the Radboud University in Nijmegen, Netherlands. His research focuses on internet art and its relationhips with traditional art history and media theory, especially notions surrounding 'musealization' and cultural heritage. Martijn has worked as a researcher, editor and media archivist at an international media art institute. He is also interested in visual and popular culture, such as comic books and music videos.

Janet Vaughan is a theatre designer – a designer of spaces, objects and environments for performance. Over the last twelve years her practice has evolved so that although theatre design currently constitutes a relatively small proportion of her practice as an artist, she feels that 'theatre' still best suggests/describes the open/collaborative way she approaches her work across a wide range of media and in a wide variety of contexts: from live performance to the web. She is one third of Coventry-based Talking Birds, and her web art has been described by The Independent as "innovative and unusual... akin to taking part in a David Lynch movie." See <www.helloland.co.uk>.

James Wallbank trained in Fine Art at Sheffield Hallam University, graduating with a Masters degree in 1992. Still based in Sheffield, he co-founded Lowtech, an organisation set up by arts group, Redundant Technology Initiative, in 1997 <www.lowtech.org>. Lowtech provides an open access space which democratises technology through the use of open source software and the rescuing and re-employment of abandoned computer equipment. James has lectured at many institutions including University of Central England (2004), DeMontfort University (1997), University of Derby (1997), Sunderland University (1996), John Leggot College (1995), Norton College (1994) and Chesterfield College of Technology & The Arts (1993).

Simon Yuill is an artist based in Glasgow where he is part of the Chateau Institute of Technology. Projects include spring_alpha <www.spring-alpha.org>, the Social Versioning System <www.spring-alpha.org/svs>, slateford (http://www.slateford.org), and Your Machines <www.yourmachines.org>. Simon is a researcher in the School of Television and Imaging at Duncan Jordanstone College of Technology, University of Dundee. He was also awarded a Research Fellowship at the Piet Zwart Institute in Rotterdam, 2005.

Index

230 // INDEX

~~~~~~
J-R
~~~~~~

Hothaus Papers
Perspectives and Paradigms in Media Arts

Edited by Joan Gibbons and Kaye Winwood
Designed by James Langdon
Printed by Specialblue, London

ISBN 1 873352 24 7

Article Press
BIAD, UCE
Margaret Street
Birmingham B3 3BX
<articlepress@uce.ac.uk>
+44 (0)121 331 5970

VIVID
140 Heath Mill Lane
Birmingham B9 4AR
<info@vivid.org.uk>
+44 (0)121 766 7876

Distributed by Central Books
99 Wallis Road
London E9 5LN
<orders@centralbooks.com>
+44 (0)20 8986 5463